THE
TENBURY & BEWDLEY RAILWAY

An evening train from the Tenbury branch drawing to a stand in Woofferton station behind the 6.25 p.m. Shrewsbury–Hereford on Whit-Monday, 10th June 1957. *M. Mensing*

THE
TENBURY & BEWDLEY RAILWAY

KEITH BEDDOES & WILLIAM H. SMITH

A steam railmotor crossing Sandbourne Viaduct, Bewdley.

CONTENTS

Introduction	1
Chapter One FROM CANAL TO RAILWAY	3
Chapter Two THE RAILWAY AGE DAWNS (The Shrewsbury & Hereford Railway)	9
Chapter Three THE SETTING UP OF THE TENBURY RAILWAY and the influence of William Norris	11
Chapter Four THE TENBURY AND BEWDLEY RAILWAY	15
Chapter Five THE CONSTRUCTION OF THE TENBURY AND BEWDLEY LINE	21
Chapter Six THE OPENING OF THE TENBURY AND BEWDLEY RAILWAY	29
Chapter Seven EXPANSION AFTER 1864	33
Chapter Eight INTO THE TWENTIETH CENTURY	55
Chapter Nine BETWEEN THE WARS	87
Chapter Ten 1940–1945	131
Chapter Eleven THE POSTWAR YEARS	139
Chapter Twelve POSTSCRIPT	201
Acknowledgements	202

PUBLISHERS' NOTE

The publishers would like to express their thanks to the following for their kind help with the production of this book: David Postle, Mike Christensen, Wendy Hinton, Brian Standish, J. W. Warren, Peter Swift and Bewdley Museum.

© Wild Swan Publications and
Keith Beddoes & William H. Smith 1995
ISBN 1 874103 27 5

Designed by Paul Karau
Printed by Amadeus Press Ltd., Huddersfield

Published by
WILD SWAN PUBLICATIONS LTD.
1-3 Hagbourne Road, Didcot, Oxon, OX11 8DP

Collection Wendy Hinton

Charcoal burners at work in the Wyre Forest in the early 1920s, by which time only a small number of men were able to earn a living from the trade. Modern portable kilns and retorts had replaced the traditional methods, as seen in this photo. Charcoal was used by the glass blowers of Stourbridge and Bromsgrove, the Teme Valley hop industry and in the iron industry of Birmingham and the Black Country.

Wyre Forest District Council/Bewdley Museum

INTRODUCTION

It is probably true to say that nothing of any great historical consequence ever happened in the little Worcestershire town of Tenbury Wells although legend has it that the fierce warrior Caradoc (or Caractacus as he was later known) was born there. After fighting a losing battle in 51 BC (reputedly at Church Stretton) against Ostorius Scapula, he was captured and sent to Rome. Later pardoned, he made his way back to his place of birth and after his death was reputedly buried under a mound now called Castle Tump.

Tenbury Wells is better known today for the excellent grayling caught in the River Teme which flows through the town, or perhaps for its unusual 'Round Market' in Market Square which comes alive with produce and visitors every Tuesday Market day. There has been a market held in Tenbury Wells ever since 1248 when the right to a market was granted by Henry III at the request of Roger de Clifford.

The casual visitor may well leave the town without being aware of another odd-shaped building tucked away behind the Crow Hotel at the bottom of the town in Teme Street. This is the Tenbury Bath House which, together with the Round Market and the Corn Exchange, were products of a prosperous Victorian age when Tenbury was at the hub of the great Teme Valley agricultural area which, with its acres of hop yards and fruit orchards, gave rise to Tenbury's Victorian nickname of 'The Town in the Orchard'.

It may be difficult to imagine that the Bath House, now in a semi-derelict state but earmarked for preservation, was once held in high esteem by Tenbury folk. The history surrounding the first Bath House and health-giving wells goes back to 1839. In July of that year a spring of saline water was discovered by accident while a well was being sunk by Mr Septimus Holmes Godson at his residence, 'The Court', near the Kyre Brook, Tenbury. From analysis, the water was found to contain health-giving salts similar to those of the waters from nearby spas such as Malvern or Cheltenham. Mr Godson, quick to realise the potential of his new-found asset, lost no time in publicising the waters and 'at great expense' set about improving and altering the well, including the provision of a small red brick bath house in which 'those desirous to bathe or take the waters could relax and be cured of their ailments'.

'On Monday June 1st 1840 the good people of Tenbury, their anxious neighbours and invalid visitors, celebrated the opening of the Tenbury Well in great style with music and rejoicing' — so read the Kidderminster paper at the time. The townsfolk of Tenbury 'were quick to open their homes for lodging purposes' which was rather surprising since all self-respecting persons then were rather reluctant to open their houses for lodgings, but it was hoped 'it would be for the public good'!

Extra stage coaches were run to and from the Swan Hotel, whence the gentry could take a pleasant stroll through the town, take the waters, then relax on the banks of the Kyre Brook whilst waiting for the cures to take effect (in 1841 Teme Street was paved with flagstones, to 'afford an agreeable promenade' for visitors to the spa).

On 19th July 1846 another spring was discovered by a Mr Joseph Griffiths quite close to the Crow Inn, fuelling speculation that Tenbury as a 'spa' would take off in a big way. Some concern was expressed, however, that comfort was just as necessary to cure a sick person as was medicine, and to achieve this aim it was felt that new buildings should be erected as soon as possible to cater for the increased number of visitors.

Hopes of expansion were, however, killed off by the grave economic crisis brought about by the failure of consecutive potato harvests in 1845 and 1846, followed by problems with the corn harvest as well, causing great hardships in the country generally, but especially to the Teme Valley people, rich and poor alike. Many speculators also lost money which was tied up in the various railway schemes for the area when these were abandoned or shelved following the collapse of the railway stock market.

By 1853 the country was recovering and economic expansion was gathering momentum, leading to great social change, for the slow and outmoded canals were being quickly replaced by the speedy and efficient railway transport system. Tenbury was passed by, a prisoner of its geographical location. It did have a canal close by which really only ran from 'nowhere to nowhere' and was all but dried up and in poor repair anyway. Tenbury did have mineral waters to equal those of Malvern, but the want of accommodation and the state of the roads in the Teme Valley could be of no comfort to those invalids visiting the spa.

The weekly produce waggons bound for the Birmingham markets were often delayed due to the difficult, hilly road to Bewdley and Kidderminster becoming impassable after heavy rains. Expenses were then increased by having to travel over a longer route through Worcester.

This state of affairs could not carry on much longer, though for a time it seemed that while every booming town and village in Britain was demanding and getting a railway line, Tenbury was lacking not only a railway to help break out of its rural backwater, but also someone with the drive to organise such a scheme. Fortunately for the town, a man did eventually come along to do just that and the railway age eventually became a reality for the Teme Valley.

A few miles north of Tenbury, just east of Cleobury Mortimer, lies Wyre Forest. The forest is now only a fraction of its former area. It is an ancient forest dating back to Roman times [Wyrecaster (Worcester) meaning the

Roman station in the Wyre] and it was once a royal hunting ground. In later times the Wyre Forest was exploited commercially for timber as a building material, for charcoal making, basket making and tanning. The forest provided much of the raw material for building the ships of the Tudor navy and, on a smaller scale, coracles used by fishermen on the River Severn were constructed by the craftsmen in 'The Forest'.

Workable coal seams of the Wyre Forest coalfield outcrop south of the Dowles Brook and a whole host of small mines produced a type of coal much favoured by the hop dryers of Tenbury because of its sulphur content. This coal could not easily find bigger markets until an efficient transport system materialised which could get across the barrier of the River Severn and reach the booming industrial growth of the Black Country and Birmingham to the east.

This history begins with the sale of a part-completed, near-derelict canal to a railway company, and records what happened in the ensuing one hundred and four years until the closure of the line. A large number of people and institutions has been involved in helping us to set down this record and it is with grateful thanks that we set out a separate list of acknowledgements.

An earlier view of charcoal burners c.1890. The charcoal pits had to be watched through 24 hours so the burners used to live by their work in temporary shelters. The charcoal pits were a framework of sticks covered with bracken and grasses which were then covered with sacks. A hole in the roof allowed smoke from the fire to escape. A 'front door' was provided too. Burners usually worked in pairs, taking turns to sleep and look after the burning. One of the long-handled tools of the trade is also featured leaning against the 'cabin'.

CHAPTER ONE
FROM CANAL TO RAILWAY

SHROPSHIRE was arguably the location of the very start of the Industrial Revolution. The Coalbrookdale Ironworks, where the Darby family pioneered so many significant developments, enjoyed outstanding success. An important factor in this was the location of the ironworks. It was one of the very few sites in Britain where deposits of coal and iron ore lay adjacent to a navigable river — the Severn.

Whilst the Coalbrookdale Company could despatch its goods swiftly and cheaply by barge, ironmasters and manufacturers in other areas, particularly in the neighbouring Staffordshire coalfield, were hindered by the need to transport their goods overland at some expense to the Rivers Severn or Trent. In the early 18th century some rivers had been made navigable and a few canals built, the latter mainly in the north of England, but the lack of substantial finance delayed any start to Midland canal building until the 1760s. Then two important canals Bills, for the construction of the Staffordshire and Worcestershire and the Trent and Mersey, were both given Royal Assent on 14th May 1766. The Trent and Mersey Canal, as its name implies, ran northward linking the Trent to the River Mersey at Runcorn. The Staffordshire and Worcestershire Canal ran south from a junction with the Trent and Mersey near Great Haywood, through Penkridge and Kidderminster, to the Severn at Stourport. Although the two canals were promoted quite separately, James Brindley was appointed engineer to both schemes.

The construction of the Trent and Mersey Canal was troubled by many engineering difficulties, whereas work on the Staffordshire and Worcestershire went forward quite smoothly, being completed by the end of 1770. Two years later the Birmingham Canal was completed, an important link connecting with the Staffordshire and Worcestershire at Wolverhampton. This junction gave access to Birmingham and the Black Country from the Severn, providing impetus to the growth of Stourport as a flourishing inland port.

The success of the Staffordshire and Worcestershire Canal had not gone unnoticed in the rural backwater to the west of Stourport, beyond the escarpments of the Abberley Hills and Clows Top, an area not only reaching down to the fertile Teme Valley, but rich also in deposits of coal, lime and ironstone. This was the western edge of the Wyre Forest coalfield where coal had been mined for centuries; indeed records of Worcester Cathedral in the reign of Richard II refer to the amount paid by the monks for coal from the Abberley area. Early mining in the region seems to have been confined to gathering coal from outcrops near the surface or from seams exposed by natural erosion by rivers and streams. In the late 18th century most workings were still of the opencast or quarry method, development being restricted by the absence of cheap power and transport, the latter especially tantalising since the River Severn was such a short distance away.

Ideas to link the area by canal to the Severn were first mooted in 1777 when Robert Whitworth, one of Brindley's assistants, was engaged to survey three suggested routes — one through Leominster to Stourport, another from Hereford to Gloucester via Ledbury and a third from the Severn, near Bridgnorth, through Corvedale to Leintwardine. These plans were not followed up, however, partly because of the likely cost of heavy earthworks which frightened off any investors.

Matters rested until July 1789, when meetings at Leominster and Tenbury prompted surveys to be made for a canal from Leominster to Stourport by way of Woofferton and Tenbury. This time support was forthcoming amongst the local landowners, principally Sir Walter Blount of Sodington Hall who owned the nearby Mamble collieries, and the Clutton-Brock family, proprietors of the Pensax mine, both of whom stood to gain extra revenue from wider markets. Following further meetings that year, it was reported in December that Thomas Dadford (Junior) had surveyed a route for a canal from Leominster to Stourport. It would be some 31 miles long, would cost £83,000, and involve three tunnels, Putnal Field 330 yards, Southnet (sic) 1,254 yards and Pensax 3,850 yards. In addition, two aqueducts would be needed, one over the River Teme at Little Hereford, the other over the Rea at Newnham. A series of seventeen locks would be required to ascend over 200 feet from the Severn at Areley Kings to the summit of the canal near Pensax.

Annual receipts were estimated at over £4,300, half of which would come from imported coal charged at 1½d per ton mile. Revenue on carriage of goods from the Black Country, Manchester, Yorkshire and elsewhere would be swelled by back carriage of local goods such as hops, perry, cider, timber (plus Welsh products like butter and flannel) presently sent to Worcester, Birmingham and London. In spite of rather unattractive financial figures, enthusiasm was high, and following a meeting in January 1790, £18,000 was quickly subscribed. At yet another meeting in April, held in Kington, the people of that town asked for a survey from Leominster to Kington, the purposes being to link with the proposed canal. The two schemes were amalgamated, the proposal now being for a canal 45 miles long.

Dadford's plans were approved in January 1791, and he was appointed engineer. Subscriptions came in swiftly and the Act authorising construction was soon passed.

The Act for the 'Kington-Leominster and Stourport Canal' (31 Geo. III Cap. 69) stated that it was to be 45 miles long. Capital of £150,000 was to be raised, with the provision to increase it by £40,000 if required. An extra tunnel 70 yards long was to be built near Newnham, and a list of tonnage rates specified. Provision was also made that subscriptions were to be first applied for the building of the section from the Severn to Milton Cross (west of Leominster) after which the residue could be used for continuing the canal to Kington. The purposes envisaged for the canal were 'to carry stone, lime, iron ore and agricultural produce to the Severn, bringing back goods and coal', including that from Sir Walter Blount's collieries at Mamble, plus that from the Pensax mine. It was also hoped to open new quarries and workings and reopen others that had closed.

Work on the canal began before the end of 1791 and proceeded quite quickly. The first newspaper report of progress was in May 1793 when a boat, *The Royal George*, 70ft long by 6ft 10in wide, built by a Mr Bird of Stourport, was reported as being launched at Tenbury Wharf. The *British Chronicle* of 22nd May stated 'This being the first spectacle of the kind on the Leominster Canal, a numerous concourse of people attended, and the launch took place amid the firing of cannon, flags, music playing and other demonstrations of joy'.

By October the following year, 1794, the section from Woofferton to Marlbrook Wharf was opened, the latter being the nearest point to the Mamble collieries of Sir Walter Blount. A tramway had been laid from the mines to the Marlbrook Wharf enabling the first load of coal to be sent to Tenbury Wharf where it arrived on 20th October, the coal being distributed to the poor through the kindness of Sir Walter, and more scenes of joy were witnessed. Six more boats passed on, over the grand three-arch aqueduct at Little Hereford, to Woofferton Wharf, where they were met with similar scenes of rejoicing.

Work on the Woofferton-Leominster section was delayed owing to difficulties with the Putnal Field tunnel, work coming to a halt on several occasions. A special meeting was held in April 1795 to consider the best method of overcoming the problem so that the canal could be completed, but the only outcome was that work had to be delayed until sufficient funds could be raised. By the end of the year, the tunnel at Southnett, near Mamble (on the Stourport section) had been built, and the canal was opened as far as the north end of Putnal tunnel. Work was started towards Stourport and foundations begun for Kingsland aqueduct over the River Lugg.

The completed Southnett tunnel suffered a sudden partial collapse (for no clear reason), reputedly burying three workmen. With the Putnal Field tunnel still not finished, the exasperated Canal Company called in John Rennie to make a full report. His findings pointed out bad design in Southnett tunnel, and mis-management in the case of Putnal tunnel. He also found faults in the aqueducts over the River Rea at Newnham and across the Teme at Little Hereford.

Another Act was obtained in April 1796 (36 Geo. III, Cap. 70) to raise further money, and by July the Putnal Field tunnel was at last completed. In December the whole length between Leominster and Marlbrook, a distance of 18 miles, was declared open. Fourteen barges laden with coal arrived that first day, the coal selling to the inhabitants of Leominster for 15 shillings per ton, about half the price that road-hauled coal had previously cost.

The 18 miles (out of a total of 45) of canal so far built had cost £93,000, putting the company heavily in debt. Many ideas were thought up to raise money, including one to raise a tonnage or lock duty on every boat passing into or out of the Severn at a basin at Stourport. However, to connect the canal to a proposed Stourport Basin would have required the completion of the Pensax tunnel and, in addition, the construction of seventeen locks to lower barges down to the River Severn at Ribbesford. According to *Philips Inland Navigation*, in 1805 the canal company was proposing to introduce inclined planes where water shortage would make locks uneconomical; this was perhaps the most logical answer.

By 1803 all construction work had ceased, the funds having been exhausted, and debts amounted to £25,000. The only traffic would appear to have been coal from

Putnal Tunnel entrance, Kington–Leominster–Stourport Canal, on the approach to Woofferton. The tunnel was 330 yards long and, although it has collapsed inside, the portals are remarkably preserved. *Kidderminster Library*

FROM CANAL TO RAILWAY

Blount's colliery, the revenue from which would not even pay off the debts, let alone help finance the vital connection eastwards to the River Severn. So yet another consultant was called in, namely John Hodgkinson, the engineer. He boldly suggested that tramroads would be cheaper than coals and that a tramway should be built from Southnett tunnel to Stourport (via Stockton) at a cost of £35,000, though £60,000 would be required to pay off debts for repairs and rebuilding the tunnel. He further proposed a branch tramway to Pensax colliery, and that no work should be undertaken on the canal or tramway beyond Kingsland (Leominster-Kington) till a later date. The proposals were put to a shareholders meeting. The directors argued that the proposal to go via Stockton would cost more than going direct to Stourport because it was 2½ miles longer, so a line from the north-west end of Southnett tunnel with the best route to Stourport should be built with a branch to Pensax colliery from Clows Top. A commission of ten members should be appointed to supervise the building of the line. After some discussion, the following priorities were agreed:

1. Money was to be raised to go in discharging debts and completing unfinished work around Leominster.
2. The railway to Stourport should be the next objective, to be pursued until complete.
3. The canal or railway to Kingsland (Leominster-Kington section) to be completed.
4. When all the other work was completed, all work west of Leominster was to be completed (together with sundry maintenance, repairs, etc.), all within 2 years.

Accordingly, yet another Act was obtained in August 1803 (43 Geo. III, C. 14) calling for more than £50,000 to be raised from shareholders, to discharge £25,000 debts, and to finish work within 2 years (£35,000). Up to £40,000 could be raised on mortgage.

The remains of the aqueduct over the River Rea near Newnham Bridge, part of the Kington–Leominster–Stourport Canal, known locally as the 'bridge of a million bricks', but now in poor condition. The canal was carried in a brick trough surrounded by puddled clay.
G. Macdonald

Nothing came of the tramroad scheme. Not even a proposal (in August 1810) to run a tramroad from the Leominster Canal at Tenbury to the Clee Hills pits, could induce subscribers to invest any cash for the completion of the canal.

Other schemes that the Leominster Canal Company advertised (perhaps in desperation) included that in 1812 for a railway or canal from the Rea aqueduct near Newnham, through the Teme Valley, via Lindridge, Martley and Wichenford to the Worcester and Birmingham Canal near Worcester, and also for a railway or canal from Morton, through Orleton, Yarpole, Kingsland, Lucton and Aymestrey, over the Lugg at Mortimer's Cross, to join the original line.

In 1826 yet another Act was obtained to repeal parts of the former Acts not now relevant, and to obtain powers to enable the company to settle with the creditors, raise money on tonnage duties or outright sale of the canal, or apply the money to creditors in equal shares. In the case of outright sale, the original landowners would have the first choice followed by present owners of adjoining lands. The Act was duly passed (Geo. IV, Cap. 94) but failed to raise sufficient funds from disillusioned shareholders. In fact, many shareholders had died in a state of insolvency or had relinquished their shares since the last Act in 1803. The extensions beyond Leominster had already become obsolete with the opening in 1820 of the Kington tramroad from Eardisley. This was an extension of the Hay tramroad opened from Brecon to Hay in May 1816 and from Hay to Eardisley in December 1818, by means of which coal was transported from South Wales pits by way of the Brecknock and Abergavenney Canal.

The tramway idea was brought up again on 2nd November 1833 when an article appeared in the *Hereford Times* promoting a line from the north-west side of Stourport bridge via Blakemore Farm, over Bayton Common, and down the valley of the Rea to connect with the aqueduct at Newnham, near Sir Edward Blount's colliery. Also proposed was a line from Leominster to Eardisley where it would connect with the Hay tramroad. In all a total of 28 miles were proposed at an estimated cost of £61,000, Edward Powell being named engineer and surveyor. Further meetings were held in Stourport and at the Royal Oak, Leominster, in January 1834. They were reported in the *Hereford Times* under the heading 'Stourport and Kington Tramroad'. This piece reported not only on the tramway schemes, but a further plan for purchasing the Leominster Canal 'which hasn't sufficient water for any considerable traffic, so let out the water and lay a tramroad on the bed to prevent inconvenience, delay and damage in loading and unloading goods'. The article further suggested that should the canal not be bought on equitable terms, then the tramroad would continue, but under the canal near Newnham, then between it and the Teme, to and over that river at Little Hereford Bridge, thence to Leominster. Acts would be applied or, should the scheme be adopted, to raise £105,000 — £65,000 for the two tramroads plus £40,000 if necessary for the by-pass line.

Two further public meetings were held, both in February 1834, one early in the month at the Royal Oak, Leominster, and another at The Swan, Tenbury, on the 27th, to consider 'the propriety and advantages of opening a communication between the Severn at Stourport and the Leominster Canal by a railway'. At this latter meeting, John Rastrick, then engineer of the Staffordshire and Worcestershire Canal, was appointed to survey the tramway from Newnham to Stourport. The *Hereford Journal* for 12th March 1834 noted that 'the project for connecting the Leominster Canal with the Severn at Stourport by means of a railway has been taken up in a very spirited manner and liberal subscriptions have been entered into to obtain a survey of the line'. On 2nd April the *Hereford Journal* reported 'a survey is now being taken of the road between Stourport and Leominster with a view to the contemplated railroad'.

According to the *Hereford Times* for 5th July 1834, a meeting was arranged for the 15th July at the 'Hundred House' near Stourport to consider the survey report from Rastrick on the feasibility of the railroad scheme. Either the meeting was adjourned or he failed to appear, for the paper eventually reported on a meeting in early August, the outcome of which seems that Rastrick's figures of cost were unacceptable. Because of this the canal company got in touch with the Staffordshire and Worcestershire Canal Company, who instructed Rastrick to look at the Leominster plans and see if 'such a railway as the Brecon and Hay railroad cannot be made at the expense of £1,200 a mile exclusive of land'. The following March (1835) his recommendations were produced. The most costly scheme would cost £69,714, the cheapest £44,394, exclusive of actually converting the canal into a tramroad, which he strongly recommended should be done. Apart from several adjourned meetings in September 1835, however, no further action or reference seems to have been recorded about tramroad schemes.

Rather surprisingly, in 1837 the Herefordshire and Gloucestershire Canal was reported to be considering a connection to the Leominster Canal from its proposed Ledbury to Hereford extension, which included the possibility of making the River Lugg navigable as far north as Leominster. In 1838, the Leominster company was making overtures to the Hereford and Gloucester, offering to help with the River Lugg scheme, but it was another scheme which came to nought, for whilst the H&G company

FROM CANAL TO RAILWAY

wished to keep the idea in mind for future development, it was not willing to release any funds for such a speculative project.

By now railways were extending over Britain, following the successful opening of the Liverpool and Manchester Railway in 1830 and the Stockton and Darlington five years earlier. The future of the Leominster Canal was looking very bleak indeed. In June 1838 the Great Western Railway began its westward expansion with the opening of the Maidenhead section. In the same year, the Midlands were connected by rail to London with the opening of the London and Birmingham Railway. The canal age was rapidly passing and the railway age was about to begin.

Wharf House at Marlbrook, near Mamble, headquarters of the Kington–Leominster–Stourport Canal. This was the furthest point east that the canal was completed on the route to Stourport, for, following the collapse of nearby Southnett Tunnel in 1795, reputedly burying some navvies and their equipment, all construction ceased. From the opening of the canal in 1794, a tramway had been laid to convey coal from the Mamble pits to Marlbrook wharf but was taken up following the canal's demise in 1858. *Kidderminster Library*

This view of Teme Street, Tenbury, shows a familiar scene for many years on cattle fair days, when the animals were walked from the station to be sold off at the cattle market in Tenbury. On occasions when 'foot and mouth' regulations were in force, cattle sales would be held in a field by the 'Rose & Crown' near the station. *Collection Brian Standish*

CHAPTER TWO
THE RAILWAY AGE DAWNS
(THE SHREWSBURY & HEREFORD RAILWAY)

AS early as January 1825 the idea of a railroad linking the Teme valley with the Severn at Worcester had been raised. In a terse paragraph in the *Hereford Journal* under the heading 'Ludlow and Severn Railway', it was announced that a railroad was contemplated from Ludlow to the Severn, and that a petition had been presented to the bailiffs of Ludlow to carry the measures into effect. Mr C. Buck had been appointed to survey the best route and a subscription had been started. A further meeting was promised on the 10th February but what the outcome was, or what form the railway would take, is not known, for there appears to be no further record. Speculation suggests it might have been a horse-drawn tramroad, similar to, or to connect with, the alternative Leominster Canal Schemes.

In 1836 there appeared to be some prospect of Tenbury being on a main line of communication between London and Dublin. A meeting in Caernarvon took place in January to consider the best railway route from London to Dublin, to further the improvement of the Irish Mail. The frequent comings and goings across the Irish Sea were tiresome for travellers, especially the politicians, and were not helped by the lengthy coach journey to and from Chester, which at the time was the main port for Ireland. Frequent silting up of the River Dee made navigation increasingly difficult and time-consuming, and by 1826, following the opening of Telford's Holyhead road, Chester's importance as a port gradually fell away, most of the Irish traffic going through the small port of Holyhead on the Isle of Anglesey.

Following the meeting of 1836, three surveys were made and reported to the government in 1837. Of the three schemes proposed, one was for a line surveyed by Brunel for the GWR and intended to be an extension of the company's broad gauge (7ft) line from Didcot through Oxford, Evesham, Worcester, up the Teme Valley to Tenbury, then via Ludlow, Newtown, Dinas Mawddwy, Dolgelly, Barmouth and Portmadoc to a small village called Porth Dynlleyn (close to Nevin on the north-west coast of Caernarvonshire) where a new harbour would be built. Another scheme (for which Charles Vignoles was responsible) was to reach the same place by a railway from the Grand Junction at Wolverhampton via Ironbridge, Shrewsbury and through the Welsh mountains via Bala and Dolgelly. Robert Stephenson, however, proposed a line from the Chester & Crewe Railway following Telford's coast road to Holyhead, and the enlargement of the small harbour there.

In view of the importance of the subject, the Government appointed a Commission of three, with two naval advisers, to report on the merits of the various projects. Brunel's line 'promised to beat all others as to speed' and was favourably regarded by the Commissioners. Vignoles' line was criticised for its steep gradients and heavy earthworks, but both were rejected on the advice of the naval experts, whose advice was that a harbour at Porth Dynlleyn was liable to silt up due to the currents prevailing on the coast at that point. Robert Stephenson's scheme was found to be the most favourable, and eventually came to fruition after the Chester & Holyhead Railway was given its Act in 1844. Both the Grand Junction and London & Birmingham Railways contributed to the scheme; the two companies were to amalgamate with others in 1846 to form the London & North Western, under which Holyhead became the principal port for Ireland that we know today.

During the 'Railway Mania' of 1844/6 many grand schemes were brought before the public, no less than thirty-six being deposited at the Shirehall, Worcester, in 1845. Three such schemes were the 'Hereford, Leominster, Ludlow & Birmingham Railway' (later called 'Hereford & Kidderminster'), the 'Worcester & Cardiff Junction Railway' and the 'Welsh Midland Railway'. They were in fact one and the same basic proposal, in that they sought to promote through lines from the South Wales coalfields to the industrial Midlands, and to varying degrees were all sponsored by the Midland Railway and its allies.

Because of duplication, both the Worcester & Cardiff and the Hereford & Kidderminster schemes quickly disappeared, the latter being amalgamated with the Welsh Midland in April 1845. Strong support for the proposals had been expressed at meetings in several towns, including Brecon, Hereford, Leominster, Ludlow and Bewdley. At a meeting held in Bewdley Guildhall on 27th August 1845, local landowners met a deputation from the London & Birmingham, Midland, Welsh Midland and Trent Railways who outlined the proposals for a line from South Wales through Hereford and Worcester (to make connection with the Birmingham & Gloucester line) and branches from Leominster to Woofferton, Tenbury, Bewdley and Kidderminster. At Kidderminster there would have been a connection with the proposed Birmingham, Wolverhampton & Stour Valley line, the Birmingham & Kidderminster Railway being a branch of the latter, and thence to the Trent Valley, Midland and Grand Junction lines. At the end of a highly informative and enthusiastic meeting, Mr W. Lacon Childe of Cleobury Mortimer proposed that 'this railway will be conducive to the best interest of the town and neighbourhood of Bewdley, and this meeting will afford its most strenuous support for the extension from Leominster to Kidderminster'. A further meeting took place, this time at Kidderminster, on 3rd September 1845, where it was noted that the engineers of the Welsh Midland were surveying the route from Leominster to Kidderminster.

Earlier in the year a provisional committee, principally made up of promoters of the Shrewsbury & Chester line, had met to discuss plans to extend southwards to Hereford

9

to connect up there with several projected routes. This line, the Shrewsbury & Hereford, would run through Church Stretton gap to Ludlow and Woofferton from where a proposed branch (the Woofferton branch) would link up to the Welsh Midland eastward towards Tenbury. Continuing south of Woofferton, it would have then formed a rival line to the latter, running parallel to it as far as Hereford.

Seeing all this railway activity surrounding them, the proprietors of the Leominster Canal let it be known that they wished to dispose of what was now, to them, a liability. What traffic there was on the canal had dwindled to only a few boats carrying mainly pit props, bricks and timber, the coal supply from the Mamble pits having fallen away. Navigation had become increasingly difficult because of weeds and constant leaks in the aqueducts, which required considerable attention. Enquiries were made by both the Shrewsbury & Hereford and Welsh Midland companies with a view to purchase, and a special meeting of the canal company was called at the Royal Oak, Leominster, in November 1845 to consider the sale. The meeting, under the chairmanship of Sir Edward Blount, expressed the view that £40,000 might be realised; however, a figure of £20,000 was fixed as the price for forming part of the Welsh Midland Railway. When it became clear, in early 1846, that terms had not been agreed with the Welsh Midland, the Shrewsbury & Hereford again pursued the canal company, eventually agreeing terms and a purchase price of £12,000, this being confirmed by the canal proprietors on 15th July 1846.

The Shrewsbury & Hereford Railway was sanctioned on 3rd August 1846 (the same day as the Newport Abergavenny & Hereford Railway), and in the same session it joined forces with the Oxford, Worcester & Wolverhampton Railway, the Great Western and Waterford, Wexford and Dublin railway companies in promoting a Bill for a broad gauge route to Ireland from Worcester via a railway, (to include the 'Worcester, Tenbury and Ludlow') to Port Dynlleyn. This was at the height of the broad gauge 'war' when the Great Western was trying to spread its seven foot gauge as far north as it could go, and it seized the opportunity to revive the proposed line of 1837. The Broad Gauge Commission issued its report and, in brief, recommended that 'although admitting the superior qualities of the broad gauge for speed and heavy hauling,' they were generally in favour of the narrow gauge (4ft 8½in) as best suited for the general traffic of the country. The Government was divided over the report and although not adopted in its entirety, the Commons passed a resolution in favour of the general enforcement of the narrow gauge in future, much to the Great Western's annoyance. In consequence the proposed broad gauge line was withdrawn, thus depriving Tenbury of the chance to be on a main line, a broad gauge one at that.

The following year, on the 23rd February 1847, the Shrewsbury & Hereford Railway shareholders met to confirm the terms of purchase of the Leominster Canal. The chairman outlined the value of the canal to the railway through its intended use as a site for the track bed and the value of the land for possible exchange purposes, though he mentioned also that there might be some difficulty in acquiring the canal because of concern in Parliament over disputes concerning land of which the canal company had been in possession for over fifty years. This was probably a direct reference to the 1826 Leominster Canal Act which required that in the case of direct sale of the canal, the original landowners would have first choice of purchase followed by present owners of adjoining lands.

Power to sell the canal to the railway was given by the Leominster Canal Sale Act (10 and 11 Vic. Cap. CCLXVI) of 22nd July 1847 in which it was stated '. . . was of little use for the purposes which it was intended and by the construction of the said railway its use would be further diminished . . .'. Section 14 of the Act gave the railway company powers to close the canal between Leominster and Woofferton wharf on giving one month's notice.

By the end of 1847 the railway boom of 1844/6 had ended following the collapse of the railway stock market, and many schemes were abandoned. The Welsh Midland project was among them and with it the expectations of the landowners in the Teme Valley area came to a sudden end. Work on the Shrewsbury & Hereford was well behind schedule due to the difficulty in getting shareholders to pay their calls, and thus a shortage of money to pay the contractors and the canal company, whose solicitors were pressing the railway company to carry out the agreement to purchase. Because of the financial situation, little construction work on the Shrewsbury & Hereford line was done until the end of 1850, when Thomas Brassey took a contract to construct the line. He also offered to work the railway at his own risk. This offer was accepted, and afterwards incorporated into a lease for eight years from 1st July 1854. The railway was eventually opened as a single line from Shrewsbury to Ludlow on 21st April 1852 and to through goods traffic on 30th July 1852.

In August 1852 the Shrewsbury & Hereford Railway engineer Henry Robertson was instructed to examine the state of the Leominster Canal eastwards from Woofferton with a view to using the bed for a possible extension to Tenbury, but the railway and canal companies were still locked in legal argument because of the railway company's failure to complete the purchase of the land, and the idea was shelved. As this legal battle had been raging since 1847, the Shrewsbury & Hereford had also dropped the idea of using the canal towards Leominster for its track bed, merely following it south of Woofferton and crossing it twice on bridges.

The Shrewbury & Hereford was finally opened throughout to Hereford on 6th December 1853, and from that date Tenbury was only 5½ road miles from a railway station at Woofferton. Shortly after the station opened, a horse coach conveyance was being advertised from the Royal Oak, Tenbury, to meet principal trains there.

CHAPTER THREE
THE SETTING UP OF THE TENBURY RAILWAY
AND THE INFLUENCE OF WILLIAM NORRIS

THAT a railway ever came to Tenbury was due almost entirely to the vision and energy of one man, Mr William Norris who, born in 1821, was the youngest son of the Rev. Thomas Norris, then Rector of Harby in Leicestershire. After being educated at Grantham School, William Norris studied law and, on becoming a qualified solicitor in 1842, joined the firm of Messrs Sewell, Escourt and Norris of Newport, Isle of Wight. In 1850, at the age of twenty-nine, he moved to Tenbury to take over the practice of Mr William Adams.

Why he came to Tenbury was revealed some years later in a speech he gave at a public dinner at The Swan in Tenbury, held to honour his services to the town. He recalled how a lady friend concerned about his welfare and success had expressed surprise that he'd chosen such a decaying place as Tenbury. His explanation was, that when he had looked around Tenbury he'd found that there existed a desire for improvement, that the town possessed the best of mineral waters, and the streets were properly paved and cleansed. All that was wanted to keep pace with other towns was a railway and that he personally was prepared to use all his efforts to get one — and he was to do just that!

Even before the opening of the Shrewsbury & Hereford Railway and Woofferton Station in December 1853, William Norris had been stirred into action by the close proximity of Tenbury to the activity going on with the construction works of that line. He had approached Mr William Davis of Dean Park, Burford, to whom he put forward his ideas for a branch line to Tenbury from the S&H. Mr Davis, a director of the Shrewsbury and Hereford Railway, was most enthusiastic about Norris's proposals and he advised him to make an attempt to carry them out, whilst Davis himself sounded out likely local influential support.

A near neighbour to Mr Davis was Captain Rushout of Burford House who was at that time not only MP for East Worcestershire, but also Chairman of the Oxford, Worcester & Wolverhampton Railway. Who better to interest in Norris's scheme? Later (having succeeded to the title of Lord Northwick) Captain Rushout was also to exert an important influence upon the coming of the railway to the Teme Valley.

By late 1853 William Norris had aroused sufficient interest for subscriptions to be raised for two surveys. One was for a line from Worcester to Tenbury, the link favoured at first by Norris and which he described as 'the first wedge'. The other, a cheaper project, was a line from Woofferton to Tenbury and then to Kidderminster via Cleobury Mortimer and Bewdley. A meeting was arranged at the Swan Hotel in Tenbury in April 1854 to discuss matters concerning these two possibilities. Although some £10 shares were pledged for the Worcester line, the scheme most favoured was to join Tenbury to the Shrewsbury & Hereford Railway at Woofferton, and in the other direction to join with the Oxford, Worcester & Wolverhampton Railway at Kidderminster, thus providing a through link between Tenbury and Birmingham and the Black Country. David Wylie, assistant engineer to the Shrewsbury & Hereford Railway, had provided the survey, and his plan for the junction at Woofferton was adopted. William Norris could now see his dream becoming a reality, but despite his own enthusiasm and the promised backing from most of the local gentry, the scheme was under-subscribed and therefore could not be started. Undaunted by this setback, he began his efforts at improving the commercial standing of Tenbury and stimulating its growth as part of the overall plan. To do this he would need to continue encouraging and persuading local businessmen that it would be to their benefit to have a railway in the town. Norris's next move therefore was to stimulate trade by setting up and becoming secretary of The Tenbury Corn Exchange and Public Buildings Company who were responsible for constructing the Corn Exchange in Teme Street and the Round Market opposite Norris's office in Market Square. In addition he formed The Tenbury Agricultural Society, also becoming secretary, in which office he was to remain until 1898.

Immediately following the opening of the Corn Exchange in April 1858, local papers were carrying reports of a proposed branch railway line to run from the Shrewbury & Hereford (S&H) main line at Woofferton to Tenbury. It was reported that surveys had been made and a provisional committee set up to investigate the possibilities. This committee, headed by the now-promoted Col. Rushout, was made up of various local landowners, some of whom were also directors of the Shrewsbury & Hereford Railway, including Sir Edward Blount, of Mawley Hall, near Cleobury Mortimer, owner of Mamble Colliery, and E. V. Wheeler of Kyrewood House near Tenbury. Later in the year (in October), a set of plans for the proposed railway was deposited at the Shirehall, Shrewsbury under the title 'Woofferton and Tenbury Railway' with William Norris named as secretary and David Wylie as engineer. The following month, Norris was a signatory to a notice giving intention to apply to Parliament for a Bill to incorporate and construct a railway, to be called 'The Tenbury Railway', 'Woofferton' being deleted from the wording of the original title.

By the end of 1858 events were beginning to move, for, following the publication of the Parliamentary application notice, a public meeting on the subject of the proposed railway was held on 14th December at the Corn Exchange in Tenbury. Col Rushout M.P. was chairman, and also noted present were E.V. Wheeler Esq., Rev T.E.M. Holland, Rev H. McLoughlin, Rev H. Brown, Rev D. Jones, Mr Field (representing the Shrewsbury & Hereford Railway) and several leading agriculturalists in the immediate district and 'a pretty good muster of inhabitants of the town'.

Col. Rushout was keen to get local farmers to become more enthusiastic about the proposed railway and therefore pointed out the advantages for them of an expanded market that the railway was sure to bring. Increased patronage of the Tenbury 'waters' would also bring with it, he said, better trade for the townspeople. To those in the audience lacking the confidence to invest in railways, since the market had become uncertain, Col Rushout had this to say: "The lines that are not paying are those that are quarrelling or continually engaged in law and those that are considered sucking or feeding lines, but the Tenbury is neither". He reminded the audience of his own involvement as a shareholder in four local railway companies which averaged 4½% payment for him — 'not a bad speculation'. He explained that enough shares in the proposed line had been taken to warrant them going to Parliament but that the total cost would be £30,000 and that a deposit of 8% would be required by 7th January 1859. After some further discussion, the chairman proposed, seconded by E.V. Wheeler Esq:

'That this meeting approves of the line of railway between Woofferton and Tenbury and also of the proceedings that have been adopted by the Solicitors, Messrs Loxdale and Peele of the S and H, and Mr William Norris for the formation of the Company and the carrying out of the undertaking and hereby authorise them to take such further proceedings as shall be necessary for that purpose. That in order to provide the deposit of 8% on the capital required by the rule of Parliament, the sum of £2 be paid before 7th January next on such share of £10 and the amount thereof to be paid to the undertaking at the Tenbury and Ludlow Bank.'

This proposal was carried unanimously.

Following the vote, Mr Field of the Shrewsbury & Hereford spoke recommending the line as a paying concern likely to realise 5½% for shareholders and hinted that if the ironmasters of Staffordshire would guarantee a tonnage on their goods, the line would soon be carried out to Kidderminster. Finally, a provisional committee was approved and appointed.

In the spring of 1859, the Tenbury Railway Bill was making its way through Parliament, but its smooth passage had been halted by an objection from a local landowner, Mr John Salwey of Richard's Castle near Woofferton. Mr Salwey's complaint was the loss of more land for railway construction, having already given up some for the route of the S&H. Furthermore, his water supply, he claimed, would be lost if that part of the Leominster Canal which ran through his land was drained for the formation of the track bed of the proposed line. He made an objection under clause 33 of the 1826 and 1847 Leominster Canal Sale Acts which required that should the canal be sold off for use other than as a canal, the present landowners should be offered first option to purchase the land. He was concerned that the S&H (now the owners since concluding the purchase and taking over the canal in March 1858) were denying him his legal right in offering the canal to the Tenbury Railway.

Consequently, a House of Commons Select Committee was convened to adjudicate on the various matters involved. Most of the inquisition was directed at the promoters, searching questions being asked of the witnesses, in particular the reasons for establishing the Tenbury Railway first rather than pressing for the eastward extension via Bewdley at the same time, thereby making it one undertaking.

By this time, Col Rushout had succeeded to the title of the 3rd Baron Northwick (on the death of his uncle in January 1859) and almost his first appearance under his new title was to attend the Parliamentary Select Committee to give evidence in support of the Tenbury Railway Bill. In reply to the question concerning the objectives of supporters of the scheme. Lord Northwick stated his desire was to get the line to Bewdley and suggested that the line to Tenbury was only a stepping stone in this plan. A prospectus for the Bewdley extension had been issued by this time, with Lord Northwick included amongst the provisional directors. Asked if he considered it true that the line between Woofferton and Tenbury would not be of great public value unless it was extended beyond Tenbury, he replied that it was his own opinion that it would not. Nor did he consider Tenbury of enough importance to support a railway on its own. However, he considered that the extension would be promoted if the Bill for the small line under consideration was carried.

Mr Joshua Peele, Solicitor for the S&H, was asked in his turn as witness if one Act of Parliament and one set of promoters would have effected the line as far as Bewdley. In his answer, he replied that the original proposal was that the line should be built by the S&H and join either the Severn Valley or Oxford, Worcester & Wolverhampton line but that money would not allow. He was then asked if there were two parties in opposition and rivalry. 'No, nothing of the sort' was his reply. 'The S&H', he continued, 'were not the original promoters of the Tenbury Railway but they, as owners of the canal in a district where landowners wanted a railway, said they would be willing to give assistance to it and allow the canal to be used if the Tenbury Railway Co thought it beneficial'.

The S&H had already closed the Leominster–Woofferton section of the canal the previous June and the remaining part of the canal at this time was described in evidence as being full of weeds, the locks and aqueducts decayed and leaking in many places. Only one boat a week passed to Tenbury from Sir Edward Blount's coal mine at Mamble, with no traffic beyond. Only sunken hulks and a few fishermen to be seen. In fact Mr Wylie, Engineer, described it as a 'mere ditch, undeserving of the name canal'.

Mr Salwey's complaint failed to sway the committee. He had already received some payment (though derisory) when the canal was sold to the S&H and he would be paid a fair price even though his land was of poor quality. It was pointed out that some compromise could have been possible like that with the trustees of Sir Joseph Bailey, who had exchanged the part of the canal that passed through Sir Joseph's park at Easton Court for a small stretch of land through which the railway could deviate, at which both parties were content.

Finally, the Bill went through, the Tenbury Railway Act receiving the Royal Assent on 21st July 1859.

The Act 22 and 23 Vic Cap XVI incorporated the company under the title 'The Tenbury Railway Co' with powers to construct a railway from a junction with the S&H at Woofferton to a point near the Rose and Crown public house at Burford in Shropshire. Capital was to be £30,000, of which the S&H might subscribe up to £5,000. The chairman was named as Lord Northwick, Burford House, Tenbury and the company secretary was William Norris.

Section 35 of the Act stipulated that the S&H should sell parts of the Leominster Canal to the Tenbury Railway including the section beyond Tenbury to Southnett Wharf, which was as far as the canal had been constructed. Under the direction of David Wylie, the Woofferton–Tenbury section of the canal was drained of water that autumn, enabling those eminent contractors of the day, Brassey and Field, to prepare the land for construction. By March 1860 such progress had been made that Miss Rushout, sister of Lord Northwick, was invited to perform the ceremony of cutting the first sod at a small informal gathering.

In August 1860 the engineer reported 'that the whole line was in the possession of the contractors and progress was well in hand at certain points. The earthworks for the Teme Bridge near Little Hereford were in a forward state, the abutments should be complete by the winter'. Heavy rain was causing some problems as well as the difficulty in finding labourers, many navvies at the time already being fully employed in building the Severn Valley line. However, it was clear that every effort was being made to complete the line as quickly as possible.

In September, plans were drawn up for a small brick station at Easton Court. As an eastward extension beyond the terminus had now become a probability after the passing of The Tenbury and Bewdley Railway Act in July 1860, it was decided, for the present, to construct a temporary wooden station building at Tenbury but to have a brick goods shed similar to the one at Woofferton. Even while the construction of the Tenbury Railway was being carried out, William Norris was still energetically trying to raise the status of Tenbury, in particular its importance as a spa. For the previous two or three years the mineral waters had not been available to the general public, the Bath House having been closed. This, he considered, was a great loss, not only to the inhabitants of the town but also to the invalids that had previously benefited from using the waters. Lengthy negotiations had resulted in securing the lease of land for a site to erect a new bath house and now he arranged a public meeting to discuss various proposals.

At the public meeting in the Board Room at Tenbury on 1st December 1860, outline proposals were presented for the formation of a new company to be called 'The Tenbury Wells Improvement Company Limited'. The company, headed by Lord Northwick and fifteen directors with Mr Norris as secretary, was to be formed for 'the establishment and the sinking of new wells for the purpose of affording to the public the use of the mineral waters discovered at Tenbury'. With this in view, the company had taken a lease for nine hundred and ninety-nine years on 1½ acres of land and now proposed to erect public baths surrounded by pleasure gardens.

The chairman, E.V. Wheeler, went to great lengths to persuade the meeting of the validity of the venture, stating 'The railway much needs the revenue the wells will bring if sunk'. It was explained that analysis of the mineral waters, blue in tincture, drawn up by Doctor Daubeny (Professor of Chemistry at Oxford) showed more chloride of sodium was present in a pint of Tenbury water, than in any other known water in Europe. Spas such as Harrogate, Cheltenham, Leamington, and even Hamburg in Germany, could not compare with Tenbury water. Some medical men recommended that taken internally it would cure all kinds of skin diseases, rheumatics, gout, neuralgia and other such maladies. It was further claimed that by advertising the River Teme, famous for its trout and grayling fishing, together with the wells, Tenbury could equal if not surpass other spa towns like Cheltenham and Harrogate. For some time there had been a guide book in circulation entitled *Spas of England* by Dr Granville in which he wrote 'no place is more calculated to be a second Leamington than this Tenbury'. The general enthusiasm expressed at the meeting reflected that statement, and a resolution was passed to issue shares, fixing the capital at £1,800 in £10 shares. At the end of December a provisional committee met to discuss tenders for sinking the first well, that for £189 being accepted from Mr Parton (a resident of Tenbury).

In the meantime, a severe winter was making life difficult for the workforce trying to make the railway ready for a promised opening in June 1861. But the Tenbury Railway was not the only sufferer as exceptionally heavy frosts were causing delays to several other railway construction programmes in the district. At the general half-yearly meeting of the Tenbury Railway on 27th March 1861, George Pardoe of Nash Court was in the chair, and in apologising for the slow progress he stated the hopes of Mr Wylie that an opening could take place on 1st July next. Mr Wylie himself was able to report that the masonry of the Teme Bridge was finished and ready to receive girders. The earthworks were all done, but ballast was having to be brought from 'one end only' (Woofferton) so was in short supply and slowing progress. Easton Court station was nearly complete; the offices there were ready for use as were ladies waiting rooms at Tenbury.

An important announcement followed when Mr Norris told the meeting that 'subject to the approval of the shareholders, a contract with the S&H would be agreed for working and maintaining the Tenbury Railway for seven years from the time of opening'. Under this contract the S&H would pay the Tenbury Railway out of receipts £500 per annum plus 40% of the balance. Finally, another piece of good news, as far as the future of the Tenbury Railway was concerned, was the understanding that the construction of the Tenbury and Bewdley Railway would proceed 'forthwith' even though there were still problems with the S&H Railway over the canal purchase.

Delays in the construction of the Tenbury Railway continued, partly as a result of the bad weather, and disappointly the opening day was put back twice. However, in July 1861, Mr Bailey was appointed station master for Easton Court in readiness for the railway to open to general traffic, set for Thursday 1st August 1861.

Colonel Yolland of the Board of Trade was able to carry out an inspection of the Tenbury Railway on 27th July 1861 and recommended opening on condition that a double junction was made at Woofferton as only the 'Eastern' line of rails was connected at the time. He also required that 'junction signals' be provided; at the time of his inspection there was only a distant signal to act as a stop indication.

The opening day, when it finally arrived, was a much quieter event than the local public had anticipated and there was a feeling of disappointment reported amongst the many visitors who had come to the town to witness the event and join in a public breakfast. No doubt much of the disappointment would have been caused by the last minute cancellation of this treat, although the public were told that it would be held at a later date when the line opened throughout to Bewdley. It was reported that at Woofferton someone had decorated the station with a few evergreens in a half-hearted fashion, but the open hostility to the railway of the horse-cab drivers, fearing the new competition at Tenbury, did nothing to create a festive air at the new station. To add to the day's woes, it was discovered that a railwayman had stolen some tickets from Tenbury Booking Office (for which crime he was later sentenced to one month's hard labour). However, there was a lighter side when a startled horse galloped off with an empty cab towards Tenbury, its driver on foot in hot pursuit, to onlookers' amusement. On the previous day, Lord Northwick, as was his habit of caring for the navvies, treated one hundred and fifty men to a 'capital dinner' prepared by Mr and Mrs Jones of the Rose and Crown Inn close by the station.

The only notification by the new Railway of the opening was the publication of the timetable in a Tenbury paper by George Findlay, Shrewsbury and Hereford Railway Traffic Manager, Shrewsbury. It read:

Class	1, 2, P	1, 2	1, 2	1, 2	1, 2, P
Woofferton dep	8.40 am	10.40am	12.00am	3.50pm	6.00pm
Easton Court	8.53	10.53	12.13	4.3	6.13
Tenbury arr.	9.5am	11.5am	12.25pm	4.15pm	6.25pm
Tenbury dep.	7.0am	10.0am	11.25am	3.00pm	5.30pm
Easton Court	7.10	10.10	11.35	3.10	5.40
Woofferton arr.	7.20am	10.20am	11.45am	3.20pm	5.50pm

Thomas Brassey was still working the Shrewsbury and Hereford with his own locos and rolling stock, and under the terms of the Tenbury lease he became responsible also for the Tenbury line. The single locomotive that Brassey supplied was kept overnight at the temporary wooden station at Tenbury, on the site that was later to become the goods yard (on the town side of the later station).

The result of all the effort was that William Norris had finally achieved his foremost ambition of seeing Tenbury connected to the nation's railway system, and plans for the extension to Bewdley were under extensive discussion.

TENBURY RAILWAY GRADIENTS

From	To	Grade	Between
0m 0c	0m 30c	150 F	Woofferton and Easton Court
0m 30c	0m 40c	143 R	Woofferton and Easton Court
0m 40c	0m 60c	Level	Woofferton and Easton Court
0m 60c	1m 10c	300 F	Woofferton and Easton Court
1m 10c	1m 50c	132 F	Woofferton and Easton Court
1m 50c	1m 60c	800 F	Woofferton and Easton Court
1m 60c	1m 70c	Level	Woofferton and Easton Court
1m 70c	2m 00c	257 F	Woofferton and Easton Court
2m 00c	2m 20c	3143 R	Woofferton and Easton Court
2m 20c	2m 30c	2063 F	Woofferton and Easton Court
2m 30c	2m 50c	384 F	Woofferton and Easton Court
2m 50c	3m 10c	384 F	Eastern Court & Tenbury
3m 10c	3m 40c	113 R	Eastern Court & Tenbury
3m 40c	3m 60c	648 F	Eastern Court & Tenbury
3m 60c	4m 00c	1229 R	Eastern Court & Tenbury
4m 00c	4m 40c	3985 F	Eastern Court & Tenbury
4m 40c	4m 60c	369 R	Eastern Court & Tenbury
4m 60c	5m 00c	347 F	Eastern Court & Tenbury
5m 00c	5m 10c	200 R	Tenbury and Junction with GWR

CHAPTER FOUR
THE TENBURY AND BEWDLEY RAILWAY

ALTHOUGH the opening of the Tenbury Railway had turned out to be a muted affair, there was no lack of enthusiasm for an extension of the line eastwards along the valley of the River Rea through the Wyre Forest and across the River Severn to Bewdley.

Much earlier, in November 1853, several local people had paid £10 each to have a route surveyed. At the time nothing developed from this initial investigation, mainly due to financial difficulties, but by the end of 1858 the idea had been resurrected. This time it was a scheme being promoted for a branch of the Severn Valley Railway from Bewdley to Tenbury with favourable opinions from the directors of both the SVR and OWWR. Between September 1858 and February 1859 trial sections were made with the consent of the landowners in order that the scheme should proceed. At the same time Mr G.A. Porter, the promoter's Parliamentary Solicitor and agent, had attended various meetings to discuss the survey and prospectus which had been jointly issued by the Severn Valley Railway engineer, John Fowler, and a Mr Hargreaves for their own line from Tenbury to Kidderminster. Following Porter's meeting with the directors of both the Severn Valley Railway and Oxford, Worcester & Wolverhampton Railway in February, it transpired that Fowler and Hargreaves had not consulted either board. Both boards intimated that they would not support Fowler's line or act with him, although a prospectus had been issued by Bewdley solicitors Marcy and Whitcombe, acting on behalf of Fowler and Hargreaves.

Porter next wrote to William Norris proposing discussions as to the best means of promoting a railway from Tenbury to the Severn Valley line near Bewdley. Various meetings involving A.C. Sheriff (SVR), Edward Wilson (OWW), Lord Northwick and a provisional committee were held throughout the spring of 1859 whilst Norris travelled far and wide around the district encouraging the population to take up shares and circulate letters to other likely supporters, including the solicitor to the S&H, Mr. J. Peele, hoping to induce that company's assistance.

One immediate positive response came from Tenbury Railway director Sir Joseph Bailey, who offered through his trustees to provide by his business connections, iron rails in exchange for shares to their value.

By the autumn of 1859, Norris had acquired yet another secretaryship, being empowered to take on that role at the first meeting of a provisional committee set up to promote the Tenbury, Bewdley, Kidderminster & Worcester Junction Railway (as it was then titled). At the meeting the nominated engineer, Mr Wylie, was asked to meet the contractors Brassey and Field to find how many shares they would be willing to take out in part payment for the construction.

In November 1859, the provisional committee met in London and directors of the OWWR, S&HR and SVR attended to discuss the cost of the line. The calculations arrived at a sum total of £110,000 including the cost of station construction and land purchase. £22,000 was noted as the correct shortfall in capital which would need to be reduced by an additional £10,000 to £15,000, in order to justify proceeding with a Parliamentary Bill. By December it was clear that further promises of local subscriptions would be sufficient to cover this amount, so the Provisional Committee, meeting in Worcester, authorised the company's solicitors to proceed with a Bill. This was on the understanding that a contractor be found who would take at least £30,000 in shares and be prepared to offset the value of locally provided materials, such as the supply of iron rails already agreed with Sir Joseph Bailey, and timber for sleepers from the estates of local landowners along the route. At the same meeting it was resolved that security should be pledged to the Ludlow and Tenbury Bank both from individual directors and from Messrs Brassey and Field, although at this stage nothing official had been concluded with the contractors.

In February 1860 the last of the Provisional Committee meetings was chaired by Sir Edward Blount, who was still keen to improve transport from his coalmine holdings at Mamble. Part of the meeting was taken up with a discussion involving Sir Edward's near neighbour Charles Wicksted of Shakenhurst House, Neen Sollars, who had written a letter at the same time as the surveyor's plans were deposited at the Shirehall, Shrewsbury, in October 1859. In it he suggested a deviation of the line towards Cleobury Mortimer, away from his own estate. The Provisional Committee felt unable to comply with this request on account of the tunnelling that would be necessary through the high ground around Cleobury Mortimer. This response prompted Wicksted's agent to write offering Wicksted's agreement to accept payment for his land in shares on condition that a station be sited at Shakenhurst with an obligation for all trains to stop. Wicksted's bargaining in this manner was not an isolated case for in another letter, Mr Pearson of Stourbridge (agent for Beriah Botfield of Clee Hill Works) stated that he would be willing to take out shares if a tramway from Clee Hill to Tenbury was formed as part of the T&B Scheme. The reply indicated that a connection had already been discussed but that only if he and Mr Botfield could carry it out would it be possible financially. As far as the provision of a station on Shakenhurst estate was concerned, the Provisional Committee came up with a proposal for a siding and to stop one train each way per day providing Wicksted paid all expenses for the station plus the wages of the signalman (who would nevertheless remain under company control). If an express train was stopped, it should only be to pick up first class passengers, their servants and luggage.

The Wyre Forest section of the planned route east of Cleobury Mortimer was to pass through very different countryside compared to the Rea Valley, not least in terms of ownership. The Wyre Forest was largely in the hands of the Crown's Woods and Forests Office, forerunners of the Forestry Commission of later years. It was arranged by the directors that a deputation consisting of Sir Moreton Peto, Mr Knight and Mr Pakington meet Woods and Forests officers to arrange for the purchase of the Crown lands and that Lord Ward, Earl of Dudley, a private Wyre Forest landowner, also involved, should be met for the same purpose.

Two obstacles were foremost in the minds of the T&B directors and subscribers alike in the early months of 1860. Firstly, no satisfactory arrangement had yet been entered into with Brassey and Field who were due to pay £3,400 towards the Parliamentary deposit, and secondly, a rumour was circulating that the S&HR were to oppose the T&B's Bill in Parliament. Norris dealt with the first problem by arranging with the Tenbury and Ludlow Bank to advance the whole £9,600 Parliamentary deposit. The second was left to Mr Davies when he travelled from Dean Park, Burford, in February 1860 to the S&H half-yearly general meeting to get an answer to the question; was it true that the S&H were going to oppose the T&B Railway? The answer from the S&H chairman, W. Ormsby-Gore, was that 'this is under discussion at Board level, the directors considering that the line would be injurious to the company and that the Board intended to keep their eyes open regarding any amalgamation'. Mr Davies was then able to explain that the line was 'entirely a local project, the promoters having not the slightest intention of rendering it injurious to any other undertaking'. It was not intended to be 'other than a mere branch line'. The possibility of a combination of railways antagonistic to and in competition with the S&H, so close to their neighbourhood, was naturally the main cause of concern for the S&H at the time. Perhaps the associations of some directors on the Provisional Committee, the representatives from the OWW in particular, had alerted the S&H to dangerous possibilities. At this time amalgamations, one of which later resulted in the formation of the West Midland Railway, were being freely discussed in railway management circles.

In the same month there was a half-yearly meeting of the OWW and in referring to money raised at the request of the Tenbury & Bewdley, the OWW meeting was told that the directors had 'agreed a subscription not exceeding £7,500 providing the SVR subscribed an equal amount and that the OWW should have the working of the railway at 5% and that no contribution should be paid until £40,000 of local subscriptions had been spent on the project so as to ensure a bona fide project supported by the local district'.

As events transpired, the S&H did indeed oppose the T&B Bill, in March 1860, but the opposition's evidence did not convince the Parliamentary Select Committee of its worth. This increased local optimism, and visible progress was being made on the Tenbury Railway — if only the cutting of its first sod.

In a further boost for the directors of the T&B, agreement was reached in March 1860 with both the Commissioner of Her Majesty's Woods and Forests and the Earl of Dudley concerning the land sought after by the T&B for constructing the line through the Wyre Forest. Part of the agreement on behalf of the Woods and Forests' Commissioner was that given notice of one month in writing, the Company 'will forthwith construct a siding from the Railway at such point on the Crown lands as shall be specified on such notice' with the siding intended for use primarily for the purposes of the Commissioners. The agreement continued with a statement that 'if at any time required that Company shall erect, maintain and keep permanently open a station for passengers, goods and merchandise at the point marked 'A' (see plan) or within a furlong of it'. Two trains per day would be required to stop at the station and the company should construct sidings and other works in connection with a station.

An Act 23 and 24 Vic Cap CXXVIII was given the Royal Assent on 3rd July 1860 under which the Tenbury & Bewdley Railway was given powers to construct a 'railway from a junction with the Tenbury Railway at the station there, to a junction with the Severn Valley Railway at Bewdley, both lines being under construction'. Capital was fixed at £120,000. The newly formed West Midland Railway would be allowed to subscribe up to £15,000 and the Tenbury Railway half that amount, though in the event the Tenbury Railway did not take up the option.

Clauses in the Act stipulated arrangements that were to be made by the company prior to the construction of a bridge over the River Severn at Dowles to join the Severn Valley Railway on the opposite bank. The bridge had to be approved and constructed to the satisfaction of the Admiralty Office. The company had at their expense to keep the bridge lit at night, both during and after construction, for safe passage of river traffic, and to defray the costs of any survey or examination by the Admiralty or in event of abandonment or decay of the work, fund the cost of the Admiralty's restoration of the site to its previous condition.

On 18th July 1860, at the first directors meeting following the establishment of the Tenbury & Bewdley Railway Company, previous appointments were made official. William Norris was now to be paid £50 a year for his work as secretary and to double in the role of company solicitor, jointly with Messrs Marcy and Whitcombe. Lord Northwick was installed as chairman with Sir Edward

Blount as vice chairman. The engineer appointed was David Wylie, although John Fowler's name had also appeared on the deposited survey plans. Wylie was also authorised to stake out the line as soon as the crops were cleared off the land. So with the contractors already in possession of the Tenbury Railway, the landscape between Woofferton and Bewdley was soon to undergo radical alterations, as the railway age dawned in this district.

The Tenbury & Bewdley held its first ordinary shareholders meeting on 16th August 1860 at the Corn Exchange in Tenbury. A resolution confirmed the appointment of the directors named in the Act, viz Lord Northwick (Chairman), Sir E Blount, Messrs E. Wheeler, W. Fenton, J. Parson, W. Davies. William Norris was to act as secretary, with J. Cranstoun (Ludlow Bank) and B. Home (a printer from Tenbury) appointed as auditors. These formalities completed, the next directors meeting in September 1860 started matters under way by authorising the company's solicitors to prepare a contract with Brassey and Field to construct the line at a cost (exclusive of land, stations and sidings but inclusive of accommodation and works) according to their offer at £100,000 of 18th September. Mr Wylie had his payment of £250 per mile ratified plus full remuneration for his services as engineer since the passing of the Act. The original supporters who subscribed £10 or more for the survey of 1853 were not overlooked and were offered equivalent shares to their subscriptions. Those who paid less than £10 were asked to make up the difference before they were included in the offer.

Meanwhile, negotiations were proceeding regarding the purchase of land for construction purposes and in particular the part of the Leominster Canal from Burford Bridge to Newnham. On 22nd October 1860, Norris wrote to Peele of the S&H offering, on behalf of the company, £20 per acre for canal and land, the value to be taken out as shares and with immediate possession. The same day he wrote to Sir Edward Blount informing him that the engineer was about to draw off the water from the canal in order to make the necessary surveys.

Lord Northwick had once confessed his ambition to be the driver of the first train between Woofferton and Bewdley but in reality it had become time to decide on the operation of the line once it was open. To this end a proposal from the recently established West Midland Railway was considered at a directors meeting in Worcester in November 1860. The offer was for the WMR to work the line and out of gross receipts, to pay the interest on the T&B's borrowed capital, then for the T&B to keep 40% of what remained. Whenever clear profits rose sufficiently to pay more than 5% to the shareholders of the T&B, the excess was to be shared equally between the two companies. The directors of the T&B expressed agreement though insisting that their company should have exemption from all payments on the WMR and also on the SVR. At the same time they checked again that they were going to receive the promised subscriptions from both these companies.

As the year 1860 closed, the eagerly anticipated surveys had been delayed because the canal had not been drained as planned. The reason was that the S&H were proving to be obstinate over the canal's sale price. Norris wrote to Peele again requesting him to authorise the engineer to start the draining procedure as only then could he survey the sections. When that request was refused, it was to prove the first of many irritating delays over the land purchase.

In spite of these frustrations the next year, 1861, began full of promise and the expectation was of speedy progress towards the completion of the T&B. The now familiar ceremony of cutting the first sod of the new railway line took place on 3rd January 1861, and newspapers as far away as Worcester carried reports.

The *Worcester Herald* wrote:

'The cutting of the first sod took place on Thursday at two o'clock in the presence of a few local dignitaries and a number of curious onlookers. Although the affair was not planned to be a festive occasion the day proved otherwise. The drum and fife band were marched from the Assembly Hall to the scene of the ceremony arriving shortly before the lady excavate of the day, Miss Rushout, sister of Lord Northwick. When she arrived she was received with cheers. Prayers were then read by the Rev J W Joyce. Sir Edward Blount then stepped forward with Miss Rushout and Mr Davies placed a wheelbarrow suitably inscribed in front of her and handed her an ornamental shovel to perform the duty.'

As the first sod was cut, the volunteers presented arms and the band struck up the National Anthem. When all the cheering had ceased, Sir Edward Blount made some flattering remarks about Miss Rushout, intimating that her pleasant disposition had made the day to be happy. He proposed a vote of thanks to her and all present. A parting volley was fired by the volunteers as they marched to Mr Davis's house at Dean Park, where they were regaled with plum cake, mince pies and hot, spiced cider, after which they took their leave with two volleys.

Ceremonial cutting of the first sod was certainly the vogue in Tenbury as another took place on 7th January. This time the 'lady excavate', to use the reporter's earlier description, was Mrs E V Wheeler of Kyrewood House and the occasion was the sinking of the new wells under direction of the Tenbury Wells Improvement Company. Hopes were expressed that the Tenbury & Bewdley Railway and the new Tenbury Well would open conjointly.

The next directors meeting of the T&B was scheduled for February when progress was found to have suffered another slight setback. Messrs Brassey and Field had intimated that they would need the addition of another £7,000 to the contract, making £107,000, before they would start working. The directors agreed to this request.

Not unnaturally, the public were expecting a start to be made on the work, and questions about the delay were raised at the first ordinary half-yearly meeting, held at the Corn Exchange, Tenbury, on 27th March. Mr Field was on hand to answer and explain. 'Construction could begin immediately from the Bewdley end where the work would be heaviest and also because the plant was there already, having been in use on the Severn Valley line. However this could not happen without at least another £10,000 more shares taken up out of the £50,000 to be paid to them in cash.' Sir Edward Blount explained to the gathering, from the chair, that a revised total had been asked for to construct the whole works exclusive of sidings. He recommended that this contract be entered into, likewise the contract with the WMR to run and maintain the T&B for ten years after its time of opening. An important reference was made at this meeting to a Bill before Parliament for the line between Bewdley and Kidderminster, 'which it was said, will bring Tenbury in direct contact with the manufacturing districts of the Midlands'. Closing the meeting, Sir Edward Blount urged those shareholders who had not paid their call to do so. Evidently (as with many local railway schemes) money promised was not as forthcoming as had been anticipated.

In May the directors travelled to London to meet Brassey at his office in Great George Street, Westminster, where they tried to thrash out the financial problems. The outcome was that they were still £15,000 short of the figure Brassey and Field required to enable a start to be made on construction. It was eventually determined to approach the GWR for a subscription of £10,000 instead of trying local supporters again. It was 15th July before it was possible to consult the GWR Board at Paddington. This was not a productive meeting for the T&B which was quite bluntly told that there was no money available to it from either the GWR or the WMR.

It was therefore resolved by the T&B that the only option was to try the shareholders again and make up the deficiency by creating preference shares. It would be necessary to obtain the consent of the shareholders for an application for an Act for that purpose. The disheartening news that the directors eventually had to give the shareholders at the September half-yearly meeting was that we 'regret the inability to increase the share list to the extent that was considered necessary before commencing construction of the line and have been unable to complete the contract that was authorised at the last half-yearly meeting.'

The contract had still not been signed by 8th October 1861 when, at a directors meeting, a letter from Brassey detailing more conditions was discussed. Before signing the contract, Brassey required that a stipulation be inserted that he should be paid extra for all occupation bridges beyond those included in Mr Wylie's estimate and any such further sums beyond the £7,000 estimated for the bridge over the River Severn. This time the directors demurred and would not agree. They asked Mr Wylie to submit his plans for the construction of the Severn Bridge to the Board of Admiralty for approval, and these differed substantially from the design included on the deposited plans, which showed a five-arch brick-built bridge.

Whilst all obstacles to the progress of the T&B were being encountered, the inhabitants of Tenbury were already gaining benefits from their recently opened railway. The line had not been in operation a month before a special train was run to take passengers to Hereford to see the famous Victorian entertainer, Blondin. This train left Tenbury at 9.30 am and departed on the return from Hereford at 8.30 pm. With fares of 3/- for 1st class and 1/6d in 'covered wagons', the special was reported filled to capacity. The *Shrewsbury Chronicle* told of another outing on 23rd August when at ten in the morning Tenbury children from the National School were lined up in twos. Then, carrying flags and banners, they marched to the station led by the drum and fife band of the Rifle Corps, to be accompanied by friends and teachers on the train to Ludlow. After visiting the annual fete held there, they returned to Tenbury in the evening and were treated to a party at Mill Meadow (Mr EV Wheeler's land) of tea and plum cake. The exciting day was rounded off with hymns and thanksgiving, before the tired company set off back home again.

It was not all one-way traffic, though, for Tenbury Flower show attracted visitors on a special train from Shrewsbury which stopped at all stations. The excursion included an omnibus trip to see the views from the Clee Hills for those who wished. Cheap returns (2/6d 1st Class, 1/3d 2nd) were also advertised for journeys from Tenbury to the Church Stretton Hills, as were through tickets to London (Euston) via Shrewsbury 13/4d third class. The traditional Worcester Hop Fair could now be conveniently visited using the train from Tenbury, leaving at 7.15 am and arriving at Worcester via Hereford at 9.55 am. The cost was nine shillings first class return and seven shillings second class return.

Receipts for the week previous to the half-yearly meeting of the TR in September 1861 were quoted as £26, of which £23 was from passengers. Shareholders were urged therefore to 'do all in their power to convey goods on the line in preference to other routes or other means'. At the same meeting, Lord Northwick took the opportunity to refer to the delay in the T&B affairs and to urge once again for shareholders to add to their share purchases.

Negotiations over the canal sale had now come to a head with a letter received from Peele on 28th November. In it he offered to refer the value of the canal and land to three parties, one of whom would be Mr Wylie, but only when the price was fixed would he allow the contractors possession of the canal. Norris, in frustration, immediately went to Shrewsbury to see Peele who, when confronted, promised to have the matter concerning possession arranged at once. Very soon afterwards the canal was drained of water, thereby ending twelve months of arguably needless delay.

THE TENBURY & BEWDLEY RAILWAY

The *Hereford Times* on 7th December 1861 reported delay of another nature for the stations at Tenbury and Easton Court were still not finished well over 4 months after the opening and 'what adds still more to the inconvenience of the public, the places are still in total darkness.' To counterbalance this criticism, the same newspaper reported that a start had at last been made to the Tenbury & Bewdley Railway. On 30th October at a directors meeting, Norris had been authorised to agree to Brassey's altered contract to which the Tenbury & Bewdley seal was affixed at long last. The difficulties with the contract having been overcome, work now commenced in a field belonging to Lord Northwick, a short distance from Tenbury. The *Hereford Times* report continued: 'In a few days it is expected that several gangs of navvies will set to work'. The line, 14 miles long was expected to be completed by 1st January 1864, i.e.within three years.

Wyre Hill was originally the main road from Bewdley to Wales, and to the towns and villages often referred to as 'those over the hill'. This view, looking in the other direction, features the Clent Hills and the Black Country beyond. *Collection Wendy Hinton*

This early photograph of Teme Street, Tenbury, gives an atmospheric view of what William Norris saw when he first came to Tenbury in 1850. The street does appear to have been 'clean and properly paved', but judging by the deserted air, the look of some of the buildings, and shuttered-up shop window fronts, there was, as he said, 'want of improvement to the town'.

Ctsy. T. Ratcliffe

CHAPTER FIVE
THE CONSTRUCTION OF THE TENBURY AND BEWDLEY LINE

IN the spring of 1862, David Wylie wrote a letter in which he took the liberty, as he put it, to call the attention of the Tenbury & Bewdley's directors to an important subject before it became too late. The LNWR were about to lease the Shrewsbury & Hereford route whilst, at the same time, the West Midland Railway was taking an active role in promoting a line connecting Leominster with Worcester via Bromyard. Wylie wrote that the LNWR, as a result of their new role on the S&HR, could theoretically stop and block all T&B traffic at Tenbury, thereby cutting off an important source of income. He suggested that the directors of the Tenbury Company should inform the S&H that they considered themselves to have the power to grant running powers to either the GWR or the WMR who would thereby still be able to collect traffic at Woofferton and Ludlow. As well as disputing the need for the WMR's Worcester–Leominster line, he considered that the WMR should be called on to complete the extension from Bewdley to Kidderminster by the time the T&B was ready for the opening and, if the WRM proved unwilling to do this, some other railway alliance should be sought by the T&B.

In the meantime, consideration of land deals was occupying the Board. James Bourne, Valuation Officer of Mawley Town Farm, Cleobury Mortimer, was engaged in discussions and negotiations with landowners on either side of the River Severn in the vicinity of the proposed Dowles Bridge and also with the agent representing W. Lacon-Childe of Kinlet Hall, owner of Hungry Hill and Nailing Coppices in the parish of Cleobury Mortimer as well as Alton Woods, Rock (at which site Mr Lacon-Childe had requested a siding be put in as part of the land deal, though this was subsequently not agreed to). Most of the line at this time had either been staked out or fenced where land was acquired and claims for compensation were received for such items as the extra expense of a farmer who had to haul hay a long distance around a road obstructed by construction work, and for straying animals which damaged hop poles and crops (beans, peas, barley and wheat), all as a result of alleged poor fencing by the contractors. One person, amongst many, who received compensation from the Tenbury & Bewdley Railway was George Smith (builder of Tenbury's Bath House) whose brick yards alongside the old Canal Wharf at Burford were taken by the T&B, who then proceeded to excavate the land to make bricks for their own use, dumping the waste in making the railway embankment at 2m 8ch. George Minton, valuer, of The Vine, Tenbury, dealt with this and other land valuation matters in the Burford district.

A year passed after the cutting of the first sod with no construction started, but at the half-yearly meeting of the Tenbury & Bewdley Railway on 26th March 1862, Wylie stated that Brassey and Field had begun work on their contract at several places on the line between Tenbury and Mawley Hall, near Cleobury Mortimer. In addition, the Admiralty had given consent for the construction of the bridge that would enable the railway to cross over the River Severn in order to reach Bewdley. Wylie also requested as a personal favour that John Fowler, the engineer on the Severn Valley Railway, be appointed joint engineer of the T&BR. It was agreed to write to Mr Fowler but to defer making a decision, and to have further discussion about this matter.

At last quicker progress could be expected, the engineering presenting no difficulty as the level bed of the drained Leominster Canal would be used for three miles from Tenbury to Newnham Bridge. From Newnham Bridge to Neen Sollars, and beyond towards Cleobury Mortimer, the valley of the River Rea also provided relatively easy terrain for the contractors and their men. However, when the route reached the neighbourhood of Cleobury Mortimer it was underlain by the rocks of the Wyre Forest coalfield and the digging became more difficult and dangerous. The deepest cuttings and highest embankments had to be made beyond this point as the line made its way through the Wyre Forest towards the River Severn. The problem was the tendency for the sandstone to slip over the newly exposed clay, producing several earth falls that hindered progress. One such landslip resulted in a serious injury to navvy John McCue, reported in the *Worcester Herald* on 5th May 1862 as having happened at Cleobury Mortimer. John McCue was one of the many navvies camped on Sir Edward Blount's land at Mawley Hall. This encampment remained throughout the summers of 1862 and '63, while the navvies opened up the way through the Wyre Forest.

In a very few instances navvies were reported for misdemeanours; one such was a John Rice who was given twenty-one days hard labour for stealing a hatchet from someone at Neen Sollars. Navvies often lived with their families and one navvy's son was found guilty of stealing apples (fined seven shillings with costs) in August 1862. On the camp several resourceful men used local ingredients to make and sell beer and cider from huts alongside the works, though as this was against the licensing laws, prosecutions inevitably followed. The *Worcester Herald* reported several incidents such as William Payne (ganger) and Thomas Jakes (bricklayer), both found guilty for selling beer and cider without a licence. The witnesses were two tradesmen from Cleobury Mortimer who had 'been to see the progress of the line' and been offered drinks by the accused. Several occurrences of this crime were reported and brought to court, with some offenders appearing more than once. On a happier note, at least one navvy married a local girl, the wedding taking place at Neen Sollars church.

The Tenbury and Bewdley directors were satisfied with the progress of the construction work and reported this at a half-yearly meeting on 24th September 1862, adding their hope that the line could be finished by 1st January 1864, the date stipulated in the contract. They also related to the meeting the agreement that had been made with the West Midland Railway to lease the line, giving a first year dividend of £2.10%, then three years at £3%, the following year at £3.10% and thereafter £4%.

The engineers report at the same meeting stated 'Earthworks and masonry and foundation between Tenbury and Bewdley Road (Cleobury Mortimer) are progressing favourably. Works in the Forest had begun where the land had been obtained. Foundations of Dowles Bridge are in hand on the West side of the River and contractors are prepared to begin on the East side as soon as the land is settled for'.

An interesting feature in the construction of two of the bridges spanning the line in the Forest involved a novel and economical plan. The ground was very rocky so the usual masonry abutments were dispensed with, the arches being sprung directly from the rocky sides. Centres were also dispensed with, the brickwork being laid on the soil, which, on completion of the arches, was carefully removed from beneath.

At that time a considerable amount of industry was to be found alongside the Dowles Brook in the Wyre Forest including several mills which would have been inconvenienced because the Dowles Brook had to be stopped up and diverted in places whilst the line was constructed. A few local well-known landmarks were demolished at the time, too, including a blacksmith's shop. A smithy operating from the site of 'The dry mill' (an old oatmeal mill), and some fireclay mines and a tramway belonging to an enterprising Bewdley industrialist named Samuel Skey, were obliterated. Many complaints were reported in the *Worcester Herald* about the high embankments then being thrown up in the Dowles area to raise the line up to the

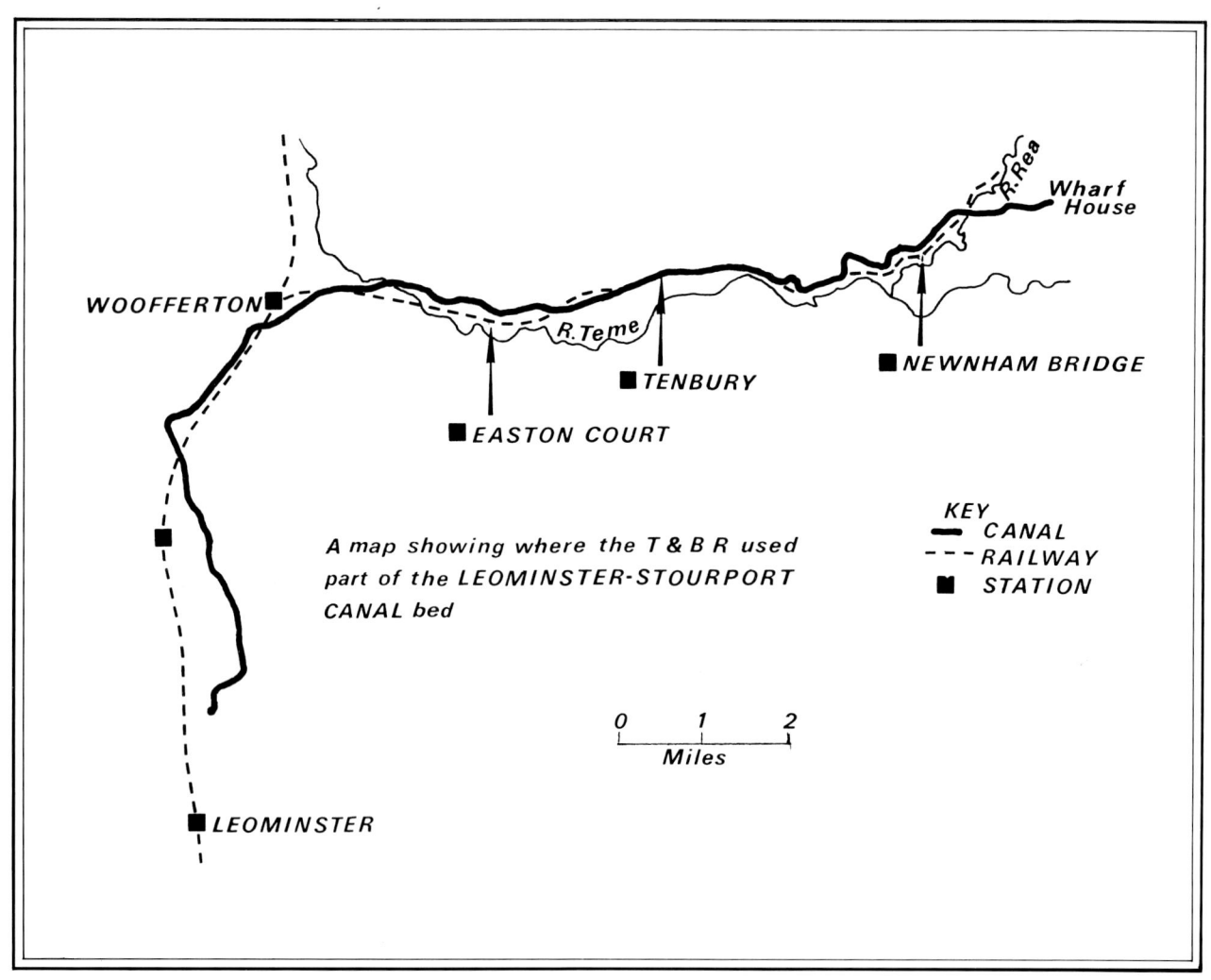

Cleobury Mortimer, looking towards Bewdley. *Collection J. W. Warren*

level of the river bridge. Some thought the view was spoilt, others complained that light was blocked out, and some naturalists feared that the work would destroy forever rare orchids and deer that were in the forest.

Throughout 1862, the Tenbury Railway had been in full operation awaiting completion of the eastern link to Bewdley. A major development that was anticipated to increase revenue for the Tenbury Railway was started in March 1862. Under the direction of the Tenbury Wells Improvement Company, George Smith (a local builder mentioned previously) began construction of a new bath house from the plans submitted by John Cranston of Birmingham. Mr Flewett was the engineer supervising the innovative use of corrugated iron work, involved in the design.

The initiative of the Tenbury Wells Improvement Company was pointed out at the fifth ordinary half-yearly meeting of the Tenbury Railway at the Corn Exchange, Tenbury, on 26th March 1862. At the same time the proposed opening of the neighbouring Clee Hill Railway was described as another source of additional traffic for the Tenbury Railway. Coal, iron and stone would be conveyed to Tenbury by road down from Bitterley where rope-worked inclines from the various Clee Hill quarries and mines would terminate. It was suggested that the mineral loads, could then be worked on by rail from Tenbury.

David Wylie, the engineer, reported that all stations and sidings on the Tenbury Railway were completed and 'in excellent order. The passenger, goods and siding accommodation at Tenbury are more extensive than originally planned, ample room being provided in offices and wharves for the use of the Tenbury and Bewdley Railway now under construction'. Wylie went on to add news of a locomotive shed at Woofferton to house the Tenbury Railway's engine: 'A small engine house and water tank is under construction at Woofferton on completion of which the contract with Brassey and Field can be closed.' Exactly how long the Brassey engine was housed at Woofferton shed after completion is uncertain, for at that time the LNWR had their Shrewsbury & Hereford leasing Bill going through Parliament, strongly objected to by the GWR and WMR. However, after withdrawal of their opposition and agreement to share the lease equally with the LNWR, the Bill was passed. The S&H (including the Tenbury Railway) becoming a joint line (half LNWR, half GWR and WMR), administered by a joint committee made up of four directors of each company.

The joint ownership took effect from 1st July 1862 and from that date the working of the Tenbury Railway was undertaken by the LNWR on behalf of the three leasing companies, Brassey's working lease for the S&H having expired on 30th June 1862. At the half-yearly meeting of the Tenbury Railway, in September Lord Northwick confirmed that the lease of the line had become vested in the joint companies and expressed the hope that the prosperity of the line would be increased.

Also in September 1862 Tenbury Bath House opened to great enthusiasm, grandiose plans being made for a new hotel and boarding house on the site, surrounded by exotic pleasure gardens fronting the Kyre Brook.

In October 1862, Easton Court station disappeared from the passenger timetable of the Tenbury Railway. This

The Tenbury and Bewdley Railway

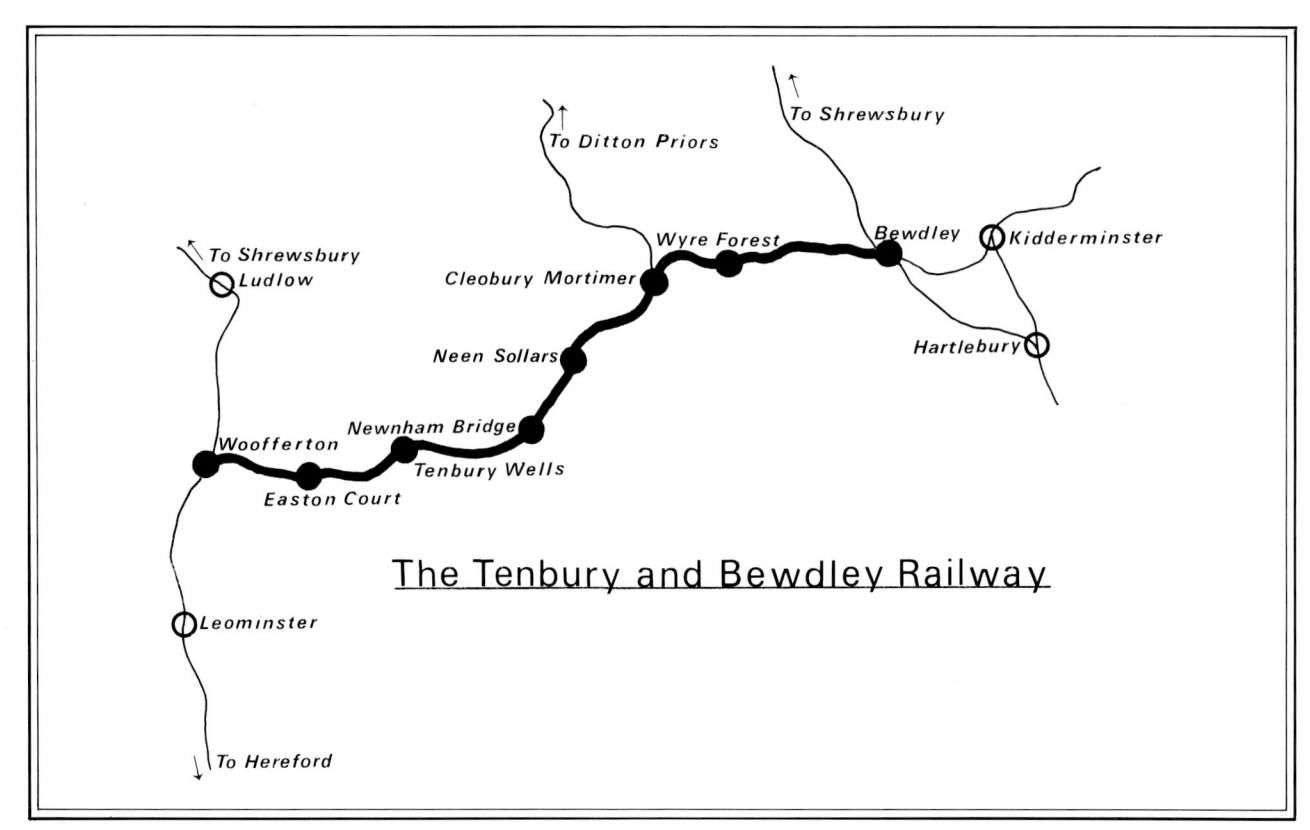

was a result of a survey of the line by officers of the Shrewsbury & Hereford Joint line. They found the receipts at Easton Court to be too low, at ten to fifteen shillings per week, to cover costs. The Tenbury Company however, was bound by agreement to keep the station open for Sir Joseph Bailey and his family. As a compromise, the officers recommended that Easton Court be closed as a regular station, that a platelayer's family be placed in the house, and the trains only be stopped for Sir Joseph Bailey dependents by signal when required. This system would save a station master's wages in addition to stores and stationery. Mrs Bailey helpfully agreed to waive the powers that she had to keep the station open and maintained by a proper staff, and consented to the station master being transferred to work at Tenbury provided that he was still allowed to live at Easton Court station house.

There were other problems, too, particularly over the train service to Ludlow. This concerned passengers using the 10am and 11am trains from Tenbury who couldn't return until 6.35pm. A request was made to the traffic manager at Shrewsbury, for the Tenbury engine to bring passengers back from Ludlow to Woofferton in time for a 4pm train to Tenbury. There was also a request for an early morning train to run from Tenbury to coincide with the Ludlow and Leominster fair days. In November 1862 it was reported at a joint lessees committee that tenders had been submitted for providing locomotives for the Tenbury branch, one from the LNWR at £1,125 per annum, and one from the GWR at £4 per day. The LNWR offer was accepted on the undertaking that it included the expenses for pumping water for the engines, presumably at Woofferton. It was later confirmed that the LNWR had taken over the locomotive working of the Tenbury Railway from 1st December 1862. During December the whole locomotive stock of the former Shrewsbury & Hereford Railway was divided between the three leasing companies, and the Brassey engine, with sixteen other locomotives, became WMR stock. Timetables show that Tenbury branch trains were now worked from Ludlow which was a joint shed housing locomotives of both LNWR and GWR but under LNWR control.

On Christmas Day 1862, Lord Northwick treated all the navvies working on the Tenbury & Bewdley to a 'bounteous and excellent meal' at the Rose and Crown Inn, Burford. Venison had been dispatched to Tenbury from Northwick Park in Gloucestershire to be added to the menu of beef and plum pudding. Three free pints of ale were allowed each man, the subcontractors kindly making this up to five pints at a later stage in the celebrations, which passed off pleasantly and without incident. Happily, there was never any trouble reported concerning the navvies around Tenbury. They were well looked after by Lord Northwick and his sister, who paid great attention to the welfare of the workforce, visiting them on the work sites and often inviting small groups to have tea with them at Burford House. In addition to the navvies brought in to provide labour, many local people found employment on the construction of the T&B. Local farms provided horses and carts, the blacksmith from Bayton made wheelbarrows for the site workers, and miners from Clee Hill and Bayton pits were recruited, especially for digging out the lengthy tunnel at Prizeley, just south of Cleobury Mortimer.

The closure of Easton Court station did not reflect a general decline in the affairs of the Tenbury Railway. On the contrary, in the first month of 1863, the WTT showed the extra train asked for departing from Tenbury to Woofferton at 8.15am, the loco leaving Woofferton at 7.30am. By March 1863, the extra traffic from travellers arriving at Tenbury 'to take the waters' was beginning to be noticed, helped no doubt by the special rate tickets advertised by the S&H Joint line in the *Shrewsbury Chronicle*.

A meeting on 25th March 1863 heard of the recent rapid progress of construction:

> 'Cuttings have been commenced with the exception of the two near Bewdley, earth works and bridges between Tenbury and Neen Sollars are almost complete and the permanent way layed for four and a half miles. The masonry of the Severn (Dowles) Bridge will soon be ready to receive the girders and the whole structure will be finished early in June. The heaviest portion of the work is at the Bewdley end but there is every reason to hope it will be completed by the end of the year.'

At this stage, arrangements were entered into between the LNWR, GWR and WMR over the anticipated increased through traffic on the Tenbury & Bewdley. 'The LNWR', it was announced, 'have brought in a Bill before Parliament under which they seek to enter into working arrangements with this company and the Tenbury Company which will, under standing orders, be submitted to shareholders at a subsequent meeting. The directors draw satisfaction in drawing attention to the fact that the big companies have changed their policy of unprofitable competition and have given way to amicable arrangements relative to traffic which will greatly affect the increase of traffic when the T&B is opened.'

The good progress and the optimistic outlook for the future were overshadowed by the announcement at the same meeting of the sudden death of the engineer David Wylie. Fortunately, the position was taken over by the then little-known William Clarke. He was an executor of Wylie's will and described as 'the late Mr Wylie's partner'. He was later accepted by the company on the same terms as Mr Wylie, subject to, at his own expense, 'looking over the line and reporting on it'. William Clarke had already assisted Wylie (who was in fact his brother-in-law) on both the Shrewsbury & Hereford and the Leominster and Kington contracts before he went to India in 1859 as engineer to the Punjab Railway. Clarke's appointment precluded any thoughts of John Fowler being made joint engineer, Clarke later settling this issue with the latter on amicable terms.

In May 1863, only six weeks after his appointment, Clarke suffered his first setback as company engineer. The tunnel which was being excavated at Prizeley, near Cleobury Mortimer, suddenly collapsed, and a local man, a miner from Clows Top named Charles Mole, had to be dug out and rescued from underneath the rubble. He suffered an injured back and was taken home strapped to a cart. He received treatment from a surgeon, Mr Jones of Foxley, who was responsible for medical welfare on this section of the works. The main cause of the disaster was that old coal workings dating from around 1835 had been cut into by excavations, and, in addition, springs had caused the tunnel to flood. Eventually the idea of a tunnel had to be abandoned and the excavation was consequentially opened out into a very deep cutting instead.

It was about this time that the only real trouble concerning the navvies occurred, and then it was only an internal matter not involving local people. An attack was made by the English navvies upon the Irish contingent with the intention, it appeared, of driving the Irish off the site. Before the police had time to arrive and restore order, a bruising battle took place. A Welsh man named Jenkins was caught in the middle of it and, mistaken for an Irish man, he ended up badly beaten and kicked. He was taken to the Union Hospital in a poor state, yet refused to name the men who had harmed him.

The specifications for the construction of the stations at Newnham, Neen Sollars and Cleobury were laid down in an agreement between the contractors and the T&B Railway Company dated 1st October 1863. The drawings were provided by William Clarke, and his station architecture blended well with Wylie's designs at Tenbury, Easton Court and other stations on the main S&H line. Newnham and Neen Sollars were designed as mirror images of each other. Cleobury included more generous accommodation and the addition of a large brick-supported water tank at the Neen Sollars end of the main building. Brickwork laid in Flemish bond was stipulated as the building material, roof tiles were to be best Lightmoor or Broseley Blue tiles, and the window sills, plinths and copings to the outer walls to be of Grinshill stone. The rail for sidings was to be of the same weight and section as that used on the S&H main line, with the rail turned up at the end of all sidings and fixed with wrought-iron straps to stayed Baltic timber uprights.

All crossings were specified to be Ransom and Sims best cast iron chilled type. The bottom ballast in sidings was to be provided from the spoil taken away from the Bewdley end of the line, with the top to be finished off with gravel from Woofferton or elsewhere and approved of by Clarke. Platforms were to be 150 feet long and 12 feet wide at their narrowest. Only a single platform was provided for at Newnham and Neen Sollars, but two were required at Cleobury. Cleobury Road (as it was also being referred to at this time) and Neen Sollars had their platform wall height set three feet above the running line, whilst Newnham was lower at two feet. Approach roads at Neen Sollars and Cleobury were to be 30 feet wide, with ditches of 2 foot, to be surfaced with Clee Hill Jew (sic) stone alongside gravelled footpaths 4 foot wide. Sharp, screened gravel was to top the footpaths and also the platforms, whilst wooden fencing and quick (hawthorn) hedges separated off the general public's rights of way. The platforms were to have paling fences fixed around them as were the fronts of the station houses.

Gates (4ft wide) were to be put in, leading from the platforms at Neen Sollars and Cleobury, whilst the goods yards at each station were to be gated. A well was required to be sunk at each station. The costs were noted at £450 each for Newnham and Neen Sollars station house, offices, buildings and fittings and £900 for similar at Cleobury. Brickwork in each weighing machine house, the platform walls and goods sheds was costed separately, and it was noted that filling for the platforms at Neen Sollars and Cleobury could be obtained from the excavation of the siding and station grounds. Station nameboards were to be provided, painted, lettered and fixed for 40 shillings each. It was also decided to place a crane at each station similar to one already existing at Tenbury.

It was decided that Brassey and Field should be given first refusal to build the stations at a cost of £450 each for Newnham and Neen Sollars and £900 for Cleobury Road. In the event of decline, tenders would be put out to other builders.

The prospect of a railway extending from Bewdley to Kidderminster once the Tenbury and Bewdley was completed, was first publicly mentioned at a meeting of LNWR/GWR Joint officers held at Paddington on 9th July 1863. There it was decided that the extension line was necessary, and, in order to make facilities available to the LNWR, construction should start as soon as possible. However, at the next meeting held at Euston in August, Mr W. Fenton (Chairman of the WMR as well as a director of the T&B) spoke to the Joint officers. He explained how instructions concerning the proposed extension to Kidderminster could not be given by the GWR until after their next general meeting when a new board would be selected following the takeover of the WMR on 1st August 1863.

Engineering work on the T&B was reported in September to have made highly satisfactory progress, there 'now being only three bridges to build'. The lattice girder bridge at Dowles was another of William Clarke's designs, possibly from a style familiar to him from his employment in India. The earthworks were recorded as having been generally completed and the permanent way laid and ballasted between Tenbury and Mawley with the remaining permanent way delivered on works. All the overbridges had been built to accommodate double track, extra land having been provided for, should doubling be required.

Ballast trains had been a notable feature on the Tenbury Railway via Woofferton ever since the Bewdley extension had been started. Brassey and Field had been charged one shilling per wagon for the conveyance of ballast from Woofferton to Tenbury and they were required 'to find and maintain all extra signals where and when necessary and to pay the wages of an additional pointsman at the ballast hole at Woofferton'. In fact, not all the materials came by railway wagon particularly at the Dowles end of the Wyre Forest. Barges also delivered construction materials. It is known Brassey and Field operated their own barges, and one described as belonging to them was boarded (and a rope was stolen) whilst moored at the Dowles Bridge site.

By October 1863, the new GWR board of directors had met and instructions were given for plans for the Bewdley and Kidderminster extension to be made. At the November meeting of the Joint Committee a suggestion was put by the GWR officers that the LNWR should become joint owners of this line. The cost was estimated at £60,000 and it was suggested that each company pay tolls according to usage. The LNWR would have running powers from Stourbridge to Smethwick, the GWR being entitled to absolute powers from Crewe to Manchester. Mr Moone (for the LNWR) was non-committal, replying that his company would give the ideas due consideration, but nothing came of this proposal.

The year 1864 began full of optimism with two reports from the local Tenbury organisations (Tenbury Wells Improvement Company and the Tenbury Corn Exchange and Public Buildings Company) noting the likely gains to the town once the new line was open. The railway's directors, meeting at Tenbury on 2nd March 1864, discussed minor matters connected with construction and in particular a landslip at Norgrove's End. The engineer reported that the GWR required a telegraph on the T&B line. This was agreed to, provided the GWR guaranteed £4 10s% on the outlay. At the same time it was decided to present a petition to Parliament against the proposed Central Wales and Staffordshire Junction line.

Further optimism about progress was shown by William Clarke who gave his opinion that he could see no reason why the line should not be open by May 1864, since with the exception of a small amount of work at Prizeley, the earthworks had been completed (over 100,000,000 cu yards were involved). The three-arch bridge spanning Prizeley cutting entailed a small road diversion and this would be completed in about six weeks. All other bridges and culverts were finished. The station buildings and sidings were almost completed, though a small length of permanent way and some more ballasting remained to be done. Arrangements had now been made with the GWR to lay down another line between the junction with their Severn Valley line at Bewdley and Bewdley station. It was learnt at this time that nothing had come of the proposal to work the T&B plus the Kidderminster extension as a GWR/LNWR joint line.

At last, on 14th June, the secretary of the T&B was requested to inform the GWR that the line would be ready for opening on 1st July and to request that a day be appointed on or before 25th June when an exchange of agreements and payment of subscriptions (from the WMR and SVR) should be made. The GWR were requested as well to 'make immediate arrangements for working the line as soon as the same shall be passed by the inspecting officer'.

In connection with the track doubling near Bewdley, Messrs McKenzie, Clunes and Co. of Worcester were contracted to supply signals and equipment needed to protect the junction with the Severn Valley at Bewdley station. The signals supplied were stated as one distant, 30ft high, and another 25ft high, one for each line. In addition there was a repeating signal 18ft high, the total cost, including pulleys, sheaves, signal wire and lamps, etc, being £111 6s 3d.

These signals were positioned about 500yds north of Bewdley and gave warning to drivers of trains approaching Bewdley. The term distant, as applied at the time, must have had a different meaning, (probably acting as a stop signal), for they were operated from a signal box at the northern end of Bewdley station; the actual cost of this signal box (£8 10s 0d) suggests it was a small wooden hut covering a ground frame.

By far the biggest alterations carried out by McKenzie Clunes and Co. at Bewdley was for the supply of new signals, fittings and labour, including the erection of a signal box.

McKenzie and Co's account, submitted to the GWR for payment, gives a very detailed list of all the equipment supplied and was as follows: two distant signals with lamps 18ft high, one junction signal with lamps 43ft high, one junction signal with three arms and lamps complete 52ft high, one wrought iron gallery and palisading with cranked valance and boards, one new arm repeating signal with ironwork and lamp, fixed to a signal 25ft high, and another the same but 17ft high, the total cost amounting to £410 7s 6d. The signal box was described as being 10ft by 12ft by 10ft, double lined with floors and glazed windows, covered in slates. Inside the box was a 'Chambers Patent Junction Signal Apparatus' with seven signal levers and four point levers, the total cost amounting to £205 8s 1d, which included £110 for the signal apparatus, £75 for the signal box and £20 8s 1d for steps, labour and timber used to elevate it, between the (south) end of the platform at Bewdley station and the entrance to the goods yard. Bewdley at this time had only one platform (the present down platform).

McKenzie Clunes and Co. also supplied and erected a 45ft diameter turntable in Bewdley yard, two water cranes at the end of the up and down platforms at Cleobury Mortimer, and three 5 ton wharf cranes, one for each new station. All the other signals on the T&B were supplied by McKenzie Clunes and Co. but no specific details have yet come to light. The single needle telegraph system put in by the GWR was to a design of their own telegraph superintendent, C.E. Spagnoletti.

All looked set for the grand opening day until disaster struck in the form of another serious landslip in Prizeley Cutting around 3am on the morning of 24th June. The *Worcester Herald* reported:

> 'An earth slip of formidable proportions occurred at Prizeley cutting on the Tenbury and Bewdley Railway. 9000 yards of soil gave way but fortunately the wagons had just been pulled out and no injuries occurred. The contractors are pushing on as rapidly as possible, the men working day and night. The opening will be delayed by at least a fortnight from the time originally planned.'

Meanwhile, bridge testing trials were carried out by locomotives still referred to as belonging to the WMR and for which £12 was charged for the services rendered.

On the Tenbury Railway at the same time, Easton Court station remained closed, but William Field, Thomas Brassey's partner, showed his faith in a future for the station by setting up a coal agency in the yard as well as at Tenbury. At nearby Clee Hill he formed a partnership with Mr. John Mackay (agent for the T&B contractors) for extracting and transporting the local dhustone rock, leading to the appearance of the Field and Mackay private owner wagons which became a familiar sight on railways many miles distant from their Ludlow base. At a Joint Officers meeting in July 1864 there was some discussion about putting in a turntable at Woofferton. The LNWR agreed, providing the GWR paid for it and a similar arrangement was made for the GWR to extend its electric telegraph system along the whole of the Tenbury Railway. There was also agreement to the proposal that the GWR should take over the working of the traffic over the Tenbury Railway on the same terms as were paid to the LNWR, subject to a month's notice and the connections of the LNWR trains not being disturbed. The S&H division of the joint Committee were to continue to supervise the working as before.

Whilst the Tenbury Railway, with installations such as the turntable, prepared for change to come, the town of Tenbury was planning for a grander celebration than they had managed for their previous railway opening day. The *Worcester Herald* reported a meeting on the 8th July in the Pump Room of the Bath House at the close of the Horticultural Exhibition when 'interested parties' met to consider the best means to celebrate the opening of the line. The Rev. T.A. Smith took the chair and various local dignitaries and members of the Board of Directors were present. A trip to Bewdley and back, followed by a public breakfast and a sham military battle plus picnic, seemed to gain favour. The meeting ended with a committee being formed to gather subscriptions for the expenses that would be incurred.

The date set for the opening was 5th August, all necessary arrangements having been made for the public celebrations. But frustrating news suddenly arrived to say that the Board of Trade inspector had cancelled his visit due a week before the opening date. The general disappointment was avoided at the last minute when the Directors decided to continue with the arrangements already made, even getting permission to run the special trip to Bewdley on the morning of the 5th.

Locomotive No. 1A on Dowles Bridge with an inspection train shortly before the opening of the line in August 1864. The 2–4–0T was built at Wolverhampton in the same year. It was renumbered 17 in 1865. This picture shows an empty train with the crew in stiff pose for the camera. The first coach was an ex-WMR third which, built in 1850 by Wright, had four doors but only two compartments (GWR No. 168) and a dog box under the centre seats. The second vehicle, a four-compartment second, was built in 1850 (GWR No. 156), whilst the third coach, a 1st/2nd Composite, was built at Worcester in 1861 (GWR No. 201). The passenger brake van was built in 1856 as one of a series numbered 69-88 by the GWR. The destination boards on the third class coach included the words 'Woofferton and Bewdley'. The two men on the bank were William Clarke (holding rolled-up plans) and William Norris, barely visible, sitting beside him. The barge probably delivered some of the materials used in building the bridge. Dowles Bridge was built in 1863 at a cost of £7,000. It was designed by William Clarke, the T&B engineer, and brought in sections from Brassey's Canada Works, Birkenhead, for erection on site. It was known as a 'Town truss' after the style of Ithiel Town, an American who claimed that Town lattice bridges could be made of wrought iron instead of his usual timber bridges, popular in America at the time of his patent in 1820. The first wooden bridge of this type had been built over Otter Creek, Vermont in 1813 and was soon followed by others over rivers and creeks running through many American estates. Town bridges could easily be assembled on site and its close lattice work, with many pinned intersections, made a safe, strong truss, the static forces being such that should some intersection be damaged or fail, there would be no immediate danger of collapse. Later proof of this was in the last war when Dr. Barnes Wallis used the design (which he called the 'Geodetic System') in the construction of the Wellington Bomber. Many of these aircraft were still able to fly home after bombing raids on Germany although heavily damaged by enemy gunfire. The brick bridge on the left beyond the figures marked the entry of the Dowles Brook into the River Severn. This bridge was later replaced.

National Railway Museum

CHAPTER SIX
THE OPENING OF THE TENBURY AND BEWDLEY RAILWAY

The contractor's loco 2–4–0 *Gipsy Lass* which hauled the navvies from Bewdley to Tenbury for their celebration dinner. It was built by Rothwell of Bolton in 1840 and is seen here at Great Malvern in 1861 with Stephen Ballard standing on the buffer beam and a driver known as 'Hellfire Jack'.
Ballard Collection/Hereford County Record Office

IT was reported in the *Hereford Times* that about noon on Thursday, 4th August 1864, a train of ballast wagons left Bewdley for Tenbury conveying the navvies who had worked on the line, bringing them to attend a dinner to be given in their honour by Lord Northwick. The engine *Gipsy Lass* was decorated with evergreens, the Union Jack was draped over the smokebox whilst on the last truck someone had hoisted a tricolour. Most of the men had smartened themselves up and appeared to be enjoying the trip, laughing and joking as the train stopped at the pick-up points along the line to pick up other groups of workmen.

On arrival at Tenbury, the men made their way to the 'Rose and Crown Inn' just a short distance from the station, where Lord Northwick and his sister Miss Rushout were waiting, along with Mr Brassey and Mr Field. The staff at the Rose and Crown were taken by surprise at the large number of guests arriving, (between four and five hundred) so the meal had to be divided, the first sitting leaving the tables directly they had finished eating in order to make way for the second sitting. At the conclusion of what was described as a sumptuous feast, the guests adjourned to a field opposite the inn where Miss Rushout presented each man with a neatly bound church service. A ring was then formed and Mr John Mackay, agent for Brassey and Field, addressed the gathering, observing that he knew of no workers more loyal than navvies, and that he knew they would receive the toast 'to the Queen, the Prince of Wales and all the Royal family' which they did to loud cheers. He concluded with toasts to 'The Directors of the Tenbury and Bewdley' and to even louder cheers, 'Lord Northwick, Chairman of the Board'.

At that point two spokesmen, John Preece and Charles Tolley, stepped forward. Turning to Lord Northwick, they explained that as this would be the last time the men would see him and his sister, they had, by a subscription amongst themselves, realised £40 and obtained for his Lordship a handsome silver goblet, and for Miss Rushout, an elegant gold bracelet set with pearls and inscribed 'presented by workmen employed by Messrs Brassey and Field on the construction of the Tenbury and Bewdley Railway, to Miss Rushout, in grateful remembrance of past favours'. Each of these gifts was accompanied by beautifully illuminated addresses on vellum.

The address read as follows:

'To the Right Honourable George, Baron Northwick. We the undersigned workmen employed by Brassey and Field in construction of the Tenbury and Bewdley Railway, in approaching your Lordship for the purpose of presenting a silver cup as a mark of gratitude for the kindness displayed towards us by your Lordship during the progress of the works of the above railway, venture to express our conviction that your Lordship's appreciation of our exertions in carrying out work of such importance, and of our conduct during its formation, will tend, not only to raise our class in the estimation of the public at large, and to impress upon them the value of our services in the course of progress, but will tend to induce a sense of self respect amongst ourselves, and a determination to return that high character which we venture to hope our conduct, (publicly approved by your Lordship) has gained for us while in the neighbourhood.'

Signed on behalf of the Committee, John Preece, Chairman. John Mackay, Treasurer.

To loud cheers Miss Rushout and Lord Northwick stepped forward to be presented with the gifts, and in replying, his Lordship said he had difficulty in finding words to express his feelings to the honour they had bestowed upon him and his sister, and it was totally unexpected and undeserved. The men had come amongst them to perform a great public service. Having been acquainted with them for some years and never having any cause to regret making their acquaintance, the least he could do was to make them welcome. Some time ago he had been asked whether he was not afraid of navvies, as they were a rough lot, and his answer was 'Come and see what they think of me'. Amidst laughter and loud cheers he held the goblet aloft. 'Still', he added, 'if I was asked how I got it I would have some difficulty in explaining' (to more laughter). Underneath the rough jackets he had found generous feelings and kind hearts.

He then offered some advice to those men who would now be seeking work, cautioning them not to be swayed by agents of the Federal Government of America, who would entrap them in the Civil War raging there. In concluding, he wished them health, prosperity, and everlasting happiness in the life to come. Mr Brassey rounded off the proceedings, and amidst loud cheering the crowd finally dispersed to make the return journey to Bewdley.

Early next morning, Friday, 5th August, special trains arrived at Tenbury from Woofferton, adding yet more people to the already crowded station and the waiting special train. The correspondent of *Eddowes Salopian Journal* described the scenes which were of a most joyous charac-

Composite No. 203 (ex-WMR Compo No. 123), built at Worcester in 1861 and condemned in June 1882. This was the same type as No. 201, the third coach behind the loco in the Dowles Bridge picture. Dimensions were 23ft 6in x 7ft 6in, with 13ft wheelbase. Note the GWR cypher on the 1st class door panels. *HMRS*

Coach No. 221 was a composite of the same batch as No. 156 on the Dowles Bridge. It was numbered 221 when it was later downgraded to third class. This photograph was taken in 1884 when the vehicle was already condemned. It is recorded as being built by C. C. Williams in 1850 (C. C. Williams was the contractor who ran the West Midlands Railway in the early years), though it is possible that J. Wright of Saltley was the builder. The dimensions were 18ft x 7ft 4in, and 10ft wheelbase. *HMRS*

THE OPENING OF THE TENBURY & BEWDLEY RAILWAY

ter, Tenbury being 'the grand central point to which assembling hosts are converging'. He went on 'the twenty-five coach train was densely packed, the directors having being extremely generous in the distribution of tickets, the station was neatly ornamented with evergreens, flowers and a host of flags and mottoes.'

After a short delay while doors were secured, the driver, Mr George Crichelow, opened the regulator at 9.45am and the train moved off, slowly winding a sinuous course around many curves to Newnham, the first station on the line. The station buildings here were also gaily decorated with bunting, and spanning the nearby road was an arch of evergreens, whilst the signal posts were crowned with pretty bunches of flowers. Similar scenes were witnessed at Neen Sollars and large crowds caused the train to be delayed at Cleobury Mortimer. Arrival time at Bewdley was just after 11 o'clock, the crowd there witnessing the second railway opening in two years.

After waiting about a quarter of an hour at Bewdley, the train set off back towards Tenbury and had just started to climb through the Wyre Forest from the Dowles bridge, when a slight mishap occurred which could have led to serious consequences had the train been crossing the bridge. The telegraph wires crossed the line soon after the bridge was cleared and, according to the correspondent of the *Wellington Journal*, the wires somehow got caught in the carriage lamp chimneys. Before, the crew were alerted to bring the train to a halt, one telegraph pole was pulled out of the ground and several others dragged from their positions. Some time was spent disentangling the wire and temporarily refixing the poles before the train could restart, eventually arriving at Tenbury at 12.30pm.

On arrival, the scene was of great excitement, the road from the station to the town was so crowded with people that it was difficult to make progress on foot. An added attraction was the arrival a short time earlier of an immense train from Shrewsbury with two companies of the Shropshire Volunteer Artillery who had positioned themselves by the station in readiness for marching to the town to take part in a revue and sham fight in the afternoon. The fife band then struck up 'See the conquering hero comes' — a tune long associated with railway openings — and with some difficulty the marching artillery set off towards the town and down Teme Street (the main street of Tenbury) which was gaily decorated and thronged with people all making their way to Palmers Field. There, a large marquee had been erected and a magnificent lunch prepared, with the finest champagne and choice wines all provided by the Tenbury and Bewdley directors. Four hundred guests in all sat down to eat.

At the top table, Lord Northwick sat, flanked on his immediate right and left by Sir Edward Blount, Thomas Brassey, Colonel Knight (M.P. for Worcester), William Field and various other directors, shareholders and dignitaries. Grace having been said, the chairman rose to give the loyal toast, adding that as time was limited he would shortly hand over to the clergy, the army, the navy and volunteers who would all do their duty in their respective spheres, but he now gave them the health of the M.P. for Worcester.

Colonel Knight M.P. returned the thanks and proposed, before sitting down, the health of Lord Northwick, the directors of the Tenbury and Bewdley and success to the railway.

Lord Northwick, in replying, went into some length about the history of the line and continued: notwithstanding the peculiar difficulties in the construction of it, it was one of the cheapest to build in England and there were several reasons for this. One was that they had taken advantage of the site of the old canal that ran from Woofferton and obtained the ground at much less cost than they would have otherwise. Another, and more important reason was they had managed to keep away from the harpies who fed on the necessities of railway projects, owners of little corners of land who, standing on the undoubted right of every Englishman to do what he liked with his own, defied the railway people to touch their land until they had paid a most exorbitant sum. Lastly they had selected a young and rising engineer, Mr Clarke, who had also given them the Severn bridge, one of the prettiest and most serviceable structures of its kind in the country. Last night, he went on, a song had been put into his hand the burden of which was:

> 'This pretty little line that makes its way
> Through river valley, coal and clay
> I wonder if it will ever pay?
> This Tenbury, Bewdley Railway.'

The answer to this song he had no desire to bring, for the solution lay in the future and, so far as he could see, considering the great agricultural and natural productions of the district, he felt every confidence of its financial prosperity. He concluded by saying he couldn't sit down without giving them one more toast and it was to the health of Messrs Brassey and Field and the workmen employed on the line (*cheers*). When the navvies first came into the neighbourhood he was asked what he should do with them as they were a rough lot of fellows. 'I will tell you what I did, I invited them to dinner, I went amongst them as respectable men and the result was they were contained as such'. He now had the peculiar pleasure of toasting them and their worthy employers Brassey and Field (*loud cheers from the assembly*).

When the applause died down, Mr Brassey arose and acknowledged the toast on behalf of himself, Mr Field and all the workmen engaged on the line, whom he said had no doubt all benefited by the kindness of his Lordship and his Lordship's sister towards them. It had been a great pleasure to him to see on the previous day, the kind of feelings reciprocated by his Lordship and the men, he believed that if they were met half way and were better treated than they usually were, they would find the workmen a class of men not to be afraid of. As to this railway which they had just opened at last, thanks must go to the directors for they had got the railway, and if it had not been for them it might have gone another way. He believed it would prove satisfactory to all shareholders. He added that when the Shrewsbury & Hereford was projected, people said 'What are those men doing, there is not enough trade to keep a coach on the road once a day?' but it was geographically right and so, he thought, was the Tenbury & Bewdley. He paid high compliments to the engineers without whom they could have done nothing, especially his late lamented friend Mr Wylie, after whose death, the engineering department had been taken up with the great talent of Mr Clarke. He concluded by complimenting the secretary, Mr Norris on his zeal and diligence in the discharge of his duties.

After a few more toasts, the proceedings were drawn to a close with prayers being said by the Rev. T.A. Smith, whereupon everyone left to watch the festivities.

By this time more Rifle Volunteers had arrived outside although there was some delay to the proceedings due to non-arrival of a train bringing a further contingent. At length, a sham fight was arranged. Ten companies of rifles, under the command of Col. Knight, would be the attacking party, whilst the Shropshire Artillery and one company of the Tenbury Rifles, under the command of Capt. Field, would be the defending army, guarding a bridge thrown across the River Teme. A series of warlike manoeuvres then took place with great spirit, the artillery guns, placed on an elevated spot, firing with great rapidity on the attacking party as they approached the defensive positions. Pretty soon Palmers Field was thick with smoke and organised confusion, and amidst it all Private Roberts of the 2nd Battery, Shropshire Artillery, was hurt and his arm severely burnt when, ramming home a charge in a cannon, the powder exploded, sending the ramrod over the heads of the startled onlookers to land some way away over the River Teme.

The final attempt to capture the defenders involved a great deal of clever skirmishing followed by a grand advance in line at the double with bayonets fixed, followed by a grand volley to the delight of the crowd. Finally, a march past the dignitaries concluded the event, all the companies then being entertained to an excellent spread in the great tent.

The next day, Saturday, 6th August, Sir Edward Blount of Mawley Hall treated the workmen employed on the section passing through his estate to a supper at the Talbot Hotel in Cleobury. On 9th August the line was inspected by the Board of Trade Inspector, Capt Tyler, who declared it fit for public use.

Apparently Capt Tyler had been over the works a few weeks earlier, for in a letter to the Board of Trade dated 21st July 1864, William Clarke, the T&B engineer, confirmed work had been carried out on strengthening the Dowles Bridge by shortening the transoms, as requested by Capt Tyler.

No details of that visit have come to light but he must have been satisfied with what he had seen, for the report of his visit of the 9th August 1864 can be given in full and suggests a very cursory visit.

In his report Capt Tyler stated,

'The line is a continuation of the branch line from Woofferton to Tenbury. It is 15 miles long to the West Midland section of the GWR at Bewdley. The line is single and worked by the train staff system. The ruling gradient is 1–70 and the sharpest curve is 12 chains radius. Permanent way is double headed rail in lengths of 21ft and 24ft, 75lbs to the yard in weight. Chairs are cast iron, 25lbs in weight secured by iron spikes to transverse sleepers. Sleepers are half round timber measuring 9ft by 10ins by 5ins. There are 10 bridges over and 18 under, variously treated in brick, iron and timber the largest span being 60ft.

'There is a viaduct over the Severn of 3 openings each of 70ft carried by wrought iron lattice girders on masonry piers and abutments. All the bridges and viaducts have been carefully and substantially constructed but there has been slight movement in places in brickwork and should be watched, but should not give any rise for apprehension. In some of the smaller bridges the permanent way is carried on wooden cross beams which is an inferior system and must be watched and will require more careful maintenance than the larger bridges.'

He recommended 'when on the spot' that an extra signal should be added south of Bewdley station, with means of intercommunication between the signal men north and south of that station, and short bolts in fish plates be replaced by longer ones. Alterations should be effected in the locking apparatus of the south signal box at Bewdley station and he went on to add that 'enclosed there was a letter from the T&B engineer stating these improvements had been carried out'.

In a letter to the Board of Trade, dated 12th August 1864, the engineer reported 'that I have been over the line and the small matters had been attended to, fishplate bolts had been substituted for longer ones, and fences and culvert mouths are now complete. At Bewdley, the new signal box communication between the signal box and the other end of the yard is fixed, and the locking apparatus is now perfected, so that there can be no cross signalling, a possibility of which, would have trains running at the same time on the same piece of track'.

Both Capt Tyler and the engineer's comments shed some light on early operating methods, for the interlocking mentioned is probably the first reference to it other than on a main line. The communication system must have also been unique for it appears to have been some kind of audible means, for McKenzie, Clunes and Co. were required to supply and fix bells to two signal arms.

The final paragraph of Capt Tyler's report stated the improvements had been carried out and he was of the opinion 'that the line may open to the public without danger to the public using it'. The report was dated 13th August 1864, the same day as the T&B finally opened!

CHAPTER SEVEN
EXPANSION AFTER 1864

A c.1900 view of Bewdley's main thoroughfare, Load Street, taken from Telford's road bridge over the Severn. 'Load' comes from the Saxon word 'lode', meaning a ford, and for centuries, before bridges were built over the Severn, Bewdley was an important river crossing to Wales. *Collection Wendy Hinton*

THREE weeks after the line opened, a public banquet was held at the George Hotel in Bewdley on the evening of Friday, 2nd September 1864. The hosts for the occasion were the Town Council, and amongst the guests were Sir Thomas Winnington (M.P. for Bewdley); Sir Edward Blount, representing the promoters of the line; Mr J Gabb, Mayor of Bewdley; the Rev Walcot, Rector of Ribbesford Church and Captain Marcy of Marcy and Whitcombe solicitors. Letters of apology were received from Lord Northwick, Mr Norris and Messrs Brassey and Field.

The Chairman, Sir Thomas Winnington, in proposing the toast of the evening to 'The success of the Tenbury and Bewdley Railway', said it was a matter of congratulation to the inhabitants of the town and district to find they had at last got a railway that linked them with the agricultural district on the other side of the hills. A long time had elapsed before this chain of communication had been completed. They had naturally looked along the Severn Valley. Now he was happy that Bewdley was placed on the main line north to south and a short distance from Tenbury, from whence, by another branch, to another main line, travellers could proceed through Herefordshire and the Welsh districts.

He trusted that the projected line to Kidderminster would soon be carried out, giving a direct line from Birmingham to South Wales. The Mayor then proposed the health of the Chairman and of Sir Edward Blount for his activities during the building of the line. In his speech the Mayor congratulated everyone concerned with the line to which he gave his utmost support. People had asked 'What's the use of a second line?' — the first almost ruined the place and this one will quite ruin it'. He wasn't surprised to hear these comments, he said, for when people got to the shady side of life they saw things in a dull light. Though times change, they stand still. He had noted houses, at one time empty, now being occupied. To him that showed people's faith in the railway and the town. He then proposed 'the Contractors', saying it was gratifying to hear from the Government Inspector that it was the best line he had ever gone over. After an excellent dinner and prayers, the assembly departed in high spirits.

The high expectations for the line were proving well founded. The traffic figures between Bewdley and

George Hotel, Bewdley, where the second public banquet was held to celebrate the opening of the T&B in 1864. Telford's road bridge, over the Severn, and toll house (now demolished) can be seen in the distance. The Severn Valley and Tenbury line was obscured by the trees in the background.
Collection Brian Standish

The same hotel, but a typical scene fifty years on from the opening of the line. The first motor cars had arrived, the first serious threat to railway transport!
Collection Wendy Hinton

EXPANSION AFTER 1864

Woofferton for the first four months operation, August to December 1864, showed a total of 31,120 passengers, 15 horses, 89 dogs, 57 cattle and other livestock, 1,156 tons of general merchandise as well as 843 tons of coal and minerals, most of the latter coming from the Clee Hill via the Ludlow and Clee Hill Railway which opened on 24th August 1864.

There had been some operating difficulties however. Two GWR trains had collided at Tenbury, fortunately with no loss of life. Trains had been delayed and connections missed due to passenger trains carrying out unauthorised shunting at the various stations.

The telegraph system had also proved defective, one train with an irate director aboard being delayed at Cleobury Mortimer for over an hour because of it. Strong protests were sent by letter to the local GWR traffic manager to draw attention to these facts and to ascertain whether station masters were fully acquainted with the use of the telegraph. Another letter, this time to the General Manager, pointed out the need for a daily luggage train, proper rates for goods and issue of market tickets to and from Bewdley, Tenbury, Worcester, Dudley and Birmingham.

Since the WMR had been absorbed by the GWR on 1st August 1863, the Tenbury & Bewdley was worked from opening by the GWR at 60% of the gross receipts and certain other payments under the agreement date 29th July 1863 between the GWR, WMR and Tenbury & Bewdley Railway.

The local company still existed however, and still held regular shareholders and directors meetings. The first meeting after the opening was in October 1864 when Lord Northwick had to tell the gathering that there was to be no dividend paid for the half-year. The reason, he explained, was the overall cost of the stations which amounted to £9,000 each instead of the £4,000 estimated. Not surprisingly, a memorial received for an extra station to be built at Nineveh, between Neen Sollars and Cleobury Mortimer, was turned down. For the future, however, the meeting heard how the Tenbury and Bewdley 'looked forward with great pleasure to the completion of the loop line between Kidderminster and Bewdley'. The advantage of the LNWR using the route was referred to with great enthusiasm and optimism that increased traffic and business would ensue.

The transfer of the permanent way to the GWR for maintenance took place in the first week of November 1864. William Clarke had earlier urged the T&B Board to have this area of responsibility settled as quickly as possible. He explained to the Board that, as an alternative, they should appoint their own P.W. Inspector, since as engineer he could not be properly responsible for the men currently working without supervision or even a rule book. Clarke was at pains to make clear also that the GWR, in taking over the permanent way, were not in any way accepting any of the others works which remained under the maintenance of the contractors for six months following the opening. In fact there was a great deal of acrimony between the Engineer and the contractors at this time. The agent, Mr Mackay, astonished Clarke, by claiming that he considered the contract had been completed. This was 'a gross absurdity' in Clarke's view. He noted the slopes of cuttings between Cleobury and Bewdley were wholly unsoiled, and what amounted to shoddy work at the River Rea diversion at Neen Sollars, where several slips had taken place. In addition, newly planted hawthorn hedges were so badly choked with weeds that replanting would soon become necessary, and the wooden fencing was so inferior that the GWR's inspector had already indicated his refusal to accept it as it stood. The road approaches to various sites on the line and use of poor quality sleepers in places (despite earlier warnings) were further criticisms levelled by Clarke at the contractors. £23,733 was all Clarke was prepared to certify in extra payments and he stated that he would 'most positively refuse entertaining any further statements until works are completed' which were now not creditable to anyone concerned.

As the year 1864 came to an end, Messrs McKenzie, Clunes and Holland had still not been paid by the T&B Company for the supply and erection of signals as a letter from Vulcan Works, Worcester pressing for payment testifies. The final Directors meeting of the year records the payment of £5 17s 6d to the LNWR for carriage of a 45ft diameter turntable from Messrs Cowans and Co. of Carlisle to Woofferton where it was installed.

One of the original motives behind the building of the T&B was to reach the markets of the expanding West Midlands. Now it had become possible to travel to the Black Country via the Severn Valley Railway's southern junction at Hartlebury. This was however, not a satisfactory connection, particularly for goods traffic of a perishable or livestock nature. A reversal was necessary at Hartlebury and long delays were experienced through the lack of siding accommodation there. The LNWR, joint partner in the old S&H line, looked now to link its involvement with the Tenbury Railway to it massive undertakings in the Birmingham and Wolverhampton districts, where its relationship with the GWR was very different.

The Tenbury Railway was small fry compared to the opportunities that lay beyond it for the LNWR. Through its running powers south of Woofferton, the LNWR would gain a shortened route between the South Wales coalfield and its network in the West Midlands. All that was needed was the completion of the Kidderminster to Bewdley connection and to be able to run (possibly via Stourbridge) from somewhere on one of its routes to the south-west of Birmingham.

A Kidderminster to Bewdley loop had been planned as far back as 1860 by the then engineer of the OW&WR, Edward Wilson. This line was also authorised (1861) but not built due to financial constraints, so the authorization became void. The opening celebrations of the T&B had

A busy scene in Mill Street, Kidderminster, around the turn of the century. The horse dray belonged to Thomas Bantock, a Wolverhampton haulier who had stables and premises in Marlborough Street. These drays were a familiar sight until the late 1960s, hauling heavy loads of carpet from the mills up to the station on Comberton Hill. On the right is the Black Horse Hotel with its horse-drawn cab, which, like other hotel cabs, plied between the town and Kidderminster station. The chimney stack in the background was one of many once seen emitting smoke and steam from the boiler houses of the carpet mills. *Collection Wendy Hinton*

hardly been completed when the LNWR directors sought to remind the GWR of the need for this planned loop to become a reality. The Joint Officers Committee met at Euston in September 1864, Euston being one of the several alternative venues used by the LNWR/GWR Joint Committees. The LNWR brought to the attention of the GWR representatives the clause in the contract which stated that the curve should be completed by 30th June 1865. (Sometimes the line was referred to as the Bewdley curve, sometimes the Bewdley loop and at other times the Kidderminster curve.) At this time the LNWR was also waiting for agreement over running powers between Smethwick Junction and Stourbridge Junction, but, in the meantime, LNWR traffic for the T&B came through Dudley or Yarnton via Hartlebury.

Paddington was the meeting place for the Joint Officers in November. Mr Grierson of the GWR acknowledged the fact that the Bewdley loop was not yet started and pointed out that time was needed for the Stourbridge Company to agree terms for running powers in any case. It became perfectly obvious that the GWR were employing delaying tactics and although their next announcement did state that instructions had been given to start, no action was taken.

Early in 1865, in February, the Tenbury Wells Improvement Company met to discuss its state of affairs particularly with regard to inducing more visitors to the Bath House. The directors decided to approach the railway companies about issuing 'Bath tickets' at reduced rates during the coming year. There was also concern because they could see nothing being done to improve hotel accommodation for visitors, and to this end William Norris, active as ever, had set up the Teme Fishing Association and the Tenbury Wells Hotel and Boarding House Company, which took over and completely refurbished the Swan Hotel in Tenbury. In April, when the half-yearly meeting of the T&B took place, the Bewdley loop was again mentioned with anticipation of improved communications. Also in April 1865, Easton Court Station was reopened to the general public, a move probably encouraged by the traffic flow originating from the Bewdley end of the line.

The Tenbury Railway held its half-yearly meetings on the same day as those of the Tenbury & Bewdley as had been the custom for some time past. Many directors were common to both boards and of course there were many people with shares in both companies. Both meetings now concerned, to a large part, the financial returns for the shareholders. At the meeting in the spring of 1866 the Tenbury Railway announced a dividend of five shillings per share which it proposed to carry over to the following half-year's accounts. There was some dissatisfaction over the dividend agreements with the S&H, and a proposal was adopted to try for better terms when the lease expired. The Tenbury & Bewdley meeting also heard that a dividend would be paid (for the first time) in October 1866. In answer to a question, the T&B shareholders were reminded of the terms of the lease of the line to the GWR. They were 2½% for the 1st year, 3% for the next two years, then 4% in perpetuity. These terms differed slightly from the first agreement with the WMR in 1862.

The disappointment of the T&B Board that the Bewdley curve had not been started was apparent. 'The directors had hopes that the Kidderminster-Bewdley line would have been long since commenced. They regret they have been disappointed in this exception but they will take every opportunity of conveying upon the GWR the importance of completing this railway line.' Traffic destined for the LNWR from Tenbury was still having to be routed via Oxford over the Yarnton loop.

At the meetings of the Joint Railway officers in late 1865, there were two references to this situation which was irritating the T&B and frustrating the LNWR. In October it was reported that the Stourbridge line (Cradley-Old Hill) should be open in November but that the Bewdley extension to Kidderminster would not be ready for twelve months at least. At the December meeting there was another complaint from the LNWR representative about the delay and yet another reply from the GWR saying that instructions had been given for the works to proceed.

Several staff changes on the Tenbury Railway were dealt with at the December meeting and it is interesting to note the wages being paid. At Easton Court the position described as station agent was taken by J Clifton (moved from Leominster) at a wage of 18 shillings per week. The booking clerk at Tenbury was paid 12 shillings per week whilst the goods porter and the goods clerk were each paid 16 shillings per week. The pointsman at Woofferton was entitled to 18 shillings per week, increased from the 16 shillings per week paid previously. No payment is noted for the new Woofferton station master transferred down the S&HR line from Leebotwood. This was Mr W. Tranter, later to become a popular station master at Tenbury.

At the start of 1866, the T&B's attention was drawn away from the Bewdley loop delay to a proposition involving another line with the title 'The Teme Valley Railway'. Despite fierce opposition, the Teme Valley Railway secured an Act on 6th August 1866. This incorporated the proprietors of the Teme Valley Railway Company and authorised them to construct a railway from the London Worcester and South Wales Railway (authorised the previous year to build a line from the East-West Junction Railway at Stratford-upon-Avon to Worcester) to a junction with Tenbury & Bewdley 300 yards north of Newnham station, the junction facing Cleobury. Also proposed was another line from a point near Lindridge in the Teme Valley to a junction with the Tenbury Railway at the east end of Tenbury station, powers to be given for running over both the Tenbury & Bewdley and the Tenbury Railway lines.

The line from Worcester followed closely the route of the proposed GWR broad gauge routes of 1837/1846, following the River Teme through Broadheath, Martley, Stanford Bridge, Stockton and Lindridge, then out through a tunnel under high ground behind the Talbot Hotel at Newnham Bridge. The No.2 route would pass through Newnham station parallel to the Tenbury & Bewdley line, forming a double track to a junction at Tenbury.

The main object of the Teme Valley Railway would seem to have been the first step by the Midland Railway in its long attempt to reach its far-flung interests in South Wales by a direct line, by hoping eventually to extend from Tenbury to connect with the Hereford, Hay & Brecon Railway.

Eventually the chaotic state of the money market caused the abandonment of both the Teme Valley and the London, Worcester and South Wales proposals though neither company was ever legally wound up, and the Worcester link was for the moment left in abeyance.

Timetable changes made to the Tenbury & Bewdley line in July 1866 did not affect the general public greatly, and there were still four passenger trains daily each way Monday to Saturday. The operating side was altered, however, in that the early morning through train from Ludlow was arranged to work from Leominster with a Leominster-based locomotive running via Woofferton and returning from Bewdley to Leominster at night with the last train on the branch. The first through train from Bewdley to Woofferton was put back to arrive at Woofferton at 11.20 am. A midday goods described as the 'Bewdley Goods' ran from Bewdley to arrive at 3.10 pm with a return working from Leominster departing at 3.50 pm.

The continued lease of the Tenbury Railway came up for discussion at one of the regular Joint Railway meetings and led to the GWR (Further Powers) Act of 30th July 1866, which gave the GWR, the LNWR and the Tenbury Railway powers to enter into arrangements for the management, use, work and maintenance of the Tenbury Railway which were to lead the way to the eventual transfer of the Tenbury Railway to the two senior companies. In June 1866 the GWR introduced a new dimension into its procrastination over the Bewdley loop. It announced at a Joint Officers meeting that it had surveyed a different route between Bewdley and Stourbridge which would take in the ironworking districts around Cookley and Wolverley to the west of Kidderminster. However, on closer examination, this new plan proved to be more costly and no shorter, so the scheme was dropped in favour of the original. In October, at the request of Mr Moone (LNWR), the GWR chairman himself (Mr James Milne) gave yet another undertaking that the curve could be constructed by 1st November 1867. Earlier that year, on 1st April, the Stourbridge Company had extended its line by connecting

Old Hill Station to the LNWR via a junction at Galton. At the same time the GWR opened the connecting line between Smethwick Junction and Handsworth, thus connecting Birmingham directly with Kidderminster for both GWR and LNWR traffic. Unfortunately, the GWR promise of a November 1867 opening for the Bewdley loop came to nothing and by now a new Parliamentary application was needed to extend the statutory powers that had already been granted.

In April 1867 the agreement made in March 1860 to provide a station for the Office of Woods and Forests, in exchange for Crown land in the Wyre Forest, had resurfaced and came under scrutiny. In November 1864 Charles Gore wrote on behalf of the Office of Woods and Forests, reminding the T&B of its obligation and requiring that the station be built. The T&B Directors responded, attempting to avoid any development by referring to the spirit in which the stipulation was originally conceded, i.e. that enforcement would only take place in favourable circumstances and that current financial restrictions and poor traffic prospects of a new station persuaded the Board that the request should be deferred for the present. The Office of Woods and Forests were not persuaded and a further request was made for a plan for the proposed station site to be submitted. William Clarke, together with two GWR officers (George Armstrong, Locomotive Superintendent and Mr C Harris, Traffic Superintendent, Hereford) sent a report to Mr Gore which, in summary, stated that it was not desirable to have a station at Lodge Hill in the Wyre Forest, a view supported in writing by James Grierson, General Manager of the GWR. In the meantime, the Office of Woods and Forests had reminded the T&B Board that money was owing to it for the price of the land sold for a station site plus legal fees accrued in the process of the present exchanges, and in September 1865 another request was made that a reply should be given 'without further delay whether the Directors are prepared to carry out the portion of their agreement with the Crown for the erection of a station upon this estate'.

The matter was deliberately shelved during 1866 by the Office of Woods and Forests in consideration of the poor financial climate of the country but in April 1867 the matter was taken up again by Mr Gore, who expressed his surprise that the T&B Company should seek to avoid the fulfilment of the agreement. He had now deduced, more importantly, that the report from the Engineer and Railway Officers, including such statements as 'the proposed site is highly dangerous for a station', referred to a site at Lodge Hill (where the Crown had only requested a siding) and not to the original proposal for siting a station, which was in reality 2½ miles away towards Cleobury Mortimer! This discovery invalidated all previous objections and led to a renewal of demand that a station should be constructed 'forthwith'. As a financial inducement, an offer was made that the money owed to the Crown could be paid by quarterly instalments over four years, provided the station was opened for traffic by 1st October 1868.

There was no action from the T&B Company and the patience of the Office of Woods and Forests finally expired when a letter dated 13th May 1867 included formal legal notice to the company to construct a station in accordance with their agreement and to have it operational by 1st October 1868. The company could not take charge of the work, but by September 1867, the GWR's engineer, Michael Lane, had become involved and had drawn up an estimate of costs. In October, the Secretary of the T&B received from Charles Gore approval of the proposed building plans but also, in addition, a demand for an immediate settlement of outstanding debts!

Without any available finances it was impossible for the T&B to make a start on station building, and by September 1868 the works were still not under way. However, in August of that year the GWR had agreed to give the T&B 'such assistance as might appear to be necessary to enable them to construct the station at Far Forest'. The GWR made this offer whilst regretting the Crown's insistence but acknowledging the T&B's liability as the important issue. The GWR also asked by what means any money advanced by them would be secured by the T&B. In the end, the Crown agreed to take a rent charge of 4% on the money owed to them and their request for a siding at Lodge Hill disappeared from the discussions, as did the insistence on the introduction of a goods service, though the right to request such a service was reserved for a later date.

After many deadlines had passed, the GWR completed Wyre Forest station building in November 1868 athough it was not opened to passengers until the following June. The plans show a single-storey station house, apparently later raised to the height seen in the photographs. The station was built on a 1 in 75 gradient, so the GWR laid a short safety spur off the gradient and blocked the end of this with a turf-covered earth stop. Later, when a goods service was introduced, this spur was used as a siding with a loading gauge and a side loading dock. The station was equipped with the Spagnoletti telegraph in a small wooden 'signal box' which also operated the points to the goods siding. A porter-cum-booking clerk looked after the station on his own, the building being let to a Mr Lovatt.

Passenger and parcels receipts for the first five months of operation at Wyre Forest were disapointing, showing a loss against expenses. Norris was quick to draw this to the GWR's attention, seeking its further support in the conflict with the Crown, whose Commissioners were now demanding the construction of a goods shed which would cost the company around £2,000. Norris's hope that the Crown would drop their demands was eventually realised after the GWR had presented the case against putting the T&B to more expense.

By 1868, the expanding cattle trade at Tenbury station was suffering delay from lack of siding accommodation

Far Forest was, and still is, a scattered settlement midway between Bewdley and Cleobury Mortimer. Although it was the nearest village to Wyre Forest station, it was never convenient for rail travel as it entailed a long walk down country lanes which public transport never penetrated.
Collection Wendy Hinton

and it was recommended at a Joint Committee meeting that a new cattle pen be provided at a cost of £15. The general maintenance of Tenbury station remained entirely with the Joint Committee who discussed a plan to improve the condition of the station drive and to build a stable for the shunting horse at a cost of £65 to replace 'the very inferior accommodation provided in the town at £6 p.a.'

The uniform for staff on the Joint stations was described at a meeting, but whether this was for a new introduction or a change from previous regulations is not clear. Dark blue cloth was provided for a station master or inspector, whilst green cord was for porters and the like. All buttons had GWR/LNWR initialled on them.

The opening of the Stourbridge line as far as Smethwick in April 1867 had repercussions for the T&B because now LNWR coaches from Birmingham could run through to Kidderminster and beyond towards Worcester and Hereford. After this there was only the Kidderminster-Bewdley link needed to complete the chain that would give the LNWR its most direct route to South Wales.

From 1st January 1869, the Tenbury Railway was transferred to the ownership of the LNWR and GWR under an agreement of 1st December 1868 and in the summer of 1869, a draft agreement set up the transfer of the Tenbury & Bewdley Company to the GWR from 1st February of the following year. On 24th March 1870, the last meeting of T&B shareholders took place in Tenbury. The directors, in taking their leave of shareholders, 'beg to congratulate them on having carried out a line which must always prove a source of advantage to Tenbury and neighbourhood and secondly on transferring the undertaking to the GWR on fair and reasonable terms'.

Thomas Brassey, a most influential figure in the affairs of so many railway schemes throughout the world, died in 1870 before his contract with the GWR for the Bewdley loop could get under way. This further delay did not seem to hurry the GWR for it was showing no sign of using the powers given to it by Parliament, but it went back to Parliament in 1871 to gain another three years leeway (three years from the date of the Act — 18th July 1872).

Early in 1871 the GWR informed all station masters on the line of changes to signalling, and issued instructions for signalling trains by the disc block telegraph in addition to the train staff in use, to come into effect from 10th February 1871.

There were four staff-and-tickets: Woofferton–Tenbury, which was coloured red and triangular; Tenbury–Neen Sollars, yellow and round; Neen Sollars–Cleobury, blue and triangular; and Cleobury Mortimer–Bewdley, white and square.

By 1872 the Tenbury Line was firmly established as a cheap means of transportation for the mainly agricultural products that lay along its route. The demise of the Leominster Canal had been a severe setback for the aspirations of the local colliery owners, who hoped to expand towards bigger markets outside the area. Now a bold attempt was made to link the southern portion of the Wyre Forest coalfield directly by rail. The owner of Pensax Court, John Higginbottom, petitioned for a Bill in the House of Commons, for a single-line railway some 4¼ miles long, from a junction with the Tenbury & Bewdley 7½ chains south of the booking office at Cleobury Mortimer station. For the first mile the line would curve up and away in a south-easterly direction on a grade of 1 in 33, running parallel and close to the road from Cleobury Mortimer to Clows Top (now the B4202), crossing the minor Bayton–Far Forest road on a bridge of 20ft span and 15ft high. The next quarter of a mile was downgrade at 1 in 60, levelling off for half a mile over Bayton Common, before a sharp rise at 1 in 43 for a further half mile, crossing on the level the Clows Top–Bewdley road (now the A456), quite near to the Colliers Arms public house. On an easier grade of 1 in 379, the line would climb for three-quarters of a mile (crossing Rock Moor), then changing to a 1 in 62 down grade for a half a mile. The last half mile or so was to be uphill at 1 in 234 (crossing the Clows Top–Great Witley road on the level between Upper and Lower Hollins farms), reaching the terminus at a point where the Pensax to Stockton-on-Teme road makes a junction with the Clows Top–Great Witley road. The former would be crossed by another bridge of 20ft span and 15ft high. It was proposed to sink shafts near the terminus at Pensax and set up a colliery, test borings having shown workable coal seams.

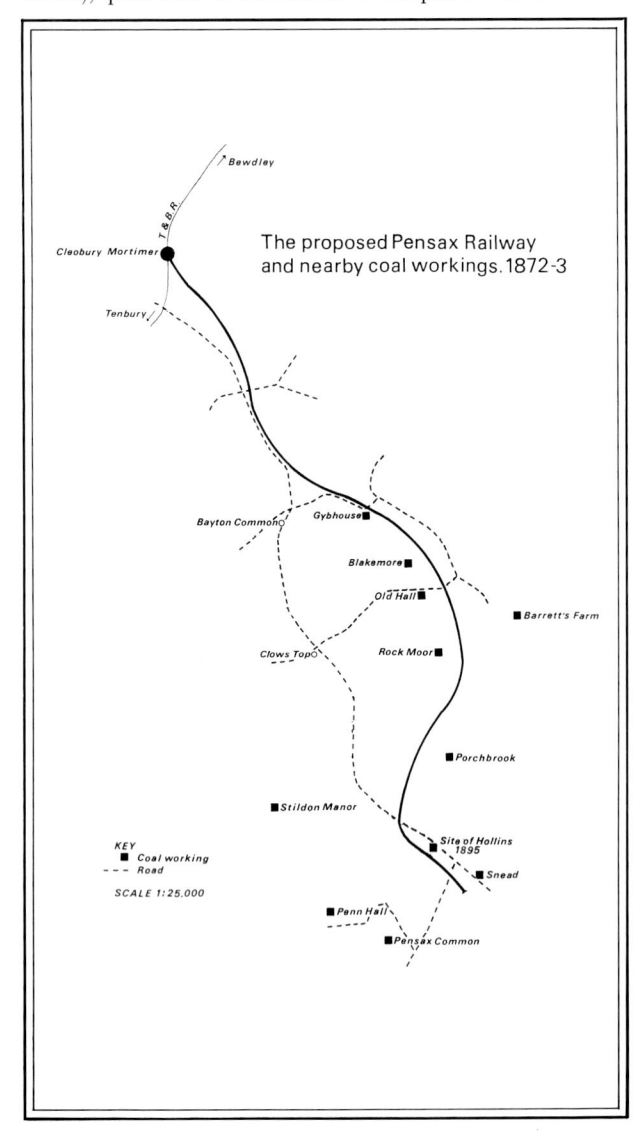

Early in 1873 an objection to the proposed line was lodged (rather surprisingly) in the House of Commons by Sir Edward Blount of Mawley Hall with the result that it was to be brought before a select committee for their judgement. The select committee convened on Tuesday, 1st April 1873. Present for the proposers were Messrs Mains and Co, solicitors; John Higginbottom; the Vicar of Pensax (Rev John Cawood); Mr William Clarke (engineer and late of the Tenbury & Bewdley Railway); and finally a representative of the GWR. The objector, Sir Edward Blount, did not attend, being represented by his son who was a practising solicitor.

Some time was spent hearing the outline plan for a direct communication with the Pensax coal mines, which up till then had no satisfactory outlet. It was felt that the yield from the mines would be sufficient to warrant the line. Initially it would carry coal from the proposed mine but also from other mines along the route near Gybhouse Farm, Blakemore Farm and the mine on Rock Moor. There was a proposal also to run a passenger service. The Vicar of Pensax pointed out the obvious benefits to the area bringing in much needed employment and better communication with the towns 'over the hill' (i.e. Clows Top). The GWR representative spoke briefly about the line, stating that although there were some heavy gradients and curves, they presented no problems to his company in working the line.

On behalf of his father, Sir Edward Blount's son put the objection, which was that the line would not be of any public advantage, being purely a speculative project to benefit the owner of Pensax Court estate. For some two miles it would pass in a very injurious and objectionable way through the Mawley estate, the promoter seeking to obtain compulsory land from the frontage of the estate adjoining the Cleobury–Clows Top road for nearly a mile. Because of the proximity of the line to the road, it would be extremely dangerous to horse traffic and the like.

Details of the proposal were:

Cleobury Mortimer and Pensax Railway promoted 1872
£33,000 in £10 shares
Engineer — William Clarke
Solicitor — James Mains, 20 Abingdon Street, Westminster
Parliamentary Agents — Martin & Leslie, 27 Abingdon St, Westminster

Length — 4 miles 8 chains
Level crossings — 4 (2 over farm roads)
Bridges — 2, 20ft × 15ft

After a great deal of deliberation, the advice of the select committee was that the Bill be thrown out, such was the influence of the powerful landowners.

In the continuing saga of the link with the West Midlands, the Bewdley to Stourbridge alternative had still not been forgotten. Another plan and section was prepared for a devious route over twelve miles long estimated to cost a huge £211,000. This time the alternative to the Bewdley loop progressed beyond mere planning and went before a House of Commons committee in June 1873. The LNWR in its evidence opposed the line, stating its strong preference for the Bewdley loop. Additional opposition came from the proprietors of the Staffordshire and Worcestershire Canal whose route the railway would follow in part and who naturally did not welcome the competition for their goods traffic. The objectors won the battle, and the GWR was told to progress with the loop. The LNWR could wait no longer, deciding to act on its own initiative and back a new project entitled The West Staffordshire Railway. This proposal was reported in the *Kidderminster Shuttle* in January 1875 and was described as a nineteen-mile long double-track line from the LNWR's Stour Valley line at Wolverhampton to a junction with the Tenbury & Bewdley near the eastern abutment of the Dowles Bridge. The route was to pass west of Kidderminster through Kinver, Cookley, Wolverley, Franche and Northwood. Landowners and ironfounders in the region gave support, as did Bewdley Town Council which resolved unanimously to support the West Staffs Railway. When the Mayor of Bewdley gave evidence before the House of Commons select committee, he stressed the importance of the proposed line for the farmers west of Bewdley who would have additional access to the cattle and corn markets at Wolverhampton and without the delays experienced with traffic via Hartlebury. He added that the proposed Bewdley loop would also end this particular evil but 'competition is essential to get the best out of railway companies'. He took the opportunity to criticize the shabby treatment which the inhabitants of Bewdley had suffered by the GWR's delay and he added his hope that the committee would sanction the Bill. Coal boring trials undertaken by Sandwell Park Colliery (West Bromwich) were taking place close to Dowles Manor near the proposed junction of the line at Bewdley and these gave active support for the proposed line although no workable coals had been found.

Whilst the West Staffs was gathering momentum, the GWR again requested an extension of time to construct its loop, and even got as far as awarding the contract to Messrs Crockett and Dickinson, with Mr C. Everest as engineer. The GWR had been finally forced into action by the LNWR's move over the West Staffs, and on 13th March 1875 the *Kidderminster Times* was able to report that 'active commencement of this long delayed railway has now been made'. In consequence of this, the West Staffs Bill failed.

In 1875 safety matters concerning the Tenbury branch connection at Woofferton were dealt with. The up home signal from the branch was moved into a position opposite the main line junction signal and the two signals made to be the same height. Previously, when viewed by a driver coming off the branch over the junction, the main line signal could appear, in error, to be the signal applying to the branch. The facing point into the goods siding was moved onto the branch down line, thereby turning it into a trailing connection. Two plans dated December 1874 and February 1875 detail these alterations and include reference to Woofferton signal box as 'new'.

The estimated date for completion of the single line beyond Bewdley was March 1876. However, true to form, work fell behind time. In March 1877, although much of the civil engineering had been completed, delay was still being caused by bad weather, in particular along the cutting east of Bewdley tunnel.

By June 1877, construction work had advanced sufficiently for discussions to take place between LNWR and GWR officers about the proposed train service over the Bewdley and Kidderminster curve. On the question of the passenger service, the LNWR representatives were unable to accept the GWR's proposed timetable as they considered that it did not provide for through traffic from their system to and from South Wales. They considered that a train was needed, leaving Birmingham at 1.30pm so as to reach Woofferton at 3.20pm to connect with the 2.25pm Shrewsbury to Hereford, and also a departure from Tenbury at 1.30pm in connection with the 12.10pm joint train from Hereford which would work through to Birmingham, arriving at about 3.05pm. The GWR officers did not consider that there would be sufficient traffic to justify running these trains but stated that their company would be prepared to put trains on under the terms of agreement, if required to do so, but on the LNWR Company's account. The question was referred to the managers but neither train appeared in the June 1878 timetable, which showed four passenger trains in each direction between Kidderminster and Tenbury, the first train of the morning originating from Leominster at 6.55am and the last train of the day terminating there at 8.32pm (thus suggesting that Leominster shed provided the locomotive).

With regard to the working of the goods and mineral traffic, it was considered that Tenbury would be the most suitable place for traffic to be handed over by the LNWR to the GWR and vice-versa. Major changes in layout and facilities would be needed at Tenbury. Two long loop lines with accommodation for engine and brake van exchange should be provided on both up and down sides of the line. An engine shed with room for four engines, coaling stage, turntables and water tank was envisaged. It was mentioned that less siding room would be needed if LNWR engines were to take traffic through from Woofferton to Smethwick, instead of exchanging at Tenbury. (It is tantalising not to know what type of LNWR locomotives worked the early schedules via the Bewdley curve noted in the 1878 and 1879 Service timetables as 'LNWR Empties' and 'LNWR Coal'.)

The officers recommended that provision should be made for trains to cross at Tenbury. A second platform would be provided, the current goods line would be utilized to form a lengthened loop, and the goods siding thus taken from traffic purposes would be compensated for by the introduction of a new siding on the down side of the line. An instruction was issued to the LNWR/GWR Joint Committee to prepare plans and estimates for properly interlocking the station at each end, for which a new signal box would be required on the up platform.

It was anticipated that the new work would be inspected at the same time as the Bewdley–Kidderminster line, but, due to delays to the latter, this was not possible. The Inspector's report of the Tenbury rearrangements (February 1878) showed some detailed alterations from the proposals discussed earlier. Two long sidings had been provided on the Tenbury side of the station, together with a turntable, a new loop in the third siding, a crossover at the Woofferton end of the station layout, an extra siding at the goods shed (not entering the shed), a new siding at the Burford side (cattle siding), and a new facing point at the Bewdley end extending the double track under the Clee Hill road bridge. One goods siding (unspecified) had been slewed. The Tenbury side station platform was extended but its new signal box, previously mentioned, was not built. A waiting shelter and gents had been built on the new down platform.

The turntable, formerly at Woofferton, had been dismantled and re-erected at Tenbury about 200 yards west of the station at the entrance to the new goods yard, the site of the original temporary station. Thirty feet from the turntable, on the turntable road, was a 27ft long locomotive pit.

The Officers of the Joint companies also reviewed arrangements elsewhere along the line. Their report concluded that at Easton Court the points and signals should be properly concentrated and locked, and the platform lengthened. It was also recommended that Easton Court be made an intermediate block station in order to facilitate the working of trains over this portion of the line. In October 1877 plans were submitted for a loop siding and second platform at Easton Court as an alternative. Although recommended, this proposal was deferred pending a statement of accounts from Easton Court from the previous year. The safety of permanent way gangs on the Joint Section was made more secure by a recommendation in the same report that the open decking of the River Teme bridge beyond Easton Court station be covered in.

For Neen Sollars, a proposed plan dated 17th June 1878 showed a new, second platform (offset in relation to the original), a crossover at the Tenbury end of the loop with a short extension to the already existing siding. A small signal box containing levers for four points, two lock bars, seven signals (and three spare levers) was detailed. The revised layout was inspected on 21st June 1878 with the anticipation that it would open for use on 26th August 1878, but Neen Sollars was shown as a crossing place in the June 1878 service timetable.

The Tenbury alterations were completed on time, and immediately on hearing this, Mr Findlay of the LNWR asked the GWR to let him have a date for the Bewdley loop's opening. The reply informed him that the GWR engineers were completing a final check on 18th March prior to the visit of Col. Rich (the Board of Trade inspector) on 22nd March 1878. The inspection train left Kidderminster in the morning carrying the GWR engineers from Hereford and Wolverhampton districts, George Armstrong (loco superintendent, Wolverhampton) the GWR traffic superintendent, the contractor Charles Dickenson, and the inspector Col. Rich. The bridges, viaducts and the tunnel (lit by candles and naptha lamps) were pronounced a credit to Mr Dickenson, but Col. Rich found fault at Bewdley.

The inspection report said:

'There is a turntable at Kidderminster and trains will run through Bewdley (where the present turntable is being removed) to Woofferton. The following works are required at Bewdley, doing away with all unnecessary facing points. Bewdley is approached from the west by two single lines. These should be connected as ordinary double junctions and run through the station as a double line of railway and the two lines from the east should be treated in the same manner. The loop lines which run round the north side of the new island platform should be connected with the double line by one ordinary double junction at each end of the platform. A bridge is required for passengers between the island platform and station building. A shelter is required on the island platform. This platform is not yet completed. The platform at the south side which is being extended requires to be fenced. All the running lines through Bewdley Station will require home and distant signals which should be placed behind locking points. Sidings and siding junctions will require safety points and ground discs. The new line generally requires packing and adjusting. I submit that the new railway between Bewdley and Kidderminster cannot be opened to traffic without danger to the public using the line in consequence with the incomplete state of the work.'

It was some time before a re-inspection was requested, mainly due to delays connected with the alterations in track formations that were required. A letter to the B.O.T. explained the GWR's position:

'Inspection of the new line from Kidderminster to Bewdley. I have to inform you that no unnecessary delay took place in commencing alterations at Bewdley station as soon as it was known what the Inspecting Officer considered necessary but owing to the peculiar character of some of the crossings required in connection with alterations of lines, a number had to be made specially and some little time occupied in consequence. The Engineer is however pushing on with the work as rapidly as possible, and will have it completed by 28th May by which date I should be obliged if you can arrange for a re-inspection between

Kidderminster station c.1917. With the opening of the loop line in 1878, Kidderminster became the terminus for most Severn Valley and Tenbury branch trains as well as giving a direct route to Birmingham and beyond. *Collection Brian Standish*

then and 31st May as we are extremely anxious to open the line on June 1st. P.S. You will be aware that we have promised to give as far as practical a week's notice of any alteration in train service and under these circumstances I hope the B.O.T. will sanction the opening line on June 1st whether the re-inspection has taken place or not or even if any small work has not been quite completed by that date.'

The Inspectorate, naturally, were not prepared to go along with such freedom of action and replied:

'I am to inform you that the B.O.T. have directed Col. Rich to inspect the line at the time requested by you but with respect to opening the line on 1st June it must rest with the Inspecting Officer as to whether he is then able to report that the line can be opened with safety to the public.'

The line was re-inspected on 29th May 1878, again by Col. Rich. The GWR had, perhaps recklessly, pre-judged his verdict by placing an advertisement in the *Kidderminster Times* on 25th May announcing the opening on 1st June. Its confidence however, was justified by the report:

'31st May, Re-inspection Report; No objection to use of Bewdley curve following an undertaking given by the Company on 15th April 1878, that the GWR Company hereby undertake that the single line of the railway between Bewdley and Kidderminster known as the Bewdley Curve shall be worked on the train staff and ticket system with block telegraph. The Shelter on the island platform and the footbridge are not completed but are in hand and to be completed as soon as possible. The name of the station is also required on the island platform and the locking frame altered in Bewdley South Cabin so that No. 16 lever shall be locked with signals 6, 23 and 21. Opening sanctioned.'

The first public train left Bewdley soon after 8.00am on 1st June 1878. There were no intermediate stations en route at this time so Kidderminster was the first stop. The 8.25am connection to Birmingham and Wolverhampton was waiting. There was little in the way of public celebrations for the first train, but no doubt relief was felt by the LNWR officers on seeing the loop at last open for their through traffic in the direction of South Wales. LNWR records show that its tri-composite carriages were put into service on the line. Two each way (commencing on Monday, 3rd June 1878) were attached to GWR trains from Snow Hill at Smethwick Junction.

The LNWR had been granted running powers for all classes from Smethwick Junction to Tenbury Joint station by virtue of articles 24, 28, and 34 of a comprehensive agreement dated 17th March 1863 between the LNWR, the GWR and WMR. (The LNWR already possessed running powers for passenger traffic between Smethwick Junction and Stourbridge, by virtue of the Stourbridge Extension Railway Act of 1st August 1861). With completion of the Stourbridge line and its opening on 1st April 1867, through passenger trains between Birmingham (New Street) and Kidderminster and/or Worcester and Hereford ran via Galton Junction (Smethwick) instead of Dudley. Initially there were seven each way on weekdays and four on Sundays. The June 1878 service timetable details six LNWR 'empty wagon', trains on weekdays (three of them run when required) and seven balancing coal trains in the opposite direction. These ran through the night, and the use of a banking engine based at

Kidderminster shed was called upon to assist these loaded trains, including the Stourbridge goods, between Neen Sollars and Cleobury Mortimer. The banking engine from Kidderminster shed reached Neen Sollars attached to the 7.45pm LNWR empties. However by March 1879, the LNWR goods trains had declined to one 'empties' and one coal on three days per week only and the Kidderminster–Woofferton passenger service was reduced to four each way. That long-lived institution, the Stourbridge and Leominster goods, was advertised in the June 1878 service timetable as a train which worked station trucks from West Midland stations to Joint Railway stations between Leominster and Condover.

Extra traffic coming on to the Tenbury line as a consequence of the Bewdley curve being opened brought the need for altered traffic arrangements. Even before the

Hotel cabs outside Kidderminster station's black and white facade, usually described as 'mock Tudor'. This lovely building was demolished in 1969 after BR declared it unsafe!
Collection Wendy Hinton

The Kidderminster and Stourport Tramway, opened in May 1898, was one of Britain's first electric tramway systems, and, as well as running between the two towns, there was also a branch to the Kidderminster suburb of Somerleyton via Comberton Hill (referred to locally as Station Hill). This view shows a tram running down the hill on its way back to Kidderminster town centre terminus. The rival 'Midland Red' bus company was one reason for the tramway's closure in April 1929. *Collection Brian Standish*

EXPANSION AFTER 1864

curve was opened, Woofferton was short of siding space. Traffic from Tenbury bound for Ludlow and Shrewsbury had to be taken down the line to wait at Leominster before moving back up line to its destination. Apart from the extra mileage involved, there were complaints from the staff at Leominster about the extra wagons taking up the siding space there. In response, a recommendation was made in 1876 for the lengthening of one siding on the up side of Woofferton and also adding a new one on the Tenbury side of the junction to hold forty wagons. The position of the signal off the Tenbury line was altered from the down to the up side, and then the following year, continuing the re-arrangements, the timber crane was moved alongside the new siding.

Tenbury, out of all the stations along the line, was most affected by the new traffic. Four new signalmen were employed to work in the two signalboxes (known as 'A' and 'B' boxes) and 'the present signalman to be employed as a platform porter'. A night inspector was also required at Tenbury so that shunting could continue for longer hours. An extension to a siding was put in so that shunting would not interfere with running on the 'main' line and in addition would free one signalman to leave his cabin and help with marshalling the goods traffic. On the matter of personnel, the news of the intending transfer of Station Master Tranter from Tenbury to Church Stretton upset the railway's customers so much that they organized a memorial in favour of allowing him to remain where he was, but the official reply briefly stated that such an alteration to the plans could not be entertained.

The diversity of rolling stock seen on the branch must have increased at this time and this is confirmed in the report of a minor accident at Woofferton in 1878 which reveals than an LNWR 3rd class brake carriage No. 242 was included in the through passenger train concerned (the 4.35pm to Bewdley). This carriage was a 22ft 6in long vehicle built in 1859 at Saltley for the Walsall to Dudley services, but by 1878 it had been cascaded to the Tenbury–Birmingham stock. The carriage was in collision with the 4.45pm empty stock to Tenbury and a vehicle from this train (GWR third class 1106 built to Diagram 738) was also damaged.

Another collision, which occurred on 24th October 1877 at Newnham Bridge station, was the subject of a Board of Trade report. The 3.15pm passenger train from Bewdley to Tenbury ran into a goods train which was shunting at Newnham Bridge station. One empty goods wagon was thrown off the rails, 3 wagons and the guard's van of the goods train were damaged. No part of the passenger train left the rails. Three passengers complained of being hurt but their injuries were believed to be slight.

The passenger train consisted of a 'tank engine with its coal box in front, a 3rd class with brake compartment, 2 passenger coaches and a brake van at the tail end of the train with the guard in charge'. It ran into the brake van and seven wagons (part of the goods train) that were standing on the main line with the van about 80 yards outside the Newnham Bridge home signal. These vehicles were detached from the engine and the rest of the train while shunting was being performed.

'Newnham Bridge is a small station on a single line of rails. It is protected with the ordinary home and distant signals which are not interlocked with points of the siding which joins the passenger line at the N.E. end of the station platform. The home signal is at the east end of the platform; the distant signal is 720 yards from the home signal and can be seen by a driver approaching from the North for about 470 yards before he reaches it. The home signal cannot be seen until the driver gets through the bridge over the line which is about 150 yards from the station. The gradient falls 1:132 from north side of the distant signal to the bridge over the railway at the NE end of the station and rises 1:590 from the bridge through Newnham Bridge station. The line is worked on the train staff and ticket system with the assistance of the block telegraph.

Evidence

Peter Dodd: Goods guard (GWR) 15 years service, worked over the Tenbury and Bewdley line over the last 10 years. I was guard of the 11.10am Goods train from Stourbridge to Leominster. On 24th October, left Neen Sollars at 3.23pm we arrived at Newnham Bridge at 3.33pm. We had a good deal of shunting to do, we picked up 8 loaded wagons and put off 3 loaded and 6 empties. When we first arrived we stopped short of the home signal to do some work. After this had been done, we drew ahead to the station and then began to pick our wagons up and put others off. When we had done this the engine drew up again opposite the platform for us to put on our roadside goods. During this time the passenger train arrived and came into collision with that portion of my train that had been left standing on the main line. The van was standing outside the home signal with 7 wagons attached to it. The effect of the collision threw 1 check wagon off the rails and damaged my van and 4 wagons slightly. I heard the collision but did not see the passenger train approaching. I cannot say what speed they were running.

Oliver Parsons: I am station master at Newnham Bridge. I have been 15 years in the Company's service, 7 years SM here. The Goods train arrived here at 3.36pm. I stopped them at the points at the up end of siding to get 6 loaded wagons out of the dock. They then drew onto this end of the station and finished shunting at 3.50pm. We were getting out some roadside traffic at the platform when I heard the collision with the passenger train. I went down the yard to see what had happened and there was one wagon off the rails, two wheels and two wagons lock buffered. The goods train was signalled from Neen Sollars at 3.27pm by two beats on bell. I replied by three beats and then Neen Sollars pegged 'line clear' and then signalled 'train on line' by unpegging instrument and ringing once at 3.27pm. I then pegged the red key down and the disc indicated 'train on line'. This should fix the instrument at Neen Sollars to 'train on line'. I did not touch the instrument again or come into the office until after the collision had occurred and then I saw that the instrument was as I had left it 'train on line'. The signals were at danger when the collision occurred. No complaint was made to me at the time by any of the passengers. Knowing that the goods train was outside the home signal I relied on the block and my distant signal for its protection or otherwise I should have sent someone back knowing the passenger train was overdue. The collision occurred between bridge and station about 80 yards from the platform.

Joseph Morton: I have been running on this section daily for the past three years. On 24th October I was driving the 3.15pm passenger train. The distant signal was at danger at Newnham Bridge, I slackened speed to about 4mph and went quietly on towards the home signal. I saw the van standing on the line as I came through the bridge. The check wagon between loaded timber trucks was knocked off the road. I thought the line was clear to the station. I never came in against signals before.

Henry Southam: In employ of GWR. 25 years in the service. Was station master from 1866–1871 and frequently been in charge of stations on a single line and am perfectly well acquainted with working the same. 24th October I was in charge of Neen Sollars I asked for by two beats of the instrument, and obtained 'line clear' by getting three beats for the goods train at 3.15pm and sent 'train on line' by one beat at 3.34pm. Red key was then pegged over to 'train on line' on my instrument. The 3.15pm arrived at Neen Sollars at 3.45pm. I then asked 'is line clear?' by pressing the key down twice. My instrument was at this time pinned to 'train on line' and this was not acknowledged but the result of my pressing the key down and keeping my thumb upon it caused the disc to hang loose which I mistook for the line clear signal and I gave the engineman of the passenger train the staff for him to proceed, the previous train having had a ticket. I had been doing stations master's duty at Neen Sollars three or four days, I had not been at Neen Sollars before but I had acted as SM at many other stations on the branch.

Milson Gwilliam: I am the guard, 3 years running over this line and was in charge of 3.15pm passenger train from Bewdley–Tenbury. I left Neen Sollars right time, 3.45pm and came into collision with the goods train at Newnham Bridge at 3.52pm. The driver checked his train at the distant signal which I saw was at danger and I put my brake on in the usual way, soon after we passed the distant signal and as the engine reached the bridge the driver whistled for the brake and we struck the goods train almost immediately. I think we were going about 6mph when we struck them and I believe we should have stopped alright at the platform. Several passengers complained of being shaken, one female said her leg was hurt a little but no one complained at being seriously hurt. When I arrived at Tenbury I left the passengers in the hands of the station master, I did not take any names. When the driver called for my brake it was on and I only had time to tighten it up a little before we struck the goods. I think the rate of speed at which we passed the distant was about 8–10mph. The driver had checked the speed before this.

Conclusion
The accident was caused by the station master at Neen Sollars who started the passenger train while his block telegraph instrument showed the line to be blocked and by the engine driver of the passenger train who passed the Newnham Bridge distant signal which was at danger and ran on towards Newnham Station at such speed that he could not stop his train when he found the line blocked with the goods train. The home and distant signals at Newnham Bridge were both at danger when the passenger train arrived in accordance with the Company's rules. The driver should not have proceeded beyond the distant at any greater speed than would enable him to pull up his train at any place if he found the line occupied. His excuse for not pulling up sooner is that he had never found the goods train at Newnham Bridge on any previous occasion and that he believed the signals were at danger against him because the line was blocked between Newnham Bridge and Tenbury not because it was occupied by the goods train at the North East side of Newnham Bridge station. I recommend that the signals and points at Newnham Bridge should be interlocked and the site of the home signal be improved so that it might be better seen by a driver approaching from the North East.

Signed F. H. Rich Col. R.E.

The goods traffic of the 1870s is brought to light from occasional references. 'Shoddy' was sent from Yorkshire to be used as a fertiliser and it is interesting to find that sugar in those days travelled by rail packed in barrels. The LNWR officers explained the reduced rates for all traffic agreed with the Burton brewers, which was politely 'noted' and 'objected to' by the officials of the GWR. Goods sent out from the stations on the line continued to follow the pattern envisaged from the early days. The movement of agricultural produce had a long high season, starting with cherries from the Wyre Forest in June, and ending with hops from Tenbury, Easton Court and Newnham Bridge in late autumn. (Newnham station had been so renamed in 1873 to avoid confusion with the Gloucestershire Newnham station). The cattle market at Tenbury produced traffic for the railway in such increasing quantities that the accommodation was found to be too limited for the numbers brought in and out on market days. A plan to provide two additional pens was approved in January 1883 at an estimated cost of £40. This improvement did not materialise for it was realised that the new construction would involve the loss of the horse and carriage landing, the replacement of which would raise the total cost to £150. The approval for the pens was then cancelled by Mr Patchett who, in spite of the demand from the customers, decided 'that traffic at Tenbury is not sufficient to warrant this expense'.

If cattle loading and unloading was being delayed at Tenbury, sorting and shunting of general goods had been speeded up, delays were being cut and the night inspector was dispensed with. Covered vans began to take the place of sheeted open wagons for some merchandise, enough now to require a landing at Easton Court to be altered in July 1883 'to admit the loading of vans'.

In 1885, with traffic continuing to increase, it became necessary for the Joint Officers to confer with the Board of Trade about introducing the block telegraph system of working between Woofferton and Tenbury with an intermediate post at Easton Court. Mr Spagnoletti was asked to submit an estimate for the work to Messrs Neale and Tyrell of the Joint Committee. The amount came to £107 6s 9d which was sanctioned with the observation that no extra wages for staff would be required. However, in May 1885 the cost was finally amended by £20 because no account had been made for working the system between the two signal cabins at Tenbury nor for the keyless disc fitted at Little Hereford level crossing. In November 1885 the system came into operation and soon it was recommended and agreed that the facing points leading to the siding at Easton Court be locked by a special staff key, and that trap points should be placed in the siding, at a cost of £30.

In May 1886 the Teme Valley and district experienced one of the area's most disastrous floods on record. By four o'clock on Friday, 14th May, Tenbury was completely under water, and a plaque in the Parish Church still shows the height of the water on that day. The damage to crops and property was widespread with the railway having its share of problems. Worst of these was the wash-out at the Teme Bridge, cutting the line completely between Tenbury and Woofferton. The Birmingham to Tenbury service was curtailed as three bridges between Bewdley and Newnham were also damaged, in

An unidentified '517' class 0-4-2T on Dowles Bridge, sometime between 1878 and 1890. The leading four coaches were GWR and appear to have had the shortlived style of class designations written above the carriage doors. The trailing coach was the LNWR through coach from Birmingham New Street.
Cty. T. Lane

addition to flooded permanent way. It was not until the first week in July that running returned to normal although the Teme Bridge was, remarkably, restored in only one week.

Despite the great flood, 1886 was a busier year than those before because of a glut in both cherries and hops. At this period there was an important cherry market at Bewdley which buyers came to from all over the Black Country. In spite of the young hops having to be replanted in May, a bumper crop resulted. In October this great hop yield posed short-term storage problems, partly solved by the use of public buildings, such as Worcester Guildhall as warehouses.

Sadly, the Tenbury & Bewdley Railway lost its major supporter in the following year when Lord Northwick died in London at the age of 76. A day of public mourning was declared in Tenbury and on the day of the funeral many local people travelled to the family home at Northwick Park in Gloucestershire, to pay their last respects to the popular landowner. The 10am train from Worcester was allowed to make an unscheduled stop that day at Blockley, the nearest station, to set down the many mourners.

By this time, November 1887, the LNWR was well into its year of responsibility for providing some of the motive power for 'short trains' on the Tenbury Railway. Patchett of the GWR had felt it necessary to remind the LNWR of its obligations under the December 1869 Joint ownership agreement to supply engine power on a biannual basis, not only for the Clee Hill branch but for the 4.15pm Ludlow to Tenbury and the return working. Nothing is known at present about the LNWR locos available then to work the latter service from Ludlow or when the agreement ceased, but two of the GWR locos used on the branch are known through being involved in minor mishaps reported at Tenbury. Both were 517 Class 0-4-2Ts, one being No. 1482 and the other 1483. The driver of 1482 was reprimanded for setting back too sharply onto the 11.07am Tenbury to Woofferton, causing complaints from shaken passengers. The nature of 1483's problem is not revealed in the report except that it happened while running round its train at Tenbury and that nobody was hurt.

Further information comes to light from another accident report involving a branch train, on this occasion at the north end of Bewdley station on 26th November 1888. The 6.30pm Stourbridge Goods from Tenbury ran into a passenger train from Shrewsbury that was due at Bewdley at 8.32pm. As a result of the collision, both engines were damaged and seven wagons from the goods train were knocked off the line, but happily no-one suffered any personal injuries. The goods train consisted of twenty-six wagons (twenty-three of them loaded), a brake van, and the banking engine which was travelling tender-first behind the train which it had banked. This was normal routine, from

Neen Sollars to Cleobury Mortimer and it was probably returning to Kidderminster shed. There were two guards travelling in the brake van of the goods train. The train engine of the goods was No. 1541, an 0-6-0ST of the 1501 class, a type which was allocated to various sheds in the West Midland districts for long periods at the end of the nineteenth century.

The train on the Severn Valley line from Shrewsbury was made up of three coaches, one a six-wheeler, and was headed by '182' Class 2-4-0 No. 184 (formerly West Midland Railway No. 23). The facts of the mishap were brought out during an enquiry conducted by Col. Rich of the Board of Trade. The signalman at Bewdley North Box had received notice of the approach of the goods train and had lowered his signals for it to pass. This was about seven minutes before he received notice of the passenger train. The goods was late, having been delayed shunting at Cleobury Mortimer and was passed by the passenger train where the two single lines run side by side on the east bank of the River Severn and close to Bewdley up distant signal. The passenger train came to a stand outside Bewdley home signal as both distant and home signals were at danger against it. The driver then drew forward over the junction, under the impression, it later transpired, that he would be given precedence over the goods. The alarmed Bewdley signalman did what he could, leaning out of the signal box window and holding out a warning red light to the driver of No. 184, who responded by setting back with the passenger train. However, by this time the goods (with signals 'all right') was getting nearer on its customary run from the Tenbury line to the back of the Bewdley up line platform. The passenger train had just started to move back when the goods train, running forward at about 10mph, came into collision with it. The driver of the goods train only had time to apply his steam brake a moment before his engine struck the engine of the passenger train. The wagons damaged were GWR Nos. 15425, 11712, 16221, and 15425 along with MR 79123.

Col. Rich came to the conclusion that the collision was caused by the neglect of the passenger train driver. The Colonel referred to the long hours Driver Robert Wright, 27 years a driver, had worked that day. The collision occurred at 8.31pm. Wright had come on duty at 6.30am, although he had four hours when he was not engaged in driving. 'I do not think it practicable for any man to remain on duty for such long hours without becoming over weary and consequently careless and bewildered'. The driver of the Tenbury train, Samuel Rollings was exonerated from any blame.

The increase in traffic continued into 1888, particularly the movement of produce out of the area. Tenbury, which was principally affected, requested an extra clerk, who duly arrived by way of transfer from Leominster. In the same period the goods shed was altered by having the bay boarded over at a cost of £10.

After the enlargement of the goods facilities at Woofferton, it was found that the passenger accommodation for the branch trains was causing congestion. The density of traffic through Woofferton increased following the opening of the Severn Tunnel and the development of the North and West route timetable. It had become clear that the Tenbury branch line trains had to be separated from the main line. Two schemes to do this were submitted by the engineer to a Joint Officers meeting of 22nd January 1889. One scheme was to provide a bay line at the back of the up platform, a junction being made between it and the branch with a connection also with the up line. The refuge siding already existing would be slewed, the platform widened and extended along the bay portion. The alterations were estimated to cost £1,950 exclusive of signalling, much cheaper than the second scheme which would have cost £6,200 exclusive of signals. This would have involved a remodelling of the goods yard in order to provide a dock on the down side of the line. The cheaper scheme was eventually sanctioned by the managers and approved by the B.O.T. inspector, along with the necessary signal alterations. Colonel Rich inspected the new works at Woofferton, which, as well the Tenbury Branch Bay arrangements, involved lengthening the platforms at the Hereford end of the station. The Inspector's approval was given on 21st October 1889, his only requirements being a nameboard facing the Bay line, and a station clock visible from all platforms. At this date there was only a barrow crossing for passengers to use for access to the branch platform.

Another improvement had been made in the first months of 1889 when Easton Court was provided with a 6 ton weighing machine, a storage hut and a loading gauge. Previously, hay, straw and grain delivered by horse and cart to Easton Court could not be weighed there and had been taken down to Woofferton for documenting, involving extra shunting movements as well as taking up room. An extra junior porter was also taken on for the additional work undertaken at Easton. From 1st November 1889, the name 'Little Hereford' was added to 'Easton Court' on the platform nameboard, for the benefit of passengers destined for the small hamlet which the station was considered to serve (in addition to the occupants of the Court itself).

A reminder of the importance of the timber trade and its traffic to the line in general — and Woofferton in particular — was a recommendation to extend the crane lines at Woofferton so that the horses did not have such a long distance to drag heavy loads of timber. Financial considerations, however, curtailed the extensions to only ten yards, less than originally called for.

In 1890, the Tenbury Goods, a regular working from Stourbridge Junction since the opening of the Bewdley loop, was worked through to Woofferton and on to Leominster if required. A sign that trade was still increasing was that in 1891 an extra carter and goods

This rather poor photograph gives a fascinating glimpse of what Tenbury station looked like between 1878 and 1911. It shows a '517' class 0–4–2T at the head of a four-coach rake of close-coupled four-wheelers bound for Kidderminster. The short down platform and signal box were put in in 1878 in conjunction with the opening of the Kidderminster–Bewdley loop line. Prior to 1878 there had been just a goods loop. The purpose of the hut to the right has not yet been ascertained. It appears on early track plans and could well have been an early signal cabin, perhaps converted to a lamp room. The station gas lamps dated from 1905, shortly after which the steps down the side of the signal box were altered to run directly out from the doorway. In 1911 the down platform was lengthened by 60ft towards Bewdley, the hut presumably being dismantled too as it would have been in the way. *Cty. Mr. & Mrs. Bevis*

checker were appointed to Tenbury during the summer and early autumn. The same year, a group of Tenbury residents approached the GWR with a number of requests, including a plea for an improved passenger service between there and Kidderminster, for a through train to Hereford between 11.00am and 6.30pm, and the issue of cheap market tickets to Tenbury on a Tuesday market day. The Market Hall Committee in Craven Arms requested that the 11.25am market train from Woofferton to Ludlow be extended to connect Craven Arms, but to no avail. The officers of the Joint Company did look kindly, however, upon the market ticket reduction and recommended the introduction of a 6d fare from Woofferton to Tenbury as a market day concession. As to trains through to Hereford, the Joint Company considered the new departure at 4.35pm from Craven Arms to Hereford would connect and provide additional opportunities for those wishing to travel in that direction from Tenbury. Complaints and a petition organised by Mrs Rawlings of Woofferton about the lack of a footbridge to reach the bay platform at Woofferton caused the Joint Company to react, and in June 1891 an estimate was produced, costing the work at £390. This was considered too much, so Mr Johnson was instructed to find a way to reduce the price. When he explained that £20 of the sum was for the expense of removing and replacing signals that would become difficult to sight with a footbridge in the way, the authority for construction of the bridge was given (April 1892).

Later that year a proposal was made to provide electric staff instruments on the Tenbury to Woofferton section at an estimated cost of £80. This was approved and

Bewdley c.1890 with a Severn Valley train in the centre and a Tenbury Wells–Kidderminster train on the right.

Kidderminster Library

Loco No. 180 (ex-WMR) 2–4–0 on Wribbenhall viaduct, Bewdley. *Bewdley Museum*

on 26th May 1892 the section was reported as being worked by the combined systems of absolute block and electric train staff. One result of this was that Easton Court ceased to be a Staff Station, and minutes recorded the 'removal of signals at Easton Court consequent to the introduction of the electric staff system'. Easton Court was placed on the Tenbury–Woofferton telephone circuit.

In the 1890s local users continued to agitate for improvements in the railway service and again this focused on the provisions for cattle at Tenbury. Although Cleobury Mortimer also held a weekly livestock market at this time, it was Tenbury, where the station was reasonably convenient to the market, that attracted the largest livestock trade. In fact Cleobury Mortimer station did not even have a cattle pen. In 1895 the siting of the cattle pens at Tenbury, close to the entrance to the 'warehouse', was such that 'only one truck can be unloaded at a time and as an engine is not always available considerable shunting delays occur'. A plan for improved pens was prepared but the cost of £895 was considered too great and the subject was again deferred. It is not clear where these additional pens were to be sited but some of the cost might have been incurred by the price of extra land which did even-

tually have to be purchased. Slow parcels delivery also came in for criticism at Tenbury, the consequence of which was the appointment of an additional junior parcels porter as well as the extra staff who, in 1896, were still being engaged for the summer seasonal traffic at Tenbury.

One factor considered important in the original establishment of the T&B had still not been fulfilled. The outlet for the products of the coalfield that existed around Pensax and Bayton, which both the Pensax Railway and the Teme Valley Railway would have tapped had they been built, was not available. In March 1897 a subscription list was opened for shares in a company that was to make another attempt to transport the coal from around Bayton, Rock and Mamble by rail to Cleobury Mortimer. This was the South Shropshire Coal, Coke, Brick and Railway Company. The prospectus explained that the company had been formed to 'acquire, develop, work and amalgamate the valuable freehold and leasehold lands, collieries, mines, mining rights and premises known as Blakemore, Culverness and Rockmoor, and also the noted and long established brick and quarry works known as the 'Bloomfields Brick Works' at Tipton, Staffordshire, and the coal mines thereunder.' The southern part of the Wyre Forest

OLD WELCH GATE

Welch or Welsh Gate, Bewdley, dates back to the time when Bewdley was the gateway to Wales. Just round the corner, at the bottom of Wyre Hill, is the Wood Colliers Inn, a direct reference to the charcoal burners of the Wyre Forest.
Collection Wendy Hinton

Another scene at Bewdley c.1890. Judging by their dirty appearance and 'snap' bags, the three figures in the foreground may have been miners from Highley or Kinlet pit on their way home after the morning shift. *Kidderminster Library*

Coalfield, it was noted, measured 6½ square miles in area and formed a roughly circular basin. Although only two seams of coal were proved, it was suggested in a survey that other workable seams would be found to exist when further borings had been taken, and in any case the seams proved were shallow and extensive. The railway project was the key to expanding the area of productive mines. An additional interest was the clay exposed at the surface on top of the coal. This clay was found, by analysis and burning tests, to be excellent for brick-making and it was suggested that a brick and tile works could be established in the area. The proposed railway was to be of a standard gauge, single line, 2¾ miles long with sidings, locomotive shed and a weighbridge which altogether would cost £9,863 to build. It would connect to the GWR at Cleobury Mortimer. Apart from supplying the local market, the company was looking to Mid-Wales to sell its products, all to be sent by rail. Sixty houses were proposed to be built on the company's land for the workmen, each with a plot of land 'to afford the means of some employment and support for the workpeople during summer or slack time of the coal trade' (10% profit to the company was expected to derive from this scheme).

Further reports on the quality of the coal and clay explained that cokes made from so-called 'Sulphur Coals' are fairly free from that impurity and are valuable for malting and especially for hop drying and brick burning. The brick and tile clays were found to be of similar quality to those used further north in Shropshire to manufacture ornamental 'Broseley Ware' and could also produce a blue semi-vitrified brick comparable to the well-known Staffordshire bricks. In spite of all these attractive possibilities, the company could not obtain the £100,000 financial support required and did not go ahead. The managing director of the proposed company was to have been Thomas Dalley of Blakemore Colliery and Works and his name appeared also on a second proposal in 1898. This was titled The Wyre Forest Coal and Clay Fields Development Company Ltd. Thomas Dalley was named as managing director of this company promoted to 'acquire, promote and work the Blakemore, Culverness and Rock Moor mines'. This time the capital requested was halved to £50,000 and, although the use of the clay for brick-making was still part of the plan, there was no mention of a housing scheme for the colliers. The railway link of the previous scheme had been reduced to a cheaper tramway and no mention was made as to whether the company or the GWR might work it. This scheme was no more successful than the Pensax Railway nor the 1897 project, so the coal and clay remained for the time being without viable transport to any but local markets.

G.W.R. BRIDGE BEWDLEY

VIEW OF THE TWO BRIDGES AT DOWLES, BEWDLEY

Edwardian views of Dowles. The wooden bridge in the foreground of the lower view crossed the mouth of the Dowles Brook where it enters the Severn and was once on the route of the Severn horse towpath to Shrewsbury. The bridge has since been replaced by a modern steel structure.

Collections Wendy Hinton and Brian Standish

CHAPTER EIGHT
INTO THE TWENTIETH CENTURY

THE Light Railway Act of 1896 was to have a major significance for the Tenbury and Bewdley line. It relaxed some of the more costly regulations involved in constructing a railway with a view to encouraging the development of isolated rural districts. A local scheme, which eventually materialised as the Cleobury Mortimer and Ditton Priors Light Railway, was first discussed as the new century began. The line, when connected through a junction at Cleobury Mortimer, would produce an important increase of traffic along the Tenbury and Bewdley route, second only to that noted after the opening of the Bewdley curve. Local landowners, Lord Boyne and Admiral Woodward in particular, were seeking to provide more efficient transport for the basalt rock, known locally as dhu-stone, quarried around the Brown Clee Hill near Ditton Priors. The rock was of a grade much in demand at that period for road making and also as railway ballast. A company was formed to explore the possibilities and Mr Everard Calthrop was employed to survey and draw up plans for a proposed route.

An application for an order to authorise construction was then made to the Light Railway Commissioners. The Board of Trade, through the Commissioners, held a public enquiry at the Oddfellow's Hall, Cleobury Mortimer, in October 1900, and, as a result of what transpired there, the application was granted. The Light Railway Order come into force on 23rd March 1901. The company then became entitled to enter into agreements with other bodies and could follow its intention of negotiating with the GWR to work the line. Enthusiastic reports were sent off to Paddington from the Secretary of the CM & DP Light Railway about prospects for the line, but they were received with little sign of encouragement from the Great Western management. Eventually, in the autumn of 1901, the GWR came up with offers to run the line for two shillings per train mile, five trains a day minimum excluding Sundays, Good Friday and Christmas Day. As an alternative it would take 60% of the gross receipts plus an indemnity not exceeding £2,000 per year, to be concluded when the line had reached working expenses of two shillings per mile for three consecutive years. A further stipulation was that the indemnity should be provided by a private person or bank and not by a company, limited or otherwise. The chief financial backer to the CM & DP was Lord Boyne, but he could not meet the Directors' financial appeal in order to satisfy the GWR. On hearing this, the Board resigned en bloc on 25th November 1901, leaving the matter in abeyance.

The *Tenbury Advertiser* reported in June 1902 that Tenbury and Easton Court stations were decorated with flags and bunting to celebrate the end of the Boer War. Later in the year, trains carrying returning soldiers arrived adorned with Union Jacks and streamers, to be met at Tenbury station by the Volunteer Band who then led processions of soldiers, their relations and friends back into town.

Dissatisfaction and unrest in the railway industry at this time did not directly affect the Tenbury & Bewdley but other changes were bringing new challenges, not least the arrival in the quiet country lanes of the motor car. The hop industry, too, was undergoing a period of slimmer profit margins for the grower, but there was nevertheless still a large seasonal demand for labour, most of it moved by train. In September 1902 details of special trains to be run from Tenbury for hop pickers returning home to South Staffordshire appeared in the *Tenbury Advertiser*. A special starting from Leominster at 3.20pm, calling at Woofferton, Easton Court, Tenbury and Newnham Bridge, was run every day except Saturday for a week, starting on 29th September. Reduced fares were available but only on these trains and no hop pickers would be carried on Saturday trains. Specials could be run on Sundays provided the party numbered over one hundred and that notice had

Dowles Road and railway bridge. In 1905 the people of Dowles petitioned for a halt to be built here, but nothing came of it.
Cty. John Farmer

55

GWR Beyer class 0–6–0 No. 334 near Bewdley with a Severn Valley freight. The Tenbury line features in the foreground.
Collection K. Beddoes

been given to the authorities by the Friday previous to the Sunday booking requested. This is the first recorded working of a passenger train over the line on a Sunday although it is likely to have occurred in the hop-picking season each year since the Bewdley curve opened.

The matter of the construction of the CM & DP was still under discussion in 1902 but financial problems prevented any start being made by J.T. Firbank and Co, whose tender had at one time looked acceptable. The project drifted on into 1903 when two more tenders were received, one from Messrs Jackson & Co and another from Kerr, Stuart & Company. Neither of these was accepted and the frustration that the directors felt over the inactivity led to resignations from the board in March 1904, including that of the Chairman, Sir Alexander Wilson.

Dissatisfaction for a different reason caused a letter to be sent to the GWR by Kidderminster Corporation in October 1904. The complaint was an echo of an earlier call from Tenbury Parish Council to improve the passenger service on the line as a whole, but the 'want of a train from Woofferton in the evenings' was complained about in particular. The letter from the Corporation was to be a strong influence in the eventual provision of a steam rail motor service on the branch. By now the GWR management had begun to look closely at the financial returns from branch lines and its pioneer steam rail motor was already in revenue service between Chalford and Stonehouse, near Gloucester.

At the close of the year, the death occurred of William Norris, described by the *Tenbury Advertiser*, as 'the father figure for the well being of Tenbury town'. He was 83 when he died on 27th December 1904, having given many years of his life as instigator, along with Lord Northwick, of both the Tenbury and Tenbury & Bewdley Railways.

The early workings of the Tenbury & Bewdley up until about 1905 were complicated; no less than six sheds were responsible for motive power. Even more complex were the changes in allocation of turns from one shed to another. Study of early timetables in some cases does not always reveal where a train started or went to. For instance, trains from Hartlebury to Ludlow may, until 1905, have come from Worcester. This would tie in with GWR records showing the Bewdley-Tenbury section being worked by 2-4-0 passenger locos of the 481 or 'Bicycle' class. Only Worcester had a 481 class allocation in 1902 (Nos 483, 484, 487 and 592, which had replaced some of the older WMR types).

Kidderminster, Leominster and Ludlow sheds were always closely connected with the working of the line, and their allocation for various months in 1902 demonstrate the selection of 517 class 0-4-2Ts for use over the Tenbury & Bewdley.

KIDDERMINSTER 1902
517 Class 0-4-2T: 220, 530, 556
1501 Class 0-6-0T: 1506, 1520, 1539, 1553
2021 Class 0-6-0T: 2092

LEOMINSTER 1902
517 Class 0-4-2T: 841, 1422, 1436, 1437, 1438, 1470
1076 Class 0-6-0T: 1147
1501 Class 0-6-0T: 1809
2021 Class 0-6-0T: 2036, 2037

LUDLOW 1902
0-4-0T: 45 (the Clee Hill shunter)
517 Class 0-4-2T: 537, 565, 574, 1422, 1438, 1475, 1477
655 Class 0-6-0T: 1778
1501 Class 0-6-0T: 1802, 1810

In March 1905, Kidderminster Corporation finally received a reply from the GWR to the letter of complaint, informing the Corporation that 'In connection with the ensuing revision of timetables for May and June next, the question of running a Rail Motor Car from Tenbury to Kidderminster at about 6pm is having consideration'.

By this time approval had already been given by the GWR for expenditure on two 'haltes' to be built between Kidderminster and Bewdley, one at Foley Park, the other at

INTO THE TWENTIETH CENTURY

the Rifle Range, the plan for which shows a platform 100 yards long, 6ft wide and 3ft high with a waiting shed 20ft by 7ft.

In conjunction with the proposed railmotor services, Foley Park 'halte' opened on 2nd January 1905 — the same day as a steam railmotor service on the Kidderminster, Bewdley, Stourport section. The 'halte' at Rifle Range opened some five months later, in June 1905.

The new through service became actuality on 1st May 1905 when the 3.48pm Kidderminster departure, due to arrive at Woofferton at 5.02pm, became the first railmotor service to operate on the line. This working left Woofferton on the return journey at 5.34pm, to arrive at Kidderminster at 7.02pm. It then ran empty to Stourbridge Junction, suggesting that the railmotor originally utilised came from Stourbridge shed.

Branch car No 29 was reported at Bewdley around this time whilst car No 35 was seen at Stourport on the Kidderminster-Bewdley-Stourport railcar service. The new T&B railmotor service did not, however, satisfy

Before the T&B opened in 1864, Bewdley only had one platform, on the main building side, and a passing loop for goods trains. The location of the original (T&B) south box was at the entrance to the goods yard, left, out of view behind the camera, and the 1½in piping seen on the platform fronts housed the signal wires from the box to the junction signals at the north end of the station.

Bewdley North Box, seen here c.1890, was built by the GWR in 1878 to replace the original T&B box, which was only a hut covering a ground frame. It had only operated the distant signals which were a few hundred yards north of the station. *Authors' collection*

Bewdley station staff grouped around steam railmotor No. 54 whilst a Tenbury train also features in the background. No. 54, built in August 1905, spent its first six months working Kidderminster–Bewdley–Stourport, and Kidderminster–Woofferton services, until it was recorded later at Oxford. By 1911 railmotors Nos. 66, 73, 77 and 98 were recorded or seen at Kidderminster, now working extended services, one car working to Stourbridge, Bewdley and Hartlebury, and another to Worcester, Bridgnorth and Woofferton. The Kidderminster–Woofferton service was taken off as a wartime economy measure in 1916, but the Severn Valley service lasted until 1918.

Collection Wendy Hinton

INTO THE TWENTIETH CENTURY

Steam railmotor No. 35 of Kidderminster shed, seen at Stourport on the inauguration of the service between Kidderminster–Bewdley–Stourport on 2nd January 1905. This service was later extended to Hartlebury from January 1911. *Authors' collection*

Kidderminster Corporation, for in June 1905, a meeting resolved that the town clerk should write again urging still more improvements and that Bewdley Corporation be asked to take action on the same question. In July, Alfred Baldwin Esq, MP for Bewdley and Chairman of the GWR, replied, promising to look into the matter, though a letter which followed from the GWR in October intimated that it felt that it had already made sufficient improvement. Kidderminster Council then resolved to thank the GWR for the alterations that had been possible but to press for an even later evening train to be put on from Woofferton to Kidderminster in the following spring. At Woofferton an unusual arrangement took place in 1905. The engine on the 4.10pm from Ludlow to Kidderminster was changed from an LNWR loco to a GWR one, and just two minutes were given to complete the operation!

The pressure from the volume of cattle traffic at Tenbury continued to trouble the railway management. Earlier the problems were mainly over the slow loading of the animals. This had been eased by the provision of a horse to shunt the cattle wagons on sale days and the use of a locomotive for the same purpose during the two large cattle fair days in April and October. In 1905 the office accommodation in Tenbury goods shed was enlarged so that the paperwork involved could be dealt with faster, and improved lighting was also put in hand. The goods yard

A steam railmotor and a '517' class 0–4–2T at Tenbury Wells c.1910. *Lens of Sutton*

had been lit by gas lamps since 1902 and now, three years later, the platforms and station approach were improved in the same manner.

In the district around Cleobury Mortimer, the wait for action over the Light Railway continued but the only change was in the Board of Directors where other resignations followed that of the chairman. Four years had now passed since the Light Railway Order had been granted.

Knowing of the opening of Foley Park and Rifle Range Haltes, the residents of the Dowles district made a request to the GWR, though unsuccessfully, for such a station to be placed for their use. The economy that the railmotors represented to the company was part of an overall cost-cutting policy which also included the Economic System of track maintenance under which the permanent way gangs were allowed daytime possession of a line in quiet periods of the timetable rather than having to work at weekends (and receive overtime pay) or for the company to employ flagmen 'lookouts'. Authorisation for the Tenbury and Bewdley branch to come under this scheme was given in March 1905.

The Railway Powers Agreement between the GWR and LNWR was altered slightly in 1905 to allow more trains per day to include through coaches from Birmingham

An early photograph of Woofferton, with the Tenbury Bay to the left.
Lens of Sutton

Woofferton station yard c.1900. The refreshment rooms were known to locals as 'Abraham's Bosum' after a local clergyman who came across the fields for refreshment. They were run by the landlord of the nearby 'Salwey Arms'. The rooms were much used by railwaymen. Clarke's shop was infamous during the Second World War for certain 'under the counter favours'.
Authors' collection

(New Street). From March there could be two through coaches on eight trains each way daily instead of six as previously.

By 1905 the challenge of road transport to the viability of branch line railways was becoming noticeable, in spite of the comment in *Worcestershire Agriculture* that 'the motor car is unpopular in Worcestershire's rural districts'. The GWR were very quick to respond to the competition by joining it and introducing a steam motor wagon into the Teme Valley. The vehicle was a Yorkshire 5 ton steam wagon delivered in July 1905 complete with large 'GWR' lettering on its sides. Officially described as a feeder service, the wagon began to operate along the route of the abandoned Teme Valley Railway scheme and was based for this purpose at Henwick, near Worcester.

The wagon was manned by an engineer and a porter who between them ran the vehicle and carried out loading and unloading en route. Officially, no goods were carried that were not destined for further carriage by rail or had arrived by rail at Henwick. Unofficially, passengers who climbed on board were not discouraged. An early report from the Teme Valley Agricultural Organisation Society suggested that a large volume of traffic was being offered to the steam wagon and that even with a trailer it could not cope with it all. A later reference in *Worcestershire Agriculture* states that up to three trailers were carried in tow by the wagon, so it is surprising to find that this early road-hauled service was not extended but, on the contrary, faded out. It is known that the wagon carried road stone in the winter months and cement for a new bridge at Stanford, so there was not just a summer seasonal demand for its use. The poorly surfaced roads, particularly in the more hilly dis-

Easton Court for Little Hereford, which lay midway between Tenbury and Woofferton. It was only a small hamlet and probably did not warrant a station. However, it was built as a concession to Sir Joseph Bailey, the Lord of the Manor, who lived in a house there called 'Easton Court'. It was opened to passengers and goods in August 1861 as 'Easton Court', then it closed to passengers in October 1862, re-opened in April 1865 and was later renamed 'Easton Court for Little Hereford' on 1st November 1889. This photograph is believed to have been taken in late 1902 and to show some of the locals waiting to greet returning soldiers from the Boer War. *Authors' collection*

An unidentified '517' 0–4–2T running into Tenbury Wells. The new ladies room at the far end of the platform was built in 1913. The notice board in the station drive proclaimed 'The Orchard Spa, Tenbury saline waters for rheumatism and gout'. *Lens of Sutton*

62   THE TENBURY & BEWDLEY RAILWAY

Tenbury station in 1913, showing the new cattle dock in the foreground, and new ladies waiting room at the far end of the station buildings. This view also features a '517' 0–4–2T arriving with a train from Bewdley. *Lens of Sutton*

The Tenbury bus outside 'The Swan' c.1910. It was the proud boast that the bus, which ran from 'The Swan' until 1930, met every train that arrived at Tenbury. Note the station master in the group. *Cty. W. E. Arnett (last bus driver)*

Neen Sollars station, 1910.

Kidderminster Library

The 1878 signal box and original waiting shelters at Cleobury Mortimer c.1880. This picture shows the up platform as built.
Authors' collection

tricts, probably became quickly churned up by the steam wagon's regular daily run, although there were no reports of this. There was news of only one accident, when the wagon overturned after running away downhill near Clifton-on-Teme. Road transport, however, was now at the start of its progressive incursion into village life and rural communications.

At Ditton Priors, however, a railway was still expected to hold the key to the expansion of the quarrying industry of the district if and when the line planned to join the Great Western at Cleobury Mortimer was constructed. In 1906 an application had to be made to the Board of Trade to extend the time allowed by the Light Railway Order since no contract had yet been let. This extension was granted and when a local firm, George Law of Kidderminster, had its tender accepted, a start looked likely once again. This time the stumbling block was not financial but a clause put into the contract by the Light Railway Company which stated that the Abdon Clee quarry must be made fully operational, by the contractors, before the line opened down to Cleobury Mortimer. George Law felt unable to agree to this and again the contract foundered but not before a new engineer, William Foxlee, had been brought in by Law as replacement for Everard Calthrop. At this time the eventual saviours of the Light Railway came upon the scene. A construction contract was signed by Messrs Bott and Stennett in September 1906, and at last work on construction could begin. Foxlee was retained as engineer and immediately changed the setting out of the junction with the GWR at Cleobury Mortimer, making a more compact arrangement whereby the Light Railway's platform would be placed adjacent to that of the GWR. In January 1907 construction of the Light Railway started at Cleobury Mortimer and by June the junction with the Great Western was made at the Bewdley end of the station.

The Abdon Clee Quarry Company were looking to the rail link to develop markets for the dhu-stone rock right across the United Kingdom and so, too, at this time was the Bayton Colliery which considered the railway still a better prospect than local roads for the movement of coal to markets outside the local district. The owner of Bayton Colliery in 1907, Mr J.A. Smallshaw, was familiar with the tramway network around the coalpits of the Madeley area of Shropshire and, in a continuation of earlier ideas, he submitted plans for a tramway to the Shropshire County Council. The Roads and Bridges Committee passed plans for a line linking Bayton to Cleobury Mortimer goods yard subject to a time limit of two years and stringent conditions for the level crossing that would have to be constructed over the Cleobury Mortimer to Clows Top road. Evidently

INTO THE TWENTIETH CENTURY

the terms and conditions were not acceptable, for the idea was shelved and the tramway not completed.

Kidderminster shed now housed a Metro class 2-4-0T No 983 amongst the 517s and 0-6-0STs but the shed's allocation in 1907 also included two steam railmotors. Stourbridge shed had for many years been associated with the working of the daily Tenbury Goods which from 1870 had worked from Stourbridge Junction to Leominster. After 1906 it worked on to Hereford via Tenbury and Ludlow and was balanced by the 1.30pm Hereford to Stourbridge which did not call at Ludlow on the return journey. A Stourbridge engine was responsible for the 9.20am working and Hereford shed provided a locomotive for the 1.30pm starting each Monday, both engines being stabled overnight at the 'foreign' shed to return next day on the alternate trips.

Such good progress had been made in the construction of the CM & DP that a goods service was opened on 19th July 1908. The contractor's locos had to be used on these first trains since the two Manning Wardle saddle tanks ordered by the CM & DP were late being delivered, not arriving until August. These two locos, named *Cleobury* and *Burwarton*, were initially housed in the contractor's loco shed at Cleobury Town (the company's headquarters) and

The embankment being constructed to take the CM & DP Light Railway on the edge of Cleobury Mortimer station c.1907. The waiting shelter on the GWR platform is visible on the top right whilst the bridge on the left spanned the Cleobury Mortimer to Bewdley road. *W. Atkinson*

The two CM & DP 0–6–0STs *Burwarton* and *Cleobury*, probably outside Cleobury Town shed. *Collection R. C. Riley*

Cleobury Mortimer from the south in 1908 with the newly constructed CM&DP Light Railway on the left and the original signal box still in situ. *W. Atkinson*

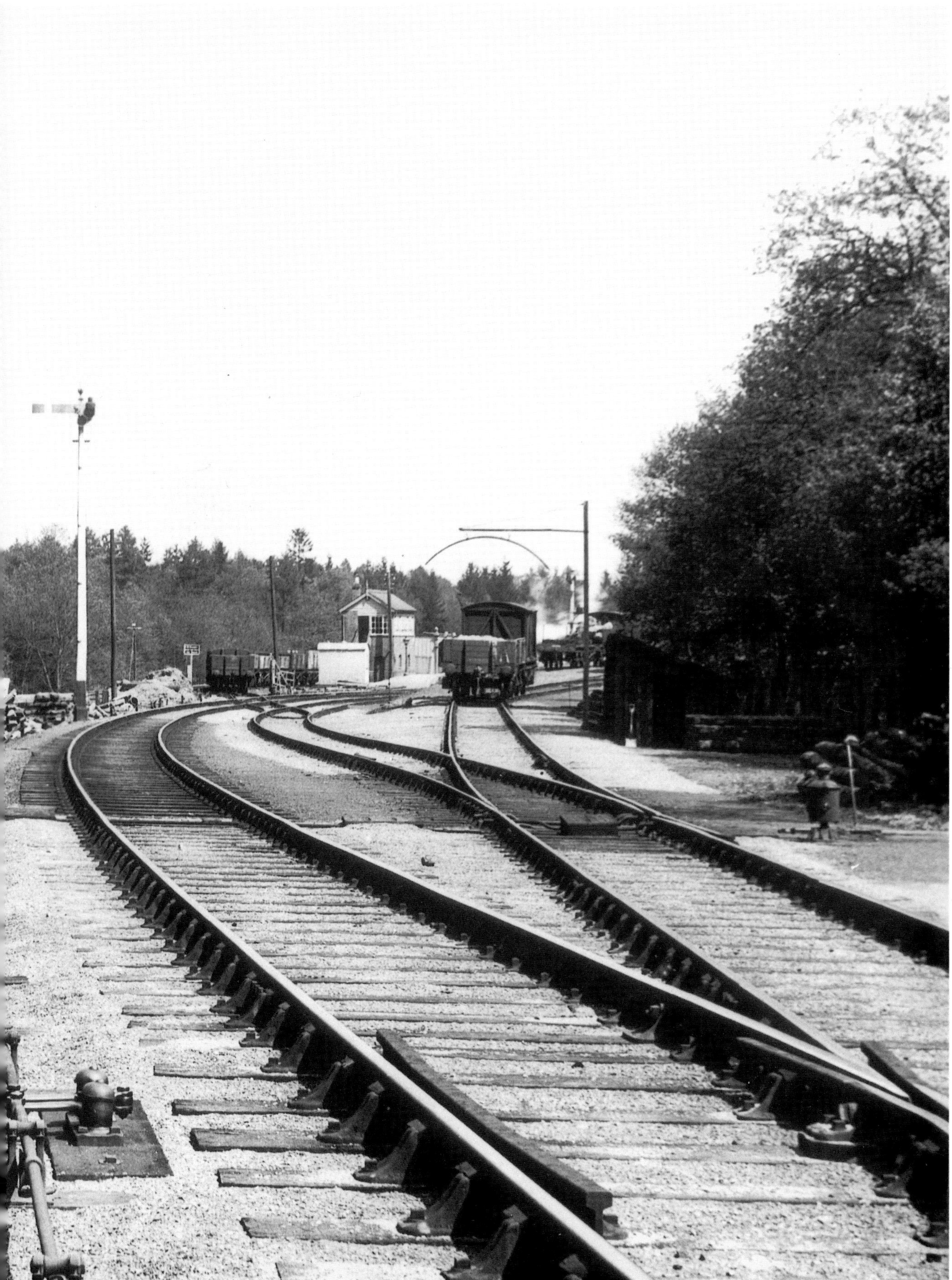

were to become a familiar sight for many years in Cleobury Mortimer station.

Following a successful inspection by the Board of Trade, the passenger service on the CM & DP commenced on 21st November 1908. The nameboards on Cleobury Mortimer station were altered to display 'Change for Ditton Priors Railway' and a new, enlarged (51 levers in use, 13 spare) signal box was opened on 18th November on approximately the same site as the previous one. The Light Railway passenger coaches to be seen at Cleobury Mortimer were ex-North London Railway four-wheelers, usually forming part of a mixed train with a CM & DP brake van bringing up the rear. The open wagons belonging to the CM & DP and the Abdon Clee Quarry Company spread much further afield and became familiar vehicles in goods trains up and down the Tenbury & Bewdley line.

The stone traffic, for which the Light Railway was built, soon increased to a substantial degree when the Titterstone quarries on the eastern side of the Clee Hills were linked to the CM & DP at Detton Ford, late in 1908. Of interest is the fact that whereas the Abdon Clee quarries were connected to the railhead at Ditton Priors by a self-acting incline, the Titterstone quarries utilised an aerial ropeway which carried buckets of stone down to Detton Ford siding where there were storage bins and a loading terminal for the Clee Hill Granite Company's rail wagons. Additional goods traffic was provided by the large quantities of round timber taken from the Burwarton estate and cattle traffic was carried from Ditton Priors for sale at Kidderminster market. The Burwarton Coal and Coke Company set up its headquarters at Cleobury Town station to add to the other traffic, such as milk, which was to be expected in the farming district.

At this time there was a depression in the hop industry which culminated in 1908 with the organisation of a mass protest demonstration in Trafalgar Square, involving hop growers and workers from Kent and Sussex, joined by those from Herefordshire and Worcestershire. Growers from the Teme Valley paid the fares of their workmen to join a special train routed to Paddington via Birmingham and Oxford. The demonstration was against the dumping of foreign hops in England. Despite the acreage under hops in Worcestershire increasing by 51% between 1874 and 1894, the prices received by the growers were now poor.

Cleobury Mortimer c.1910, showing platform extensions and new signal box to accommodate the CM & DP Light Railway. *Cty. T. Davies*

INTO THE TWENTIETH CENTURY

Long before the CM&DP opened in 1908, stone from the Clee Hills had been transported over the Tenbury and Bewdley via the Ludlow and Clee Hill Railway. Although not directly connected by rail to the T&B (as was the CM&DP), the Ludlow and Clee Hill was opened in August 1864 to serve the quarries on Titterstone Clee, some miles south of the Brown Clee quarries near Ditton Priors. It was also engineered by David Wylie and William Clarke. A company was also formed by William Field of Brassey and Field, the railway contractors, and John McKay, their agent, to extract and transport stone all over the country from the quarries via a standard gauge incline plane down to the Clee Hill line at Bitterley. In this view, taken of Bitterley yard around the turn of the century, Field and McKay waggons can be seen waiting to be loaded with stone from the wharf to the left. The locomotive shunting appears to have been an open-cabbed Ramsbottom LNWR saddle tank. The bottom of the incline can be seen in the right background. The brake or runner waggon in the foreground was attached on the down side of trucks on the rope-worked incline. In later years there was also a narrow gauge incline terminating here and a signal box to control movements. The standard gauge incline between Bitterley and Clee Hill Top closed from 7th November 1960 and the line from Ludlow to Bitterley on 31st December 1962. Stone is still quarried on a small scale but now goes out by road.
Authors' collection

By 1910 Kidderminster shed still housed two or three steam railmotors, some of which were used on the Tenbury line services, but no fewer than eight came and went at one time or another in 1910, Nos 10, 11, 19, 37, 53, 54, and 77. On occasions these were exchanges with vehicles from Worcester shed and from Stourbridge. Stourbridge shed however, still kept the connection of the Tenbury Goods which in 1910 was now routed on the return journey from Hereford to run via Ludlow before returning to Tenbury and on up the line.

In 1910, two recurring complaints concerning delays to traffic were heard when Messrs Cooper & Baldwin, (auctioneers in Tenbury) brought their weight to bear on the problem of delays in dealing with cattle at Tenbury station on sales days. On this occasion the Joint Officers felt compelled to look at the possibility of providing more cattle pens. Six extra were suggested with the rider added that the provision would require the GWR to purchase a small amount of land. Another report called the attention of the Joint Officers to delays occurring at both Tenbury and Woofferton as a result of inadequate siding accommodation at Woofferton. It was recommended, as a result, that extra sidings be provided for 115 wagons, with a shunting neck for 30, and also provision of a dead end to the run-ning-round loop on the up side, together with the replacement of the crossover on the main line.

Around this time a memorial was received from the traders of Tenbury asking for assistance in unloading goods conveyed at station-to-station rates and suggesting that such traffic should be stored in the goods warehouse until called for. The Joint Officers agreed to the employment of an extra porter but pointed out that the Joint Company was not obliged to provide warehouse accommodation for such traffic which, in any case, had dropped between 1900 and 1910.

The general public had also petitioned for an improvement in the timetable, the *Tenbury Advertiser* in April 1910 reporting that Mr S.F. Bentley of the Peacock Inn, Boraston, had received a letter from the GWR Superintendent's office at Chester giving details of a change in the summer 1910 timetable in response to the public's request. The 9.10am from Tenbury was subsequently altered to leave at 8.54am to reach Kidderminster to connect with the 9.50am express to Birmingham arriving at 10.25am. This allowed for a walk across to New Street in time to catch the 11.25am luncheon express to Euston, arriving at 1.25pm.

Bayton Colliery, 1900.   *Authors' collection*

It was in this summer that the final remnants of second class travel on the GWR were withdrawn, the 'divisions' along the branch line still being dealt with separately; the Woofferton-Tenbury section 2nd class was withdrawn from 1st July whilst the Tenbury to Kidderminster section became the very last example on the GWR, 2nd class not being withdrawn until 1st October 1910.

Although the Tenbury & Bewdley Railway was being used as an outlet for raw materials — stone and coal in particular — it had not attracted the siting of any new industry. In 1910, adverts appeared locally for the products of The Tenbury Wells Aerated Water Company. Founded in 1895 to sell fruit juices and cordials, it was an industry destined to have a long association with the town and to be more successful than the other water-based enterprise at the baths.

Whilst stone was being successfully moved by rail from Ditton Priors and Detton Ford on the CM & DP, coal from Bayton and Pensax was still not being sold in large quantities outside the immediate locality. In 1911 this was to alter. Bayton Colliery had changed owners and now belonged to Mr Francis Whitworth Wright of 'The Snead', Pensax. Perhaps influenced by the aerial ropeway bringing dhustone down to Detton Ford, Wright engaged Messrs R. White and Sons, Widnes, Lancs, to carry out a survey for something similar. This firm of engineers of ropeway and railway systems reported favourably about the possibility of a ropeway from Bayton Colliery to a terminal at the Neen Sollars end of Cleobury Mortimer goods yards, at an estimated cost of £3,000. An application was submitted to Shropshire County Council and passed in 1911, after an agreement had been entered into with the GWR for a siding connection to be put in. There was a slight delay in progress when the Highways Committee insisted on a safety net or bridge where the ropeway crossed over the Cleobury Mortimer to Clows Top road. The installation engineers, having great faith in their equipment, declined to do either. They then discovered that by deviating the line of the ropeway and putting in an angle station, they could take the line across the same road but in a different county! This neighbouring county, Worcestershire, did not insist on the safety precautions so the ropeway was built with a 104½° turn in it, passing back over Shropshire fields down to Cleobury Mortimer Station.

The ropeway was ready for use by 1913 and was of interest in being the first one R. White & Son had erected using a positive grip rope saddle on a single rope used to both haul and carry the tubs, instead of the two ropes generally in use at that time.

The length of the ropeway from the screens at Bayton to the sidings at Cleobury was 7,030ft, with a descent of some 200ft. The rope was carried above the fields by steel pylons or standards of heights varying between 25ft and 50ft to suit the contours of the ground. Each standard had six wheels or sheaves, four on the loaded side and two on the return side, over which the rope passed. These were greased by means of 'Stauffer' grease cups which could be attended to by means of ladders fixed to the standards.

The main coal bunker at the pit screens had four sections for different grades of coal, each with a grading or shaking screen. Here the buckets were guided off the slowly moving rope onto a shunt rail for loading from an eight-section gravity chute. The ropeway was driven by a horizontal cross-compound steam engine made by Pearcy &

INTO THE TWENTIETH CENTURY

Bayton Colliery ropeway sidings, Cleobury Mortimer in 1913, with buckets visible on the ropeway. *Authors' collection*

Unloading terminal at Cleobury Mortimer in 1913, showing a loaded Bayton Colliery wagon under the coal chutes.
From R. White & Co's catalogue

BAYTON COLLIERY SIDINGS 1913 (not to scale)

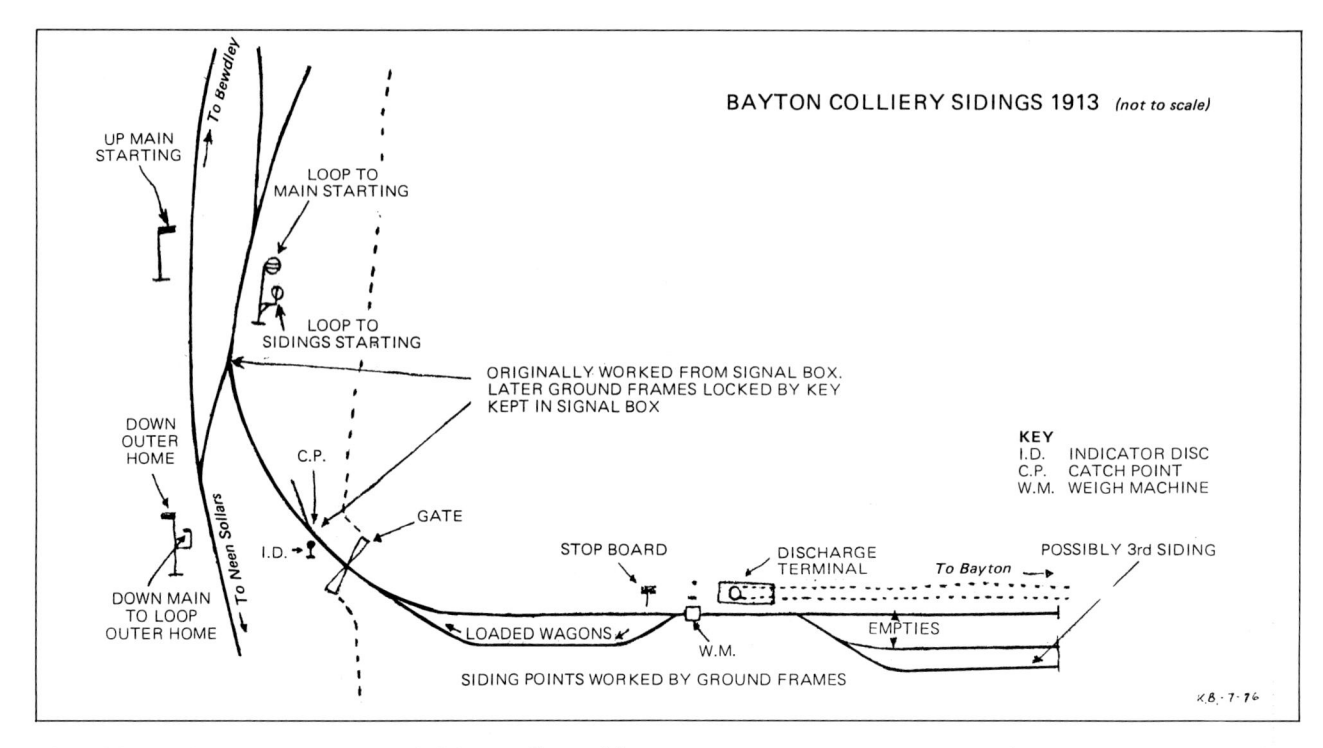

KEY
I.D. INDICATOR DISC
C.P. CATCH POINT
W.M. WEIGH MACHINE

Co of Broad Street, Birmingham, fed from a Lancashire boiler. Close by, the pit winding gear was driven by a two-cylinder engine of 12in bore by 24in stroke.

Midway in the ropeway was the angle station close to the main road, where two men were stationed to see no mishaps occurred as the rope traversed the sharp turn. Loaded buckets could also be shunted off here for a landsale yard, adjacent to the road, where coal was sold to the general public.

The discharge terminal at Cleobury Mortimer was a staging 76ft long, allowing three railway wagons to be loaded simultaneously without the need for shunting. Buckets ran onto a shunt rail over chutes fitted with anti-breakage shutters to minimise the amount by which the coal was broken when discharged to the wagons below.

Automatic tensioners at this point continuously maintained the working tension of the rope, and a private telephone system operated between the terminal and the pit head via the angle station. Thirty-five tons an hour could be carried but this could be increased by the addition of extra buckets. Equipment such as pit props, could also be carried in specially modified buckets.

The agreement with the GWR for a siding connection was signed on 17th August 1911 and contained no less than 17 clauses, most of which favoured the GWR. A selection of the clauses were as follows;

1. Colliery Company to pay £120 10s 0d (half the estimated cost of the siding) the balance due to GWR to be paid when the siding is completed.
3. GWR to pay half yearly to the Colliery Company a sum equal to 5% of traffic from and to the Colliery until such time that the cost of siding is repaid to the Colliery Company.
3A. GWR will maintain the siding but all costs are payable by Colliery Company. The Colliery Company siding (protected from the GWR siding by a gate) to be kept in repair by Colliery Company sufficiently to enable GWR Co's engines or vehicles to run in safety.
4. Colliery Co. to be responsible for all fences etc GWR to be indemnified against all actions or claims involving trespass on GWR property through neglect of Colliery Co.
5. The sum of £1 to be paid to GWR every January for easement (right of way) over GWR sidings.
6. Wagons and vans on Colliery Co. property to be marshalled by them but under direction of GWR Goods depot. A payment of 7s 6d per hour after the first 15 minutes is to be made for the services of GWR locomotives shunting to and from sidings.
11. GWR can at any time, should they wish, construct lines for their own use on the land that their siding is on or remove the siding on one month's notice and shall not be liable to relay a siding until land had been made available to GWR suitable for the purpose and free of charge by the Colliery Co.
14. If monies are not paid (under the terms of freight and carriage agreement) on demand, GWR Co. can enter the property of the Colliery Co. and remove and sell sufficient to pay for such monies owing.
16. If after three consecutive months, other than due to a strike or lock out, the Colliery Co. fail to send a substantial amount of traffic over GWR or should the Colliery Co. be bankrupt or in liquidation, or fail to pay monies regularly, GWR may terminate the agreement and lift their siding.
17. Colliery Co. to pay the cost of the agreement (2s 6d) and also that of a duplicate.

The agreement was signed for the GWR by Thomas Henry Rendell, Chief Goods Agent, and for the Colliery Co. by Francis Whitworth Wright.

A gate in the boundary fence gave access to the colliery sidings from the GW goods yard, GW engines being allowed to work in only as far as a stop board 112 yards

INTO THE TWENTIETH CENTURY

from the gate. On GW property the siding was protected by catch points and an indicator disc, all worked from the signal box. In later years a ground frame was substituted, operated by the shunter.

Whilst the first excursionists from Tenbury were content to walk on the Stretton Hills, the travelling public were now looking further afield. The seaside day trip had become very popular and the *Tenbury Advertiser* of 18th July 1911 announced the running of a grand 'chair trip' on Wednesday, 26th July, to Blackpool, departing very early in the morning at 4.40am. Specials for race meetings at Ludlow (where the racecourse was handily situated alongside the railway) became a regular feature of the line, other trains coming from as far away as Birmingham, but race specials from Tenbury were advertised as stopping only at Easton Court and Woofferton.

Wyre Forest station. This was the only one not opened with the line in 1864. It was a later addition brought into use for passengers on 1st June 1869 and goods between 1900 and 1904.
Collection Wendy Hinton

A third bedroom was added to the station house in 1896, adding one shilling per week to the rent. *Lens of Sutton*

An early view of Wyre Forest station, looking over the Wyre Forest towards Cleobury Mortimer. The line followed the valley of the Dowles Brook from here eastwards to Bewdley. In July 1896 an application was granted by the GWR to Messrs. Morris and Mason, contractors building the nearby Birmingham water pipeline, to extend the siding for their use and provide a 5-ton crane at a total cost of £42.
Collection Wendy Hinton

TATION. 98 ALFRO

Other changes occurred in the social order of the day and a strike of railwaymen took place for two days, on the 17th and 18th August 1911. The *Kidderminster Times* reported that on the first day, only the station master and an inspector remained at work at Kidderminster, the inspector acting as guard on the motor train to Bewdley. Happily, the return to work was in time to transport hop pickers. Picking commenced on 23rd August when hundreds of people were reported making their way from Newnham Bridge station to Lindridge, a little distance down the Teme Valley.

Earlier that month the projection of Tenbury as a spa town (an idea that would not rest) was begun again. The Tenbury Wells Improvement Company formed in 1860 had folded in 1872 due to financial problems and since then the baths had opened spasmodically. In 1911, the Tenbury Baths Company Ltd was formed, headed by Mr G.E. Godson, a relation of Septimus Godson who had owned the site leased to the Improvement Company. The Bath house reopened on 3rd August 1911. It had been completely refurbished and modernised, and a bottling plant set up enabling those people unable to visit Tenbury to obtain the health-giving waters via mail order. As the proprietors announced in the *Tenbury Advertiser*, 'the merits of this esteemed water will enable us to compete with any other spa in the United Kingdom'. A survey conducted at the time discovered visitors were arriving from a wide area to take the waters, Dover, Surbiton, London, Cardiff and Stoke on Trent to name a few from the list supplied by the Baths Company. Though having no connection with this increase in visitors, a joint officers meeting in April 1911 had recommended the extension of the down platform at Tenbury by 60ft and that additional platform lamps be provided.

The Light Railway running into Cleobury Mortimer was performing very well financially with an operating surplus of £2,214 announced in 1911, double that of 1910. Stone was moving down the line, limited only to the number of loaded wagons that could be hauled at a time. Encouraged by this success, Mr Foxlee put before the Board ideas for extending the line northwards to one of three possible outlets; the GWR's Severn Valley line, the LNWR's Coalport branch or the GWR's Much Wenlock line. None of these projects ever materialised and the Tenbury line continued to be the beneficiary of the traffic produced by the Light Railway. The two locomotives belonging to the Light Railway were serviced for repairs at Worcester GWR works from 1911 although Cleobury Town shed continued to deal with day-to-day running requirements.

Wyre Forest station c.1914-18 war, with round timber and baskets of fruit, typical Wyre Forest traffic on the loading bay. The shed beyond the station building housed the ground frame controlling the siding. The second storey of the station building was an addition to the original plan.
Lens of Sutton

INTO THE TWENTIETH CENTURY

An unidentified 0–6–0ST near Dowles Manor c.1910. Fires caused by sparks from passing engines were a constant hazard in dry weather. For example, in April 1905, the GWR received a claim of £637 for damage caused. After arbitration this was reduced and £309 18s 9d was awarded to the claimant.
T. R. Perkins

In a memo from a Joint Officers meeting of January 1912, it was stated that Tenbury booking office was no longer large enough to deal with the volume of parcels traffic and that bicycles were having to be placed in the general waiting room. The recommendation was that the Ladies room and the General Waiting room be converted into one office for booking and parcels and a new waiting room be added to the Newnham Bridge end of the main building. The cost of the improvement was to be added to that for the proposed cattle pens, making a total of £1,576 (not including the cost of 35½ poles of land required for the pens). Improvements were needed at Easton Court too. There was no Ladies waiting room there and a plan was put forward recommending the conversion of the booking office and waiting room into one enlarged booking office, and having two rooms built on, one for the Ladies. This improvement, recommended by the Joint Officers, was turned down a little later on account of the cost. The other recommendation for improved siding accommodation at Easton Court is yet another reminder of the importance of timber traffic on the line at other stations besides Wyre Forest. Some of the timber apparently had to be placed in a field adjoining the goods yard, for which the owners of the timber were paying rent. However, as the additional siding would have involved the Joint Company in land purchase, it did not happen.

When it transpired that the use of eight-wheeled stock in the bay platform at Woofferton was creating dangerous difficulties for passengers because of a gap left between carriage and platform, alterations were put in hand immediately.

The passenger traffic passing through Cleobury Mortimer from the Light Railway had evidently reached a peak in 1911 and the falling off in 1912 concerned the Light Railway's directors. The goods traffic, however, was not faltering. Stone was still in huge demand, particularly from railways using it as ballast (the GWR and MR in particular) and the cattle train specials to and from Kidderminster market on a Thursday, were now fortnightly (previously monthly) and could consist of as many as eighteen cattle vans per train. A warning note was sounded, though, at one Board meeting in 1912 when Mr Ernest Morris, manager of the CM & DP, referred to the growing number of road carters operating around the local villages and taking light goods traffic once carried by the railway.

Mr Charles Wesley Rogers was signalman at Cleobury Mortimer in 1912 and recalls:

'In 1912 I was moved from Much Wenlock to Cleobury Mortimer junction box; this was quite an important job as it was a 65-lever box. For this job I was paid 21s a week, so you can see why we went on strike for more money in 1926. Wages were calculated on a points basis; there were so many points awarded for the number of levers, the number of trains,

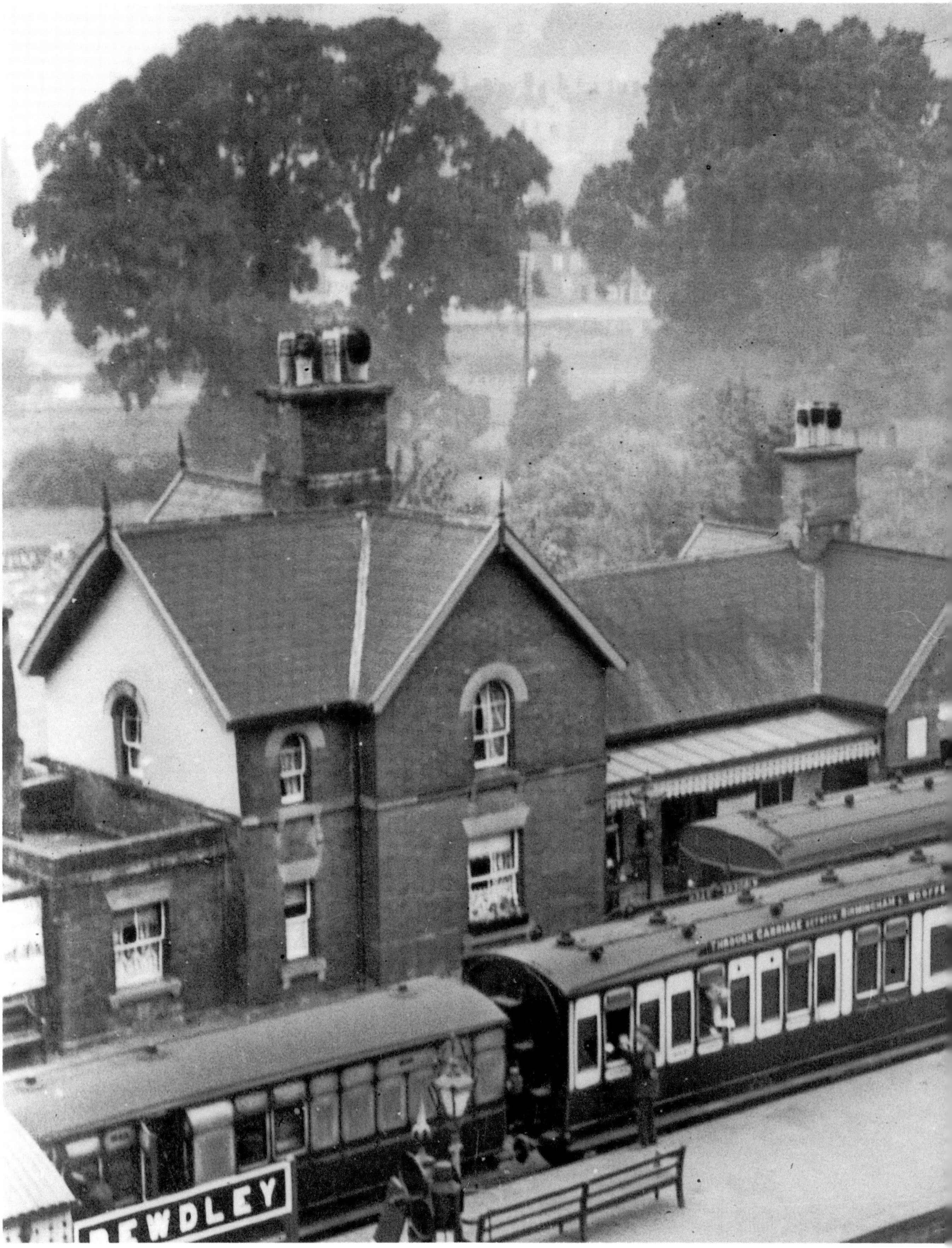

BEWDLEY

View taken at Bewdley between May 1908 and February 1911. The coaches nearest the camera were the rear of a Woofferton–Kidderminster–Birmingham train which included a through LNWR coach to Birmingham (New Street) via Smethwick. The LNWR coach can clearly be seen, complete with destination boards on the roof. It was a Diagram 229 42ft radial brake composite No. 637, built in December 1885, renumbered to 5815 on 14th February 1911. All seven of this LNWR diagram coach are shown as allocated to the Tenbury route. The GWR coach coupled to the through coach was a brake third Diagram T27 or T28 depending on whether the centre pair of the original six wheels were still in place. The GWR steam railmotor was a 70ft, Diagram R, possibly No. 91, which was completed in February 1908 and is seen here in early single colour livery of either lake or brown. The through LNWR coach working was taken off the Tenbury route in 1917 as a wartime economy measure and not reinstated.

Lens of Sutton

'517' class 0–4–2T No. 835, '850' class 0–6–0PT No. 2001, and '1501' class 0–6–0ST No. 1525 outside Kidderminster 'old' shed c.1914. These types were typical motive power on the Severn Valley and Tenbury branches until the advent of more modern classes in the late 'twenties and early 'thirties. In 1914, No. 2001 was loaned to the CM&DP Light Railway to assist with the additional traffic that resulted from additional demand for dhustone from the Army authorities. The loco is seen here with a strengthened front buffer beam, probably to enable it to carry out these wartime duties.
A. G. Ellis

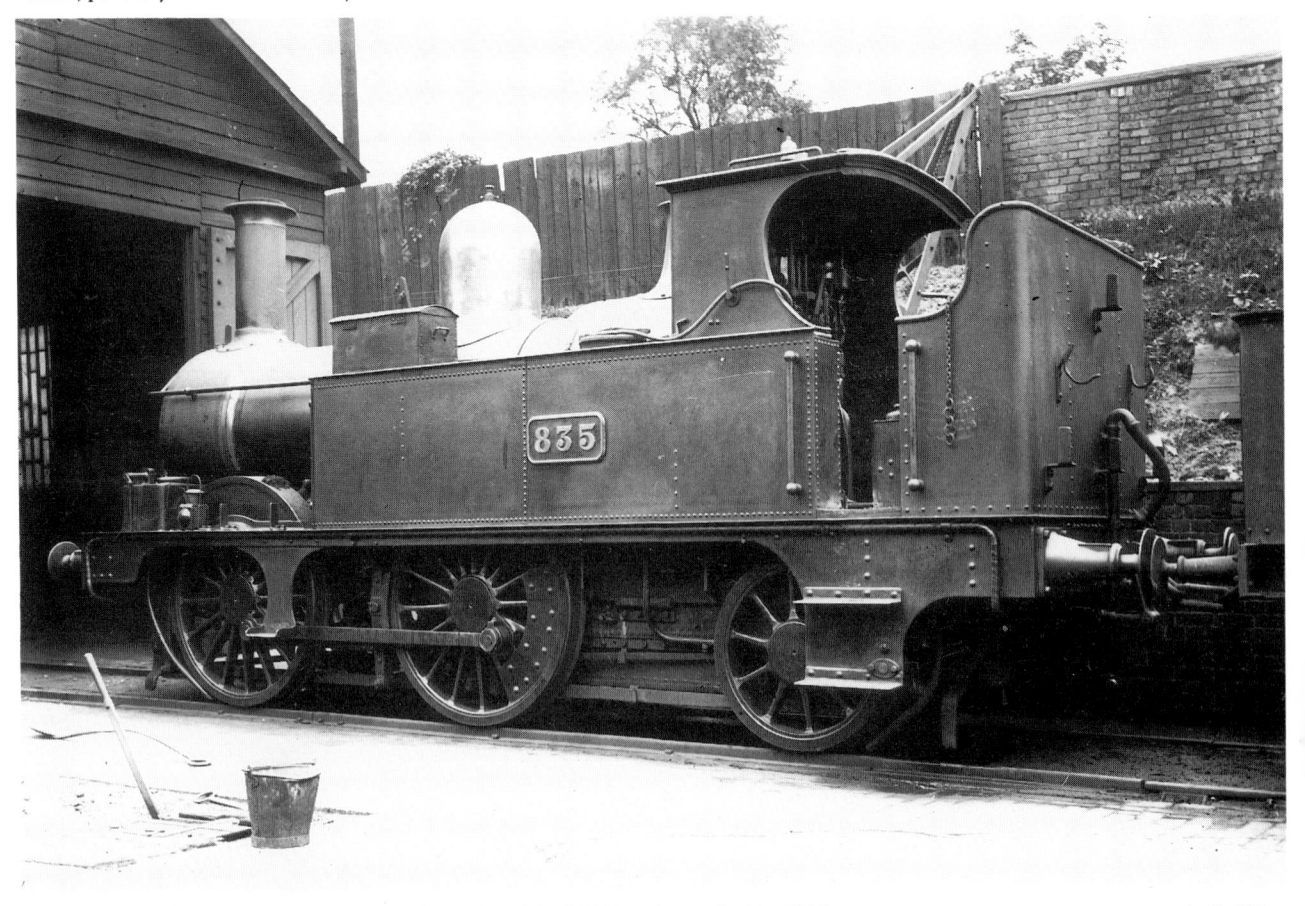

A closer view of '517' class 0–4–2T No. 835 at the original Kidderminster shed in 1914.
A. G. Ellis

gates and other complications. I put up the case that Cleobury Mortimer box was underpaid, and, after a recalculation of the points, I obtained a rise. There used to be three loads a day of stone from the quarries of Clee Hill, and a load of coal from Bayton Colliery. On one occasion the anchor wheel of the Bayton Colliery overhead railway broke adrift, and the coal was dropped all along the line of pylons. With a friend I hired a horse and dray, we gathered up this coal and made a good sale of it, with permission of course. On another occasion we had a landslide between Cleobury Mortimer and Wyre Forest which left about fifteen rails in the air, and it took a lot of truck loads of ashes to fill it up. When the war came, I decided, in March 1915, that I ought to join up, and after the war I returned to Hampton Lovett signal box.'

Another change of station name was made in 1912 when, on 4th November, Tenbury became 'Tenbury Wells' in connection with the long-felt wish to achieve spa town status. In conjunction with the refurbishment of the baths, the Tenbury Wells Advertising Committee had been established through the local council and getting the railway authorities to agree to the new name was one of their first successes.

By 1913, the ropeway from Bayton Colliery had settled down to work after a few earlier teething problems and 8,369 tons of coal passed through Cleobury Mortimer station that year compared with only 500 tons in 1903 before the advent of the ropeway. Bayton Colliery Co by now owned their own open wagons, bought second-hand, possibly from the GWR. They were painted grey with the inscription 'Bayton' in large white letters on each side.

The cattle pens at Tenbury Wells were finally built during the last year before the First World War, thirty years after they were first thought necessary. The work incidentally involved a slight alteration to the signalling arrangement with a new disc signal at 'B' box to protect the shunting spur into the pens. At the same time, the request for a ten-ton gantry crane to handle timber at Tenbury Wells was turned down, but the employment of an additional clerk was agreed, making the total seventeen staff employed.

Around the same time, a new goods loop was provided at Newnham Bridge station to allow trains to cross one another. A new 2-lever ground frame, locked by the key on the section electric staff, controlled movements at the western end whilst at the eastern end there was a larger 14-lever frame (five of which were spare), possibly inside a shelter.

The branch was soon involved in the war effort, and on Wednesday, 5th August 1914, the Tenbury contingent of 'B' Company 7th Battalion of the Worcestershire Regiment left by rail for Kidderminster to join the rest of their battalion. Up until 1914 the Royal Engineers had held their annual camp alongside the CM & DPR at Weston Farm (which involved special troop trains) but Neen Sollars became the favourite destination for officers of the Royal Scottish Signal Battalion based at Tenbury. The Railway Tavern, close by the station at Neen Sollars, was used by the officers as lodgings for rest and convalescence after a tour of duty during the war.

In 1914, the Bayton Colliery became a limited company and with this change the Bramall family started their long association with the enterprise. The first year of wartime running saw little change on the T & BR, unlike the local roads where according to the author of *Highways and Byways of England*, 'the motor car has not only resuscitated the whole of our highway system but strangled the railway monopoly which will never dominate the country again'.

The demand for dhu-stone accelerated in 1915, with increased tonnages coming off 'the Ditton Priors' onto 'the Tenbury' going to military depots across the country The work on the CM & DP had become more than the Light Railway's two Manning Wardles could manage, so a third loco was hired from the GWR. This was an 850 class 0-6-0PT No 2001 which came within the 14 tons axle weight. It came up the line from Kidderminster shed to help out, arriving in November 1914 and remaining until May 1915. From this time economy measures began to show up in the running of the Tenbury line as did shortages of staff as more men went away to the services. According to a petition of the time, the Joint Company's decision to close Tenbury goods yard early on a Saturday (at 1pm) caused much inconvenience to farmers and traders in the town. The only goods train from the Birmingham district on a Saturday arrived in the yard between 1.30pm and 2pm, leaving goods unavailable for collection until the following Monday. This was brought to the attention of the railway authorities in June together with the problems that would arise for the fruit growers who would expect to pick fruit on Saturday morning for despatch on the afternoon train.

There were other problems also for the fruit growers, namely an acute shortage of labour, so short in fact that people from as far away as Holland were being brought in to help gather in the harvests.

Later in the year, the hop season had to be extended for the same reason due to the many women and young girls normally employed in the season, now working in the Black Country munitions factories at far better wages.

In March 1915 the passenger service was cut: the 4.10pm motor train from Kidderminster to Woofferton and its return working were suspended. The 9.40am Tenbury Wells to Woofferton now had no Hereford connection until 11.26am, as trains to and from Hereford had also been taken off so that the last train back from Hereford was the 5.12pm which, through lack of a connection, did not allow passengers to reach Tenbury Wells until 7.30pm. The last train to Tenbury Wells from Kidderminster departed now at 7.53pm, arriving at 8.47pm. The Tenbury Parish Council were still planning for tourists, however, and confirmed that the station name change had been noted by all the railway companies. The council also approached the LNWR with a request to have a locomotive named *Tenbury Wells*. (There is no record of a similar and perhaps more likely attempt to interest the GWR.)

Mill Street, Kidderminster, from the Bridge Inn. The open-top double-deck bus was probably an early 'Midland Red' on its way to Bewdley.

Collection Brian Standish

INTO THE TWENTIETH CENTURY

This view of Worcester Cross, at the bottom of Comberton Hill, has strong railway connotations, for the LNWR (later LMS) goods depot was behind the odd-shaped building known as 'the fountain'. The white-faced building on the right was the West Midland Railway Inn, named after the company that briefly existed before being taken over by the GWR in 1863. Today only 'the fountain' still stands, the rest having been swept away with the building of Kidderminster's inner ring road. *Collection Brian Standish*

Mr A Rogers kindly supplied information about operating Little Hereford crossing:

'My father retired about the commencement of the First World War, but was called out of retirement to operate the crossing gates at Easton Court for Little Hereford, where I went to school. The crossing gates were of heavy oak, and quite large, with red lamps in the centre, they were opened when the telegraph system operated inside the house. This had a gong and 3 symbols, Down Train on Line, Line Clear, and Up Train on Line. The gates were opened from a small cabin by the track containing 3 levers. The two signal levers were normally at danger and the centre lever was over towards the signalman. The centre lever had to be pushed to normal first (this locked the gates) and, until this was done, neither the Up or Down Line signals could be pulled off. The crossing gates were situated about half a mile from Easton Court station.'

RATES OF PAY 1915

WOOFFERTON
Station master Class 3 £140 p.a. £10 allowance included.
1 Clerk } paid according to age
1 Junior
2 Porters — 17/- per week
1 Porter Shunter — 20/- per week
1 Yard Foreman — 23/- per week
1 Lad in Weighbridge (not given)

LITTLE HEREFORD CROSSING
1 Gateman — 19/- per week including rent

EASTON COURT
Station master Class 2 paid according to age
1 Porter — 17/- per week upwards

TENBURY WELLS
1 Station master Class 3
1 Chief Goods Clerk
2 Clerks — £55 p.a. up to £80 according to age
1 Junior Clerk
1 Yard Foreman — 23/- per week
1 Carter (Horse) — 24/- per week
1 Goods Porter
1 Porter Shunter — 20/- per week
1 Weighbridge man — 20/- per week
1 Junior Porter
1 Junior Parcels Porter

Signal men at Tenbury
1 'East or West', 10 hours duty — 22/6d per week
2 Porter S/Men, 10 hours duty — 21/- upwards

Figures kindly supplied by Mr G.R. Roberts, clerk at Tenbury Wells station 1924–29.

At the end of 1915 the *Tenbury Advertiser* carried warning of notice from the GWR of further reductions in the passenger timetable for next year, blaming shortage of staff and hoping that the public would adapt to the change. A new goods train entered the timetable in September 1915 to work between Cleobury Mortimer and Hereford, presumably for stone traffic, a diagram which remained throughout the war. A photograph of station staff taken in 1916 shows that women were coming forward at least in Tenbury Wells, to take the place of absent men at this time. Steam railmotors were omitted from the timetables but it was not until 1917 that wartime curtailments really became noticed. 'The railway timetables are so revised that their best friends wouldn't recognize them', wrote the *Tenbury Advertiser*.

The working timetable commencing 1st January 1917 shows five passenger trains over the whole line discontinued and the end of the LNWR through coaches, a feature of the branch since the Running Powers Agreement had come into force in June 1878 (the LNWR goods had ceased from about 1903). The withdrawal of the 7.50am Tenbury Wells to Woofferton hit particularly those farmers wishing to get to Hereford market in good time and schoolboys who were attending Ludlow Grammar School. The alterations also caused changes in the shed diagrams at Leominster and Ludlow. The so called 'short section' trains continued to be worked by Ludlow shed which was in addition responsible for providing motive power for the new 8.20am from Woofferton right through to Kidderminster. Leominster shed, on the other hand, lost the working to Kidderminster when the 6.40am Leominster-Woofferton was cancelled. A diagram by which the Leominster engine had returned home on the 7.52pm from Kidderminster was also discontinued.

Huge fare increases throughout the country, as much as 50% for distances over forty miles, came into effect, aimed at stifling the public demand for rail transport. Reductions, such as on market tickets, were also stopped, causing vexation to those farmers used to travelling by train to three markets per week. The cheap travel concession for fruit and hop pickers was to go, too, but such were the implications of this change for the Teme Valley that the Worcester branch of the N.F.U. decided to bring the problem to the notice of the Railway Executive who were responsible for administering Britain's railways in wartime. The Executive were sympathetic and passed the matter to the Food Production Department of the Ministry of Agriculture, Food and Fisheries, who advised 'It has been decided that seasonal workers can travel on railways at the rate of return ticket at the cost of the single fare plus one quarter without the 50% increase. This concession will not be confined as hitherto to fruit and hop pickers travelling in parties of not less than eight but will apply to all bona fide seasonal workers travelling singly or in parties'.

In 1917, the GWR was in correspondence with the newly formed Tenbury Fruit Growers Society. The secretary of the Society, Mr J Beaman, informed the members that negotiations were in progress to secure the field close by Tenbury Wells station opposite the Rose and Crown Inn and to have a private siding laid to a jam factory which was to be built on the site. However, when the cost was worked out, the fruit growers were forced to reconsider their ideas.

Traffic off the CM & DP through Cleobury Mortimer continued to increase, timber carriage being added to the wartime demand from the military authorities for stone. A new engine shed at Cleobury Town opened in 1917 which no doubt eased the Light Railways servicing problems, but there was still the requirement for the loan of an 850 class 0-6-0T from Kidderminster shed to help out with traffic. The 1917 season produced a tremendous crop of fruit in the Teme Valley and no-one on the railway needed reminding that the size of the fruit and hop crop affected the takings on the line by a considerable amount, measured in thousands of pounds. The Government, through the Food Production Department, made it policy to secure premises in the fruit growing districts to convert the excess fruit to pulp or to have it dried in order to conserve the glut of cheap, nutritious food for the nation's winter use. One such 'station' (as they were described) was sited in Bewdley at the rear of shops in Load Street. Tenbury growers were put out by this decision, and the newly formed Fruit Growers Society sent a petition to the Government to persuade the Food Production Department to site a pulping station at Tenbury as well. The Bewdley location would have pleased the railway, however, for it meant gaining the carriage receipts to Bewdley from the Tenbury and Newnham Bridge area in particular. Tenbury fruit growers were to remain disappointed because the Food Production Committee's reply to the petition was to inform the Society that it would not be possible to establish a pulping station at Tenbury that year. Much of the surplus fruit traffic, therefore, continued to be taken along the line to Bewdley which helped compensate for the contrasting poor hop harvest which followed the bumper one of fruit.

The hard work put in by the Tenbury Advertising Committee was brought to the public's attention by chairman G.E. Godson at a meeting held on 17th November 1917 at the Baths Hall, Tenbury. As far as the railway was concerned, the benefit came from three specials run in August Bank Holiday week for visitors returning to the Birmingham district, but there was a sting in the tail of the secretary's report when he reported correspondence with the Birmingham and Midland Motor Omnibus Company (later known as the Midland Red) with a view to a service between Tenbury and Kidderminster. The reply gave the railway a little breathing space from the possibility of direct competition for the passenger traffic as restrictions in force meant the bus company could not start a service for the time being.

By 1918, in spite of having no turntable, Kidderminster shed had acquired 0-6-0 Deans Goods tender engines. No doubt they were there to assist the war effort on the lines serviced by the shed. In November 1918 850 Class No 2016 was recorded as on loan to the CM & DP, which was obviously still short of motive power.

A bitter national railway strike that involved Kidderminster shed took place before the Armistice was signed, causing the general public to refer to the men on strike as 'German lovers' and 'traitors'. The *Kidderminster Times* of 28th September 1918 reported, 'Last Tuesday, 24th September, all employees of the railway at Kidderminster, about 70, were out on strike until Thursday morning (26th). No trains were run in the district. At Stourport, as a result of the strike, blackberries could not be taken by train'. Luckily for the growers, the Teme Valley fruit crop was in between main consignments and the hops were late ripening, but the importance of Tenbury market was emphasised when the lack of transport for cattle and sheep from Tenbury market was blamed for a meat shortage in Birmingham and even as far away as Leeds!

Despite some animosity towards the railwaymen, they came in for some praise, at least locally. Since the end of 1914, regular consignments of fruit and vegetables had been donated and sent from Newnham Bridge and Tenbury to be distributed between the officers and men of the Grand Fleet, and in a letter sent to the *Tenbury Advertiser*, the secretary of the Newnham Bridge branch of the Vegetable Products Committee expressed his thanks, and those of the Navy, to the railway staff of both stations and to the railway companies, for forwarding the produce free of charge to the naval bases. He also hoped that they would reach a target of over 46½ tons of produce sent, before the end of 1918.

In the late autumn of 1918, a meeting of the Tenbury Wells Advertising Committee noted that the Government was offering to sell surplus light rails once the war was over. In the discussion which followed, the idea of the Teme Valley Railway was born again; on this occasion a light railway was considered appropriate in order to take advantage of Government offers. The meeting also considered it an important step to 'get Clee Hill people to bring a railway to Tenbury'. With this in mind, a public meeting was held at Clee Hill on 30th October 1918 with representatives from Tenbury attending. Mr J.E. Roberts of Tenbury presided and introduced Mr Mackay, well known at Clee Hill from his association with the stone industry, to speak on the advantages to be gained by the organization of light railways in agricultural districts. The scheme he outlined was to use the surplus 2 foot gauge track from the Military in France, possibly widened to 2ft 6in, and include passenger traffic as well as goods and minerals. He could not say whether the enterprise would be carried out by the Government, or by private means, or with Government help. The discussion concerned a light railway from Clee Hill to Ludlow through Knowbury and Doddington, but representatives of the Tenbury Wells Advertising Committee (Messrs Morris, Bentley and Dukes) took the opportunity to remind everyone of the value of a link to Tenbury, particularly as so many residents of Clee Hill did business in the town. Further meetings on the same theme were held later in Hereford where Mackay was actively backing a proposed Hereford light railway in addition to the Clee Hill scheme. There are no clear-cut reasons why these proposals did not materialise, but cost was a factor and it was never obvious who would fund what; local authorities appear to have had a suspicion of the Government's motives. In any case, yet again the Teme Valley, Tenbury to Worcester railway link failed and the idea was lost. As the war came to an end on 11th November 1918, engine whistles and exploding detonators along the line were added to the sound of pealing church bells signalling the news that the Armistice had been signed.

Hop pickers at Tenbury gathered round a hop crib. They all appear to have been in their 'Sunday best' so there is little doubt that it was one of the final cribs of the season, the proceeds from which were traditionally donated to a local charity or good cause, hence 'The Hospital Crib' written on the back of the photograph.

Collection Brian Standish

Looking towards Bewdley. The building nearest the camera was the stone-built vicarage, and the brick building next door with the decorative quoins formed part of a terraced row of Victorian and Georgian houses opposite St. Mary's Church.

Collection J. W. Warren

CHAPTER NINE
BETWEEN THE WARS

PEACE returned but was not officially celebrated in Tenbury until July 1919. Not all was peace on the railways however, for another strike broke out on 26th September almost a year to the day after the previous one. Unlike the 1918 strike, this one did clash with the busy fruit harvest time in the Teme Valley. Some growers had their crops go rotten, others looked elsewhere for transport. For the first time ever in the district, damsons and apples were moved in quantity by road. The milk traffic, too, went away on lorries and it was not until Saturday, 4th October that a train service was reinstated on the Tenbury and Bewdley. Road competition was now to become even more intense, for in 1919 a local bus service became operational. A bus to Birmingham was advertised to run from the Market Square, Tenbury on 18th December at 9.30am, arriving back at 9pm, for a fare of 7/6d. The route to Birmingham was via Bromsgrove and Northfield. At first timekeeping was a problem, the first trip arriving an hour and a half late back in Tenbury.

In 1919 the CM & DP management was unable to regain independent control of its affairs, for like all other railways in Britain, it came under the two year extension of Government control which was exercised under the Ministry of Transport Act. The company had, however, already forged links with the GWR. In addition to hiring locos, their own *Cleobury* and *Burwarton* travelled to Worcester works in 1919 for repairs. Furthermore, the annual permanent way inspection was carried out jointly with a GWR engineer. At the other end of Cleobury Mortimer station, the Bayton Colliery siding had been extremely busy throughout the war; a new rope costing £500 was necessary in 1918 to maintain the movement of buckets down for offloading into the GWR wagons.

In 1920 Mr C.R. Clinker recorded travelling on the joint section of the Tenbury line in a train consisting of LNWR 6-wheeled coaches, hauled by a GWR 0-6-0T. He also noted an LNWR loco working to Tenbury Wells when a Hereford-Shrewsbury local freight worked a trip from Woofferton hauled by an LNWR 18in 0-6-0 goods. Another observer from the early 1920s, `Mr R.G. Higgins (a GWR fireman at Ludlow shed) recalls that the Ludlow to Kidderminster turns were composed of four-wheeled GWR carriages, usually four in number but at times up to seven were used. However, in the May 1920 Service Timetable there is noted the introduction of a short-lived autocar working of three trips each way per day between Woofferton and Kidderminster, using the Ludlow-based auto-fitted 0-6-0PT No 2120. In these early post war years, passengers alighting at Cleobury Mortimer would travel to the town, some two miles distant, in a model 'T' Ford Bus operated by Dudley's, the local ironmonger which superseded the former horse bus.

A much more drastic and widespread change on the railways was to come, for the year 1922 ushered in a new partnership on the Tenbury Railway and new ownership of the light railway line to Ditton Priors. The grouping brought the LMS into being as the successor to the LNWR on the joint lines, though the LNWR influence continued to be strong. Ludlow retained its usual allocation of two engines (an ex-LNWR 2-4-2T and an 0-6-2 Coal Tank) for working Shrewsbury local trips. At the same time the CM & DP was absorbed by its giant neighbour the GWR, and from mid 1922 a start was made on improving and renewing the track, particularly replacing the flat-bottom rails on the CM & DP side of Cleobury Mortimer station.

The long established Stourbridge to Hereford goods trains of the period have been recalled by Stourbridge driver Jack Smith who worked on them as a young fireman. Typical locos remembered were ancient 0-6-0 tender types, Coal Engines Nos 945 and 946, Standard Goods No 702 and also the relatively modern Dean Goods 0-6-0 No 2325.

By the early 1920s Leominster shed's passenger working to Kidderminster had been reinstated following the war, but diagrammed to run from Leominster to Woofferton and back as empty stock. Regular locos on the branch at the time of the grouping were still the long serving 0-4-2T

A Bewdley train at Neen Sollars c.1920. Authors' collection

'517' Class, particularly Nos 517, 555, 1474 and 1477. A 'Metro' 2-4-0T No 3512 was also frequently observed up and down the branch. These were Ludlow engines recalled by Fireman Higgins, who also remembers the Shrewsbury shed practice of borrowing locos from Chester and using them from Ludlow. Thus the unique GWR 2-4-0T No 1 came to work the branch for a while. The Ludlow engines not only worked the 'short section' and Kidderminster trains, but sometimes worked right through to Birmingham (Snow Hill). The 2-4-0T wheel arrangement became more common over the branch in the early '20s when Kidderminster shed was allocated six 'Metros' at various times until 1924 and these, along with 2021 Class 0-6-0STs and 0-6-0Ts, began to ease out the ubiquitous '517s' that were used from the Worcestershire end of the line. 0-6-0 tender engines, seen mainly on the Stourbridge-Hereford goods, included Standard Goods Nos 116, 146 and 32 (this was the loco which had been used to stress-test Cleobury Mortimer bridge in 1895) and '131' Class No 132.

1923 saw the emergence of the local bus as a severe threat to the railway, as public entertainments and other events returned to normal after the war. One local bus proprietor was Messrs Critchleys of Teme Street, Tenbury who advertised that their 'Ever Ready' saloon bus would run to Worcester for the Point to Point races on 18th January 1923. The Tenbury Baths Company (TBC) had also branched out into the motor trade on acquiring a garage, also in Teme Street, and, as well as offering the usual facilities, also ran the Bluebird Motor Services. Their first timetables included a return trip to Worcester on Mondays; a roundabout route on Tuesdays taking in Easton, Little Hereford and Brimfield (the village for Woofferton Station); on Thursdays there was a run to Kidderminster for the market, and on Friday the bus went to Leominster and back. Special trips were advertised to Stratford-on-Avon and to five small local race meetings that were popular at the time. Reduced single fares were announced, and other concessions for returns and season tickets must have alarmed the railway authorities. The response was a special excursion train with a 10.30am departure from Tenbury Wells to Bridgnorth steeplechases on 24th April, calling at all stations to Bewdley and arriving at Bridgnorth at 12.05pm. On 25th April there was a special train to Malvern from Tenbury Wells for the Music Festival, leaving Tenbury at 7.40am and costing 5/- return. Critchleys 'Ever Ready' bus also offered a return trip to Malvern for 5/- but leaving at 9.00am. In May, Bluebird Motor Services added a new route to Bromyard on a Saturday and announced more fare reductions and trips in their char-a-bancs to the same destinations as those advertised on the railways but at cheaper fares. Their 'Emperor' coach offered to take visitors to the Three Counties Show at Malvern for 4/10d return whereas the railway fare was 5/- to the same destination and required a change of train at Woofferton. The next 'day out' was advertised by the railway when cheap fares (2/3d return) were offered to Stourport for the June regatta. Ever needful of providing what the public wanted, the railway quickly responded to complaints that the thirty or so boys and girls in the district attending Ludlow Grammar and High Schools were having to leave Tenbury too early at 7.30am. Mr Williams, Joint Line Superintendent, agreed to start the train at the later time of 8.00am when the summer alterations came into force in July. At the same time a new early morning service to Birmingham was unveiled, with tickets at reduced rates. By travelling on this train, the railway's passengers could be in Birmingham by 9.02am, having left Tenbury Wells at 7.15am, the empty coaches leaving Kidderminster at 5.55am. In addition, on Thursday (market day in Kidderminster), a train from Birmingham would

No. 1 at Chester, a locomotive that was 'borrowed' on occasion for use on the Tenbury & Bewdley line. Built as a 4–4–0T in May 1880 as a running test bed for some of William Dean's ideas, it was rebuilt as a 2–4–0T in May 1882 and lasted until July 1924.

J. N. Maskelyne

An early competitor for the railway companies came from the introduction of bus routes through the rural parishes. Here a group pose outside the New Inn at Knighton on Teme. The bus travelled via Newnham Bridge and on up the Teme Valley.
Cty. S. Underwood

arrive in Tenbury Wells at 8.44pm and then form a return working departing at 8.55pm, very late in the evening by previous timetables' standards. So the railways learned to live with the opposition and compete with the bus companies, whilst no doubt watching the increase in commercial vehicles carrying livestock, etc, and the growing numbers of private cars.

In the early twenties, coal transport was still the preserve of the railway companies and the GWR looked hopefully for the increased demands of the 1914/18 war to continue into the 1920s. On the Tenbury line, the hope was for continued transport requirements from the Bayton colliery siding at Cleobury Mortimer. This was not to be, however, as it became apparent that the mine workings were becoming exhausted and that new shafts would have to be sunk elsewhere. The Bayton Colliery Company had already leased the Mawley mineral rights from the Blount Estates in 1919 and this allowed them to search for minerals over a wide area. Boring was commenced in Mamble Village in 1922, and after some time coal seams were found and a shaft was sunk. Meanwhile the tonnage of coal passing by rail through Cleobury Mortimer had fallen dramatically and by the end of 1923 Bayton pit had closed and the ropeway stopped. The pit winding engine was sold to Capt. Astley Jones for his sinking at 'Newlands', near Clows Top, but was never used again. Further borings carried out at Hunthouse Wood, near Frith Common, revealed good seams of coal, and in 1924 the Hunthouse workings were opened. Very little coal was being produced at Mamble so work was abandoned and the shafts filled in the same year.

In June 1924 came a great summer flash flood in the valleys of the Teme and Severn, which affected the Severn Valley line quite severely with wash-outs at Arley. Although much of Tenbury town was under feet of water, the trains here continued to get through.

In July 1924, the loop was extended at Neen Sollars. The Inspector's report of 18th September 1924 gives the details:

'The crossing loop at this station has been extended by 40ft in a southerly direction and 380ft in a northerly direction. The north end of the down platform has also been set back to suit the alteration in alignment. Worked facing trap points have been fixed on the up and down loops respectively in addition. In addition to these two, runaway spring trap points have been fixed at each end of the down loop, those at the north end being slotted. These sets of facing and trailing points have been laid with the object of protection against overruns or runaways. The spring, slotted points in the north end of the down loop will be of service against vehicles running backwards, provided the loop points at that end are (in accordance with instructions) maintained in their reverse position until a train proceeding in the direction of Cleobury Mortimer has been cleared back. The new points and signals are worked from Neen Sollars Box which contains a new frame with 20 working levers and 1 spare.'

A new station master was appointed at Tenbury Wells in succession to Mr J.D. Roberts who retired after 17 years at Tenbury on 31st August 1924 with gifts and grateful thanks from his customers in the district. The new appointment was Mr Maurice Bott who had entered railway service with the Cambrian Railway at Oswestry before joining the LNWR/GWR Joint Company. Mr Bott kept a diary which gives an interesting insight into his time in charge of Tenbury Wells and one of the first events he recorded was the demolition of the old cattle dock on the up side of the line. Large consignments of timber were then being taken from the Northwick estates — so great an amount that the Tenbury yard crane could not cope and a steam crane was often sent to help out. Mr Bott's son John recalls how milk was brought to Tenbury by rail, and how loco drivers were reminded to stop the train with their Siphon milk van opposite the station entry gate from where the milk churns were delivered and collected. To get this right, the station staff would shout 'milk!, milk!', to the loco crew as they prepared to come to a stop.

After 1924, when Mr Bott came to Tenbury Wells, Leominster trains ceased and Ludlow shed took over the majority of the workings on the branch, a situation which continued until 1941. Ludlow shed had four GWR crews and two LMS. Crew No 1, the senior link, began their day with the 7.20am passenger from Ludlow to Tenbury Wells, returning to Ludlow with the 8.00am school train from Tenbury Wells. Then they worked two morning passengers, Woofferton to Kidderminster and return, arriving back at Woofferton with the 1.50 ex Kidderminster. No 2 crew were on duty after this and on into the early evening, back in Ludlow at 9.16pm with empty coaches. Ludlow No 1 and No 2 turns used 'Metro' 2-4-0Ts Nos 5 and 617 or '517' 0-4-2Ts at this period, or in exceptional circumstances a 1016 class 0-6-0PT. No 3 crew worked the 6.55am Ludlow-Shrewsbury goods, changing over with the crew of the corresponding Shrewsbury-Ludlow goods at

Tenbury Wells from the western end, in August 1928. Blakes of Hereford were a well-known local coal factor and some of their wagons feature on the right.
John Bott

Tenbury staff in August 1924 on the occasion of Mr. Roberts' retirement. *Back row, left to right:* Harold Gibbs, Charlie Jones, Reuben Martin, Jack Pussey (linesman), – Holland, – Hardisty (linesman), Eric Morris, Nip Tipton, Tom Lucas (goods foreman), Charlie Jones (signalman). *Front row, left to right:* Fred Jones (drayman), Mr. Foster (local factory), John Morgan, Mr. Roberts (station master), Mr. Bowers (booking clerk), two relief clerks. *H. Heath*

Tenbury Wells staff, winter 1928, with (*back row*) Harold Gibbs, Ernie Morris, 'Nip' Tipton, G. Roberts, Noel Bowers; (*front row*) Chas. Bradley, Mr. Bott, and John Morgan. *G. Roberts*

THE TENBURY & BEWDLEY RAILWAY

Church Stretton at 9.50am. After disposing of the train at Ludlow, the engine and crew worked the 1.10pm mixed train to Tenbury Wells. The same engine then took up the working of the Tenbury Wells-Ludlow 'Joint' goods which was run when required and was timed to leave for Ludlow at 3.40pm (weekdays only). On Saturdays the working varied to a return Tenbury Wells-Woofferton-Tenbury Wells passenger working, leaving the engine to run light back to Ludlow. The 1016 0-6-0Ts usually worked this turn, Nos 1027, 1045 and 1047 being regulars. On occasions, however, 0-6-0 tender engines (Beyer goods, Dean goods or Armstrong goods) would be pressed into service. They were usually from Salop shed or borrowed from elsewhere, for instance Chester. No 4 crew worked the Clee Hill branch with 0-6-0Ts such as Nos 2104, 2109 and 1949 and the LMS crews worked their tank locos on passenger trains to Shrewsbury. These LMS tanks often ventured into Tenbury Wells to work specials up to the Shrewsbury district, especially when the popular annual Flower Show was on, and another ex-LNWR type, an 0-6-0 'Cauliflower'

Tenbury station forecourt, Whit Sunday 1929. The LMS adverts include one for Blackpool Tower and seaside. The hitching rail for horses can be seen on the right. *J. Bott*

This late 1920s view shows the Joint Railways' hand cart used for delivering small parcels to the town. *J. Bott*

Fruit and rabbit traffic were a regular seasonal feature sent to local markets by passenger train in purpose-built wicker baskets. The round type for fruit were called 'sieves' and can be seen by the waiting room, whilst returned empty 'pots' for dead rabbits can be seen below the station nameboard. August 1928.
John Bott

Tenbury Wells West ('B' Box) with station master Maurice Bott in August 1928. Known as an LNWR Type 3 box, it was built in 1878 and controlled the original double running lines between it and the east (Station Box) and the entrance to the goods yard and turntable. It closed on 12th October 1928 and was replaced by ground frames.
John Bott

'Civilian' driver Lampitt, guard Riley and clerk Bailey at Tenbury during the 1926 strike.

John Bott

Tender loco would appear in Tenbury Wells on a ballast train from time to time.

Two Kidderminster crews worked from that end of the line, No 1 crew taking the 8.48am Kidderminster-Woofferton and returning with the 10.15am Woofferton-Kidderminster-Birmingham. Later in the day No 2 crew would work the 4.40pm Kidderminster-Woofferton and the 6.55pm Woofferton-Kidderminster-Stourbridge, and on to Birmingham (Snow Hill) when required. Up until 1928 the '3521' class 4-4-0s, Nos 3527, 3555 and 3557 were used on the No 1 turn whilst on No 2 a whole range of 0-6-0Ts (1501 class or 1854 class) were used. Alternatives were 'Metro' 2-4-0T No 979, also 1076 or 1016 classes or even the unpopular rebuilt ex-MSWJ 4-4-4T No 27 which ended her days at Kidderminster. The Hereford-Stourbridge goods was still regularly worked by a Dean Goods 0-6-0, but as the older 0-6-0s went away for scrap, 'Bulldog' 4-4-0s and 'Aberdare' 2-6-0s were used even though the line had not been uprated to a 'Blue Route'. Kidderminster or Stourbridge 0-6-0PTs were usually used on cattle trains and cattle empties, but the hop pickers specials were often worked by Dean Goods or a '3232' 2-4-0, inevitably hauling a collection of very old and run-down rolling stock.

In 1924, the Manning Wardle 0-6-0ST *Burwarton* of the CM & DP returned from Swindon works rebuilt as a pannier tank, minus nameplates and looking every bit a standard GWR type, at least above the running plate. The CM & DP coaches were still to be seen at Cleobury Mortimer, now renumbered in the GWR fleet, as were some of the ten ton CM & DP wagons which the GWR had also inherited. The two Light Railway brake vans continued their useful service with the Ditton Priors branch train, usually referred to by railwaymen and local residents as 'The Gadget'. The Tenbury Wells brake van at this time was older than those on the Light Railway, an outside-framed wooden type with the allocation written on its sides as 'Tenbury' (still without the additional 'Wells').

Newnham Bridge featured in the interesting diagram for the Hereford-Stourbridge goods working in Mr Bott's years at Tenbury Wells. This train arrived at Tenbury at 4.05pm, having left Worcester sidings, Hereford, at 12.05pm and calling at Moreton on Lugg, Dinmore, Ford Bridge, Leominster and Woofferton, arriving 2.18pm. After a 1½ hour wait here, the train went forward to Tenbury, arriving at 4.05pm. Engine and crew took up the working of the 4.35pm joint passenger Tenbury Wells to Woofferton and 5.15pm return using the coach or coaches left behind at Tenbury Wells by Ludlow No 3 crew off the 1.10pm Ludlow to Tenbury mixed train. At 6.00pm the Stourbridge goods then worked forward only as far as Newnham Bridge. In the fruit season the engine and van, when required, would take perishable goods back to Tenbury Wells at 7.35pm and return to Newnham Bridge, arriving at 7.56pm to take the goods on to Stourbridge, departing at 8.05pm.

The timing of the corresponding goods train from Stourbridge to Hereford was as follows:

Stourbridge	dep 8.36am	
Kidderminster	arr 9.40am	dep 10.50am
Tenbury Wells	arr 2.22pm	dep 5.47pm
Woofferton	arr 6.10pm	dep 6.57pm
Ludlow	arr 7.12pm	dep 8.55pm
Leominster	arr 9.47pm	
Hereford (Barton)	arr 10.34pm	

Sunday excursion working was introduced in 1925, the first excursion being arranged to Wembley for a visit to the British Empire Exhibition. Strangely, that very weekend a minor earth tremor was recorded around Tenbury. The local newspapers reported chimney pots falling off and wagons being derailed in Tenbury station yard. Some said this was divine retribution for the railway violating the Sabbath, but this first Sunday outing led the way for many more to follow. Some excursion trips came from Birmingham and the Black Country on their way to Ludlow whilst others began to bring town dwellers to Wyre Forest and Neen Sollars stations in particular, to take part in the increasingly popular pastime of rambling.

As far as the Tenbury-Bewdley line was concerned, the opening in the autumn of a sugar beet factory (called the West Midlands Sugar Company) opposite Foley Park Halt, Kidderminster, in 1925, was an important event. This was under the auspices of the Anglo-Scottish Sugar Beet Corporation Limited. The factory development, promised since before the 1914-1918 war, soon brought traffic by way of large consignments of beet carried to the factory by rail from around the growing areas.

At a distance of 270 yards to the west of Kidderminster Junction Signal Box, a connection facing traffic from Bewdley was laid in, and a signal controlling movement over the new connection was provided. Later, as the volume of sugar beet traffic increased, another connection and a two-lever ground frame were installed to give access to wagons otherwise trapped in refuge sidings.

If May 1925 produced a tremor in Tenbury and district, May 1926 heralded a shock felt across the nation in the form of a General Strike called in support of the mine workers who were being threatened with cuts in pay and longer working hours. Although the events of 1926 are well documented, the part played by the railways is sometimes ignored by historians even though it was a notable if not unusual event in railway history. On Tuesday, 4th May the nation awoke to an unfamiliar hush in the streets as thousands of workers stayed at home. Many of them could not get to work anyway as the transport system was virtually at a standstill, with very few services operating. No trains were running at Kidderminster where practically every railwayman was on strike, leaving Station Master Pascoe in solitary charge. However, the men at Tenbury, under Station Master Bott, reported for work, even with no trains running, and occupied their time playing cricket in the station drive! The Government's immediate response

The horse-drawn Tenbury 'bus' outside Tenbury Wells station in 1928.   *J. Bott*

to the strike was to set up centres for the collection and distribution of essential supplies, and Major F.D. Burcher, Managing director of the T.B.C. Garages Ltd, was appointed food and fuel officer for the Kidderminster and Bewdley district. To keep these supplies moving, a function normally largely carried out by the railways, volunteers were asked for, and appeared in their tens of thousands across the country., Whilst some drove trams and buses, many were selected to drive the trains, being passed as competent to do so after only half a day's instruction! One such volunteer on the Tenbury line named as Col Cornwallis-West, whilst assisting on the footplate, stopped his train (so the story goes) between stations for his butler to deliver a change of clothes to the cab of the engine!

On 12th May 1926, the General Council of the TUC called off the strike and passenger trains began to run again, if only spasmodically at first. The miners, however, stayed out on strike for another six months which naturally resulted in a great decline in coal traffic, especially from the mines on the Severn Valley line and a curtailed passenger timetable was worked for a while. Milk traffic suffered, too, for it had been imperative for it to be taken away by road when the trains were not running and some of the regular local consignments from Tenbury never returned to rail carriage after the stoppage.

The events of May 1926 were traumatic, too, for the staffing arrangements at both Wyre Forest and Easton Court. The post of station master at Wyre Forest was withdrawn and the station was placed under the supervision of Cleobury Mortimer's station master, Mr Pugh. At Easton Court, John Sumner Bott (younger brother of Maurice at Tenbury) had been taken ill just at the time of the strike and was made redundant while off sick. As an economy measure, the LMS/GWR Joint Committee decided that Tenbury staff could run Easton Court as well, with Mr G. Roberts as booking clerk and G. Colley as porter making their way from Tenbury each day by train. Mr Edgar Price, one of the Tenbury signalmen moved to live in Easton Court station house when it became vacant following this altered arrangement. Before Mr Roberts was moved to Easton Court, he was booking clerk at Tenbury Wells, and recalls the holly and mistletoe sales at the nearby market in the weeks before Christmas. These brought in dozens of buyers by train from all over the country and resulted in large consignments of best quality holly going by train to Manchester and district in particular. Every Tuesday the 10.15am ex-Kidderminster conveyed an empty parcels van to Tenbury which was detached at the platform before the rest of the train proceeded to Woofferton. During the day, the van was loaded with hampers of fruit, rabbits and live and dead poultry brought from the market. The van would then be attached at the front of the 3.35pm Woofferton to Kidderminster passenger. On one occasion, a lapse of memory caused a slight collision involving this vehicle. The signalman had not protected the van and accepted a local goods train from Cleobury Mortimer. Luckily the goods approached Tenbury under the road bridge at a very slow speed, and, although the van was derailed, the damage to it and its contents was minimal. Mr Roberts remembers, too, that although Cleobury Mortimer's horse-drawn omnibus had long been retired, there was still one in use at Tenbury. Travellers arriving by rail were met at the station by the Swan Hotel's horse-drawn cab, known to all as the 'Tenbury bus'. The hotel boasted that it met every train!

The idea of train travel for leisure purposes had grown remarkably since the end of the war and excursion trains were offered in greater numbers than ever before. On the Tenbury & Bewdley the first Sunday seaside excursion to run off the branch was on 15th August 1926 to Barry Island with many others of similar kind in the following years.

In September 1926, the GWR's pattern of electric key token was noted by Mr Bott as having been introduced in place of the electric train staff.

By the early months of 1926, the four ex-North London Railway coaches taken over from the CM & DP and used until then by the GWR on the Ditton Priors line, had been sent to Swindon for scrapping. They were replaced by four older but standard GWR gas-lit four-wheelers which were usually stabled on the short length of siding at Cleobury Mortimer known to railwaymen as the 'Monkey Road' due to the use of the coaches to make up the local school train, presumably with some unruly children on board! It had also become quite usual for replacement engines on the Ditton Priors line to be provided by Kidderminster shed when either *Cleobury* or *Burwarton* were unavailable. Both of these engines had now been given GWR numbers (28 and 29 respectively), and in 1926 No 28 *Cleobury* came back after overhaul at Worcester factory displaying several GWR modifications including an upward extension to the coal bunker.

At Cleobury Mortimer the following year the well-liked station master, Mr Pugh, suffered a tragic death which shocked railwaymen and the local public alike. It happened early one morning when Mr Pugh, purposely waiting alongside the running line in Prizeley cutting, sadly committed suicide under the wheels of a passing goods train.

The use of the Tenbury-Bewdley line for diverted passenger trains is recalled by John Bott. The engine of one such train, a northbound express off the S & HR through Tenbury Wells to Bewdley and beyond, was remembered as having been a 4-4-0 of the 'Bulldog' class.

Changes in operation at Tenbury Wells continued. The turntable at the western end of the goods yard was deleted from the turntable list published by the LMS in 1927, though it was apparently still available for use if required. The Ditton Priors trains at Cleobury Mortimer station increasingly came to look 'Great Western' with 2021 class 0-6-0ST No 2101 being used for many months in 1927 in place of one or the other ex-CM & DP locos. Late in 1927, Kidderminster shed was allocated its first 'modern' class when four brand new 55XX 2-6-2Ts arrived from Swindon; these were numbers 5505/6/7 in late October

Easton Court from the road c.1924, with station master John Summner Bott. He left through illness around the time of the General Strike and was not replaced. In 1926/7 Mr. G. Roberts became booking clerk, with Mr. G. Colley as porter, both travelling from Tenbury Wells each day. Mr. Edgar Price, one of the Tenbury signalmen, then moved into Easton Court station house. Mr. Price was succeeded by Mr. Morgan, goods agent at Tenbury, who lived in the house for several years.
J. Bott

Hop-pickers at Blowers Green, near Dudley, in the heart of the 'Black Country' in 1928. The hop fields were a dramatic contrast to the gasometers, foundries and the slag heaps of the industrial Midlands. *Dudley Library*

Hop-picking time brought a big increase in special traffic to Tenbury Wells. This picture, taken c.1928, shows hop-pickers at Blowers Green, near Dudley, waiting for Tenbury Wells specials. Typically, the stock used would be old gas-lit, non-corridor clerestories. The working timetable included a note that 'all doors be kept locked for the duration of the journey'. *Dudley Library*

followed by 5508 on 27th November 1927. They went straight to work on the Kidderminster crew No 1 early-turn diagram on the branch, taking over from the 3521 4-4-0 tender class. The 55XX class were ideally suited to branch lines routes of this type with quick acceleration and ability to make light work of the heavier gradients. The demise of the 3521 tender engines on the branch was one reason that Tenbury turntable was no longer needed. Previously, the engines, after running tender first with the 10.15am Woofferton-Birmingham as far as Tenbury, were turned at Tenbury to run engine first to Bewdley, the W.T.T. allowing 8 minutes to complete this manoeuvre. In 1928 the GWR followed the LMS by leaving the turntable off its list even though it was still in place and, from local evidence, used for a while afterwards. The signal box at the same end of Tenbury yard as the turntable was closed down at this time, too. The GWR referred to this box as Tenbury West whereas the Joint Committee always called it Tenbury 'B'. It was closed on 12th October 1928. The crossing loop at the western end of the station layout was reduced in length by 18 chains as a result of moving a crossover, and was converted to a refuge siding with a connection from the single line worked by a ground frame at the west end. An additional home signal was provided with telephone communication to the remaining signal box (which had been known as Tenbury East or Tenbury 'A' in April 1903 but which had become Tenbury Wells) and which now had 20 working levers. The cost of all this work was estimated at £1,665, with a saving on signalman's wages of £278 p.a. On the subject of wages, Station Master Bott was now paid £10 extra p.a. by the GWR for supervising the running of Easton Court station.

Stone traffic off the Ditton Priors, was badly affected in 1928 by the closure of the ropeway and loading terminal at Detton Ford, north of Cleobury Town. Clee Hill Granite Company abandoned the quarry operations that fed the aerial ropeway as a result of falling demand for the dhu-stone rock which caused eventual bankruptcy of the Clee Hill Granite Company. The last of the ex-CM & DP open wagons disappeared that year and GWR 850 class 0-6-0PT No 1962 was in regular use on the Ditton Priors trains from Cleobury Mortimer.

The competition from road traffic continued to increase with the growth of private motoring, and the lorry was slowly replacing the horse and cart for the carriage of goods in and around country towns. The GWR decided in October 1929 to establish a Country Lorry Service in the Tenbury Wells district to replace the then current horse team. A 30 cwt Thornycroft lorry No 1459, was to be used for an experimental period of six months. This trial was reported as having produced satisfactory results for an estimated initial cost of £416, and so the official service was begun earlier than anticipated in February 1930, under the supervision of the LMS/GWR Joint Railways at Shrewsbury and with Reuben Martin as the first driver. Although Joint Railway property, the lorry was painted in GWR livery.

Fortunately for the line, the long established carriage of fruit and hops was still very much in the hands of the railway. Newnham Bridge was the railhead most convenient to many farmers in the Teme Valley, especially around the Lindridge and Menith Wood districts from where hops grown for Bass were sent to Burton-on-Trent. Problems often arose when Newnham Bridge station was swamped

Hop pockets from Lindridge would be destined for loading on a train at Newnham Bridge station. Here the hop farmer, family and kiln men display the results of their labours. *Authors' collection*

Woofferton Junction with its well-kept station flower beds, looking towards Ludlow. The station building on the right was typical of the style favoured by the Shrewsbury and Hereford Railway.
C. L. Mowat

Beyer or '322' class 0–6–0 No. 355 crossing the S&HR main line at Woofferton Junction with a Tenbury–Woofferton train to gain access to the branch siding in 1929.
M. D. England, cty. R. C. Riley

Ludlow 0–6–0 No. 355 on a midday train from Ludlow to Woofferton and Tenbury in 1929. Built by Beyer Peacock & Co. in 1866, and rebuilt at Wolverhampton in 1883, No. 355 lasted until 1931 when it was withdrawn in April of that year.
M. D. England, National Railway Museum

by this seasonal traffic, and roads became blocked with queues of lorries sometimes stretching as far as the Talbot Inn 200 yards down the road from the station yard. Messrs Firkins, hop growers of Eardiston, began to send teams of horse-drawn wagons to Cleobury Mortimer station with their hops to avoid the congestion and delay at Newnham Bridge. It became clear that there was a case for enlarging the siding and loading facilities at Newnham Bridge and this was carried out in 1930. To gain more siding space within the land owned, the GWR removed the original brick overbridge and replaced it with a much lengthened steel girder bridge in June. This structure, costing £832 8s 7d, was supplied by the Horsehay Company of Dawley, Shropshire. This allowed the GWR to place a double siding below the bridge and to provide an extra line in the goods yard. The new layout was controlled by three ground frames, the middle frame having an intermediate electric train staff instrument to enable a train to be shunted into the sidings and dealt with, leaving the running line clear. The 'elevated cabin' shown on plans as a signal box, but which only contained levers to operate the yard points, was removed and ended up at Droitwich station as a greenhouse cum potting shed!

At this date there were normally four regular staff at Newnham Bridge station where, as at Tenbury, extra staff were drafted from around the district (even from as far as

B. H. Goode

B. H. Goode

Bridge replacement at Newnham Bridge in July 1930. The top photos show the temporary structure employed while the new bridge was being built. Mr. B. Goode, landlord of the nearby 'Railway Tavern', was also a carpenter for the Newnham Estates and was employed by the GWR to help build the temporary wooden bridge. Some of the GWR men lodged with him until the work was completed. *J. Bott*

Worcester) for the busy fruit and hop season. One important task for the extra staff was to make sure that the fruit vans were swept out before loading took place to avoid getting dust on whatever was in transit. In June 1930 a notice in the newspaper to fruit growers announced the opening of Newnham Bridge fruit growers warehouse as from 1st July. On some days trains were run as required from Tenbury Wells to pick up fruit from this warehouse. However, it was not all fruit and hops at Newnham Bridge, for timber, sugar beet and cattle all came in from surrounding districts to be sent on by rail.

Cherries were still the important fruit crop around Wyre Forest station in the early 1930s and extra staff were sent to help from Cleobury Mortimer or Bewdley. Wyre Forest station was badly laid out for shunting, and in practice goods from Wyre Forest for stations in the up direction were taken first to Cleobury Mortimer and then forwarded. Even more time-consuming and costly was the operation whereby goods destined for Wyre Forest station in the up direction had to travel first to Bewdley (past Wyre Forest) then returned on the next available down train!

The railways in the early 1930s were constantly looking for attractions to keep the public travelling by train. The excursion was one idea that proliferated from the late 1920s onwards. Horse races and agricultural shows were among destinations advertised in the local press in addition to the ever-popular seaside outing. In March 1930 there was a trip to Dunstall Park (for Wolverhampton races) from Tenbury Wells, departing at 8.45am. The fare was four shillings, and one to Shirley races cost three shillings from Cleobury Mortimer (departing at 9.15am). In April there was a Bridgnorth steeplechase meeting which cost, for example, three shillings from Neen Sollars (departing 9.03am). In the summer holiday months, the LMS advertised many seaside excursions to the Lancashire coastal resorts via the Shrewsbury & Hereford main line. For these trips Messrs Critchleys of Tenbury advertised a bus connecting with the specials at Woofferton when the normal Tenbury-Woofferton train service was not suitable. In the autumn it was the turn of the agricultural and horticultural shows to provide the destinations for excursions. The Shrewsbury Flower Show excursion and Ludlow race day specials were still run by the LMS and hauled by an LMS 2-4-2T or 0-6-2T from Ludlow, Craven Arms or Shrewsbury sheds, working direct from Tenbury Wells. Birmingham Onion Fair and Kington Horse Show each prompted an excursion and reduced fares.

In Tenbury, the Swan Hotel's horse bus came to an end in the early 1930s after many years of service. Ben Mitchell was the driver in 1930, followed by Mr W. Arnett who took over just before the end. At the same time, the lorry service that superseded the railway horse team had proved itself. Receipts in the first year of operation were £138 which, after deduction for running costs, left a balance of £47 profit from the motor vehicle.

In the 1929-30 period, larger engines began to appear on the Hereford-Tenbury-Stourbridge goods trains and also on some of the seasonal fruit specials run when required. 'Bulldog' class 4-4-0 No 3442 *Bullfinch* of Hereford shed became a regular on the Stourbridge goods. Other members of the class used on the working included No 3353 *Pershore Plum*, 3402 *Jamaica* and 3409 *Queensland*. The crews on this train changed at Tenbury Wells to work back to their respective home sheds, but Stourbridge men reportedly did not like the 'Bulldogs' which, they said, were prone to stall on the gradients between Neen Sollars and Cleobury Mortimer. Stourbridge shed provided 'Aberdare' class 2-6-0s Nos 2615 and 2650 but the Stourbridge enginemen's preference for the work remained the 0-6-0 Dean goods class.

A letter in the *Tenbury Advertiser* in July 1930, concerning the attractions of Tenbury for visitors, criticised the local trains as 'not the fastest nor the most comfortable'. The letter commented that it was 'not easy to get to and from Birmingham' but 'thanks to the buses, Tenbury is now of immediate access from that district'. New ideas came to the fore again in Tenbury in an effort once again to revive the town's potential as a spa to rival Malvern and Cheltenham, but despite a campaign to sink more wells and build more houses, nothing ever developed. As well as operating the baths and a garage in Teme Street, the T.B.C. had also supplied parts of the town with electricity until this undertaking was transferred on 30th May 1930 to the Shropshire, Worcestershire and Staffordshire Power Company. The new company operated on a different voltage but gave consumers new light bulbs free of charge to accommodate this change. Signs of the times were the announcement by the Regal Picture House at Tenbury of their new talking sound system, and mention of encouraging holiday visitors to spend money in Tenbury in order to combat the rising unemployment. The Bayton Colliery Company was still active in 1930, supplying best house coal by road from the new pit at Hunthouse, Frith Common Lane, Clows Top.

The introduction of the new 87XX 0-6-0PT engines to Kidderminster shed continued the process of updating motive power which had begun in 1927. The Tenbury & Bewdley had already been used by 'blue route' engines for some time, but now as a result of the GWR's bridge rebuilding and restrengthening programme, the line could take the heaviest in the group. The neighbouring Severn Valley line was not apparently considered important enough to warrant any major renovations and remained for the time being a 'yellow route'. Consequently, 'blue route' engines were only seen at Bewdley on Tenbury trains or on Kidderminster triangle workings (Kidderminster-Bewdley-Stourport-Hartlebury-Kidderminster).

The Ditton Priors engine No 28 *Cleobury* followed its sister engine to Swindon for rebuilding into a pannier tank in

September 1930, but the '850' class 0-6-0PT No 2001 sent from Worcester to replace it was most unpopular on this exposed stretch of line in winter as this engine was still running with a half cab. After a brief interlude with '2021' class 0-6-0PT 2101 on the line, 0-6-0T No 803 was dispatched from Swindon as a substitute for No 28. This locomotive (formerly *Ravelston* of the Llanelly & Mynydd Mawr Railway) was not liked by the divisional permanent way department, which considered it the cause of much extra maintenance work and it was soon replaced by No 2187 *Pioneer*, another 0-6-0T absorbed by the GWR from a South Wales railway. Formerly No 8 of the Burry Port & Gwendraeth Valley Railway, this engine worked the Ditton Priors line for the rest of 1931. No 28 arrived back at Kidderminster shed from Swindon, in its rebuilt state, in December 1931, leaving *Pioneer* to return to Neath in February 1932.

An unpleasant accident happened in September 1931 to a hop-picker, who suffered leg injuries as a result of falling between train and platform edge at Tenbury Wells. The train was a hop-pickers special about to return to Wellington, Shropshire, a reminder that not all seasonal hop-picking labour came to the Teme Valley from the Black Country. The trains from the Wellington area mainly came via the Ketley Branch, to Lightmoor and Buildwas, then down the Severn Valley line, reversing again at Bewdley. These specials were usually hauled by 0-6-0PTs or 0-6-0 Dean Goods, but on one or two rare occasions older 2-4-0 tender engines, such as the '3226' class or '3232' class, were provided by Wellington shed. The late Edgar Price, signalman at Tenbury Wells box in the 1930s remembers 'hop-pickers' friends' specials arriving on Sundays — with double-headed trains, sometimes with as many as fifteen coaches. These coaches would have to be taken to Ludlow until they were wanted for the return journey if Tenbury was short of storage room. Most of the coaches used on these hop specials were old, gas-lit, non-corridor clerestory stock. The working appendix stipulated that all doors be locked and kept locked throughout the journey and this had to be strictly adhered to. In the case of the Wellington trains where reversal was necessary at Buildwas, the coaches were run into the Much Wenlock branch sidings while the engine ran round, to avoid possible abuse and confrontation between the hop-pickers and other rail users. A similar movement took place at Bewdley.

The year 1932 was poor financially for the line, mainly due to the failure of the fruit crop. The official 'comments on traffic compared with previous years' for Tenbury Wells

'Aberdare' 2-6-0 No. 2615 at Stourbridge shed on 24th April 1932. This loco was one used by Stourbridge on the Tenbury goods.
H. C. Casserley

Outside-framed 0-6-0 PT No. 1254 of the '1076' or 'Buffalo' class, photographed outside Kidderminster new shed in July 1932. This class of engine was a familiar sight on both the Severn Valley and Tenbury lines in the 1930s. No. 1254 was an auto-fitted engine and more commonly seen on the Kidderminster 'triangle' and Severn Valley auto turns. It was withdrawn in 1937.
Authors' collection

and Easton Court tell of decreased takings. Tenbury Wells noted 'passenger decrease £331, parcels decrease £570, due to curtailing of train service and competitive bus service, WI outing to Blackpool last year. Complete failure of fruit season and market produce to Birmingham and milk traffic now sent by road. Goods decrease £2,547, less round timber to various stations and failure of fruit season'. Easton Court recorded 'passenger decrease £25 due to fewer local passengers owing to restricted train service. Parcels decrease £28 due to failure of fruit season. Goods increase £14 roadstone traffic for road repairs'.

The excursion traffic from stations along the line continued to be a source of extra revenue throughout the early 1930s, but always in competition with the bus and coach companies. The modernisation taking place in the branch line motive power continued. From 1933 48XX 0-4-2Ts were allocated to Kidderminster shed followed by 64XX 0-6-0PTs. Both classes replaced older auto-fitted engines, particularly those of the 517 and 1076 'Buffalo' classes, on the Severn Valley and the Kidderminster 'triangle' workings. From time to time, however, each of these new types strayed onto the Tenbury branch workings, albeit on non auto-fitted trains, particularly the 4.38pm Kidderminster to Tenbury Wells. The 87XX panniers were put to work alongside the Dean Goods 0-6-0s on the branch freight services, as the older Kidderminster-based panniers of Dean's era were reaching the end of long and useful working lives. Ludlow shed also had new motive power. 0-4-2T No 5813, built in August 1933, arrived at Ludlow shed brand new from Swindon and quickly became a regular performer on the early morning and late evening school trains between Tenbury Wells and Ludlow. Ludlow at this time had also a 45XX 2-6-2T, No 4539, which was used on passenger turns to Kidderminster alongside two older panniers, Nos 1741 and 1783 (655 class). The better fruit harvest of the 1933 season turned the goods receipts around at Tenbury and Easton Court and increased income was noted at both stations. Slightly improved passenger income at Easton Court was due to more excursion bookings but the gloomy picture from Tenbury was of decrease in long distance passenger bookings (for example to Birmingham and Paddington) and of milk traffic lost to road competition.

Along with the attempts to develop Tenbury as an important spa town for tourists, another recurring scheme

This photograph, taken in 1936, shows the site of the old Kidderminster shed after it had closed in 1932. *W. A. Camwell*

in the area was the commercial development of the Wyre Forest Coalfield. The Hunthouse pit workings of the Bayton Colliery, opened in 1924, had reached output figures of 15,000 tons per year by the time of the 1926 General Strike. The strike had had little effect on the pit as it remained open and even supplied the Kidderminster Co-operative Society with coal when its usual suppliers were unable to do so. The distribution of coal since the closure of the aerial ropeway to Cleobury Mortimer station in 1924 was necessarily by road, initially with one Model 'T' Ford lorry and one Foster steam tractor conveying coal over a wide area around the coalfield. The brickmaking potential for the clay which was associated with the coal deposits had been recognized for some time and a small brick-making plant was at first envisaged around Hunthouse Wood. Later it was considered more practical to site the works actually at the old ropeway terminal at Cleobury Mortimer station where similar high quality clays were discovered. The original sidings were still in situ and could be utilised for direct loading of bricks into wagons. By 1931 the brickworks were in full production dispatching bricks to many parts of the country. At the site of another previous scheme to link the coalfield to the Tenbury & Bewdley branch, fortunes were at a low ebb and the Hollins Mine at Pensax was put up for sale in 1931. A bid of £750 was accepted from the Bayton Colliery Company of which it became part. The Hollins Mine, sunk in 1895, had been owned by Mr S.W. Yarnold and was on the proposed site of the Pensax Railway terminus of 1872. It was well known for producing a coking or 'sulphur coal' which was suitable for use in the process of drying the hops in the nearby Teme Valley hop yards, and at one time (unofficial) road signs gave directions to Pensax at the height of the hop season from as far away as Bromyard and Leominster. Queues of lorries could be seen along the Pensax road waiting to load the coal, which was measured in baskets or 'whiskets' as they were known locally.

In 1933 the brickworks sidings, as the Bayton Colliery sidings had become known at Cleobury Mortimer station, were relaid and given a new lease of useful life.

Passenger figures continued to drop; the summer season decrease was singled out in the Tenbury Wells report of 1934 whilst Easton Court reported a general decrease in local bookings for that year. Excursions, meanwhile, continued to be offered. One advertised from Tenbury Wells in

A Bayton Colliery lorry negotiating the floods on the banks of the Severn at Beale's Corner, Bewdley, in the 1930s. Authors' collection

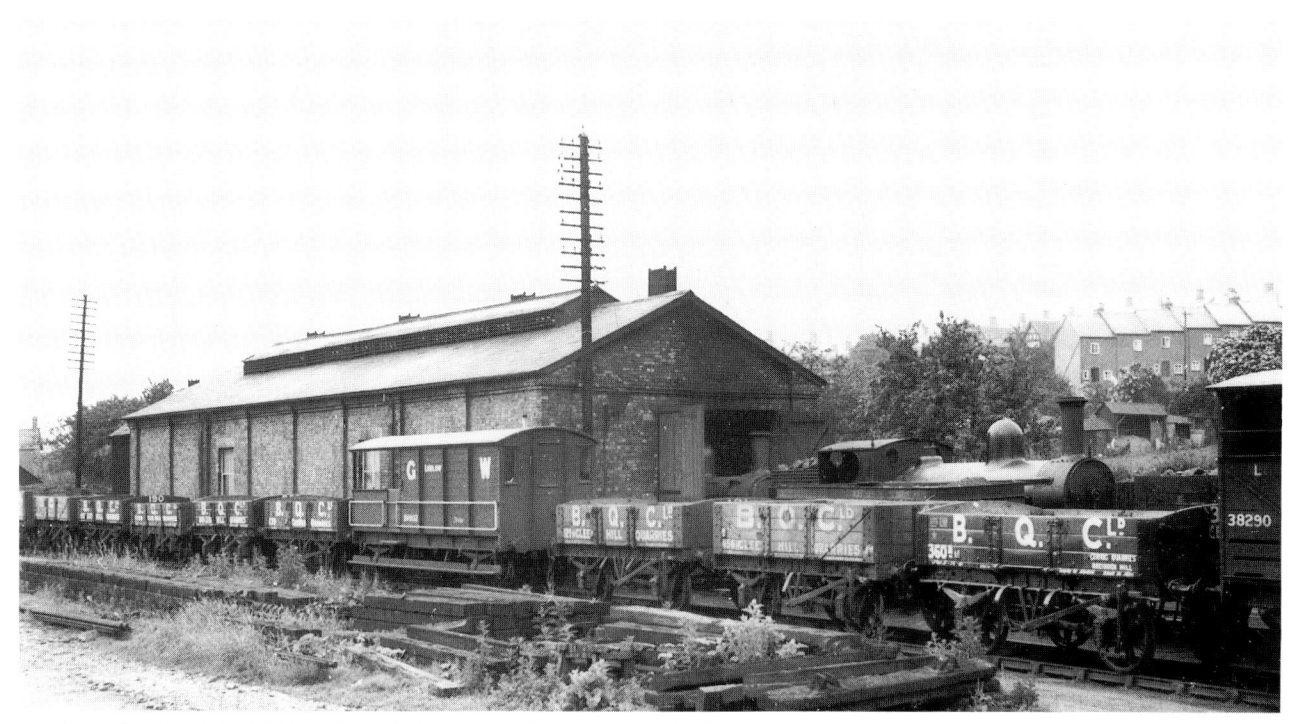

Built by the S&HR in 1857, Ludlow shed played an important role in the operation of the Tenbury & Bewdley line. Until its closure in 1951 it was always a sub shed to Shrewsbury. When this photograph was taken in June 1936, its GWR allocation was 'Metro' 3563, 0–6–0PT 9714, 2–6–2T 4527, whilst the LMS was Webb 2–4–2T and LMS 'Sentinel' 7164 for shunting work on Clee Hill. Note the Ludlow 'Toad' between a line of British Quarrying Co wagons from the Clee Hill line. *W. A. Camwell*

March 1934 was to Hereford for the steeplechases, departing at 9.40am for a cost of 2/6d return. In the autumn of 1934 there was an LMS excursion to Blackpool to view the illuminations. This was a Sunday departure, 12 noon from Tenbury, 12.05pm from Easton Court, departing from Blackpool for the return journey at five minutes to midnight. The return fares cost 7/6d including lunch, or 12/6d for supper as well. Unfortunately, the motive power for this trip is not known but obviously it would have required a larger type than one of Ludlow shed's ex-LNWR tank engines. However, on one occasion, a Blackpool trip in the 1920s was delayed at Woofferton because the ex-LNW engine about to bring the connecting coaches from Tenbury failed with a loose valve spindle and it is known that the excursion engine, a 2-4-0 'Jumbo' class, had to go to Tenbury from Woofferton to take over the train. The inclusion of a restaurant car in the formation of a train departing from Tenbury Wells would, in any case, be a novelty. The more usual passenger stock on local trains were the clerestory third and third brake coaches which had been based at Ludlow since the mid-twenties. Kidderminster also normally provided a train of two carriages, one third and one brake third, but sometimes borrowed two from a Birmingham set that arrived in Kidderminster and were uncoupled from the 8.55am ex-Birmingham, Snow Hill. These two carriages would then form the 10.16am Kidderminster-Woofferton and the 11.50 Woofferton return to Kidderminster. Later in the day the same carriages would be in use on the 4.40pm Kidderminster to Woofferton. They came back as the 6.55pm Woofferton to Stourbridge Junction and worked straight through to Birmingham if required. If not, they would be attached to the 8.35pm Stourbridge Junction to Birmingham, Snow Hill. On other occasions one coach of the Birmingham set would be used to strengthen the local pair.

Goods receipts at Tenbury and Easton Court show a very variable pattern in 1934. From Tenbury, there were increases in fruit and mushroom traffic to Yorkshire and Lancashire, but a decrease in local fruit carriage with the exception of cider fruit to Hereford. Livestock transport increased from Tenbury in the year whilst incoming tar products arriving from Langley Green, Stourbridge and Ellesmere Port declined. 1934 must have been a year of plentiful mushrooms, for Easton Court figures also record an increase in this traffic and also rabbits to the Birmingham market and sugar beet to the Kidderminster factory. Decreases were noted in traffic bringing slag as a waste product from the Hollinswood iron foundries near Wellington, and manure in the form of shoddy from Bradford.

From 1935 passenger figures for all stations along the branch dropped without exception. Particularly noticeable was the decline at Cleobury Mortimer. The Midland Red had developed its bus service from the centre of the village to Kidderminster on Thursday, Saturday, alternate

Kidderminster shed in 1936 with the Kidderminster–Bewdley line on the right. Typical loco stock allocations at Kidderminster in the mid-1930s were: 1934: 28, 29, 1169, 1254, 1898, 3557, 4586, 4816, 5524/44/72/74, 8701, 8731. 1935: 28, 29, 1254, 2040, 4564/86/94/96, 4845, 5112/4/23 and 8727. The 'stop board' and south-facing siding connection to Whitehouse's Sand Siding can just be seen as the line curves away out of sight.

W. A. Camwell

The building for Kidderminster 'new' shed was secondhand. It came from Bassaleg, South Wales, from where it was dismantled in 1929. It was rebuilt at Kidderminster and opened in February 1932. This picture was taken in 1936. *W. A. Camwell*

Former CM&DP Manning Wardle 0–6–0ST *Burwarton*, after rebuilding by the GWR in 1924 and renumbered 29, is shown here at Kidderminster shed on 13th September 1936. This loco worked the ex-CM&DP Light Railway branch to Ditton Priors, sharing the duties in 1936 with fellow Manning Wardle 0–6–0PT No. 28 and GWR 850 class 0–6–0PT No. 2001. *F. K. Davies*

GW/LMS Joint Thornycroft lorry in Cross Street, Tenbury, in 1933. These lorries, which had replaced horse-drawn drays on local deliveries around the Tenbury area, were later superseded by Austins. *Authors' collection*

Tuesdays and Wednesday, and even on Sunday! Even more competition had come from Messrs Charles Brothers, based in Cleobury Mortimer and running to Kidderminster for the market on a Tuesday. Cleobury Mortimer station suffered more and more as time went on from its situation so far from the centre of the village.

The availability of the turntable at Tenbury Wells was still detailed in the February 1935 supplement to the Chester, Birkenhead, and Shrewsbury & Hereford section W.T.T. appendix: 'Turntable accessible by means of ground frame to yard if light engine required to turn. Driver to be in possession of Tenbury Wells-Woofferton electric train token, porter to accompany engine to help movements etc'. However, since the turntable was now so rarely needed, it was finally taken out around this time.

The demand for storage accommodation in Tenbury yard was still apparent with the Clock House, a busy Tenbury grocery shop arranging to have its own grounded carriage body to be sited alongside those used by Messrs Lever Brothers and the Cement Marketing Company.

Figures for 1935 and 1936 not only show small decreases in passenger and parcels receipts at Tenbury Wells but that LMS excursion bookings to Blackpool, Scotland and Rhyl (Sunday school outing traffic) were noted as falling off in 1936. The poor summer weather resulting in a smaller than average fruit harvest, was again to blame for a drop in income from Tenbury Wells in 1935 but fortunately the position improved as a result of a better season in 1936.

In 1936, the 2-6-0 63XXs, began to appear regularly on the branch on the important and well-used Tuesday Tenbury cattle specials. In June 1936, Ludlow had 57XX 0-6-0PT No 9714 amongst its allocation as well as 'Metro' 2-4-0T No 3562 and 2-6-2T No 4527, whilst their LMS tank was Webb 2-4-2T No 6738, with LMS Sentinel No 7164 for the shunting work on top of Clee Hill.

For one year only, in 1936, Wyre Forest station reversed the downward trend of passenger traffic along the line by showing an increase in custom of 101 passengers. Neen Sollars attracted some hikers and ramblers as a starting point for a ramble, but Wyre Forest station was ideally situated to cater for the outdoor enthusiast of the day who could step out of the station virtually straight onto a forest footpath. Both Wyre Forest and Neen Sollars stations were at locations where local bus services did not closely compete (or indeed reach) and at neither of the stations did passenger bookings decline as steeply as at Cleobury Mortimer or Newnham Bridge at this time.,

The Worcester District GWR Traffic Research Committee noted from census returns that livestock traffic was passing by road from farmers in the Burwarton and Stottesdon area, and that farmers, when questioned, stated that unless cheaper rates counterbalanced the inconvenience caused by having to walk their stock to the station, they would not return as railway customers. In July 1936 a comprehensive report had been submitted to the Traffic Research Committee about the advisability of providing a

BETWEEN THE WARS

Country Lorry service based at Cleobury Mortimer. However, as far as collection and transport of livestock from farm to station was concerned, the Chairman of the Committee pointed out that the area around Cleobury Mortimer was 'exceptionally wild and the roads bad'. It was agreed after discussion that the loss of livestock traffic could not be remedied by means of intermediate road haulage from farm to station. There was, however, the distinct possibility that a GWR lorry based at Cleobury Mortimer could compete successfully for the collection and delivery service already being offered by 'C and D, Goods and Parcels', for whom Mr Dudley acted as agent. However, a complication here was that Dudley's Buses currently provided the link between the GWR station and the

The Board of Trade never stipulated that station footbridges be built on the T&B, although in 1908 there were plans for one at Cleobury Mortimer in conjunction with the opening of the CM&DP. These plans were never implemented, so at Cleobury, as at other stations, passengers still had to cross the running lines. This view of a clear line dropping downgrade to Wyre Forest, is what passengers would have seen as they were about to walk over the line by means of the timbered crossing. A better view of this is seen in the photo below.
Authors' collection

'517' class 0–4–2T No. 1442 entering Cleobury Mortimer on its way from Wyre Forest on 11th May 1935. The building in the background was the 'Blount Arms'.
V. R. Webster

Cleobury Mortimer, looking towards Bewdley, on 22nd August 1936. The two-coach train on the left of the pagoda shelter was for Ditton Priors. A 4-wheel composite coach to Diagram U4 was normally paired with a T34 or T36 brake third. Composites 6482 and 6308, with brake thirds 954 and 2657, were the regular stock in use in 1936.
S. W. Baker

0–6–0PT No. 6430 drifting into Cleobury Mortimer with the 4.40 p.m. Kidderminster–Woofferton passenger train which connected with the 5.20 p.m. to Ditton Priors. This particular auto-fitted loco was delivered new to Kidderminster in March 1937. It was normally used on SVR line and Kidderminster triangle auto services. 10th September 1938.
W. A. Camwell

BETWEEN THE WARS

town centre of Cleobury Mortimer. The GWR feared that if Mr Dudley''s reaction to parcels competition was to discontinue his buses, they could stand to lose around £150 per annum in passenger receipts. One other view was that if the problem did arise, the Midland Red Company's buses might be able to make a small detour from their route along the Bewdley road to the top of the station drive in order to make a connection for the 2½ mile journey down to the town. All this became theoretical when it was ultimately decided that Newnham Bridge station would be more suitable as a base for a Country Lorry Service at that time. This decision was not implemented until 1938, since demands on cartage resources at that time for sugar beet haulage meant there were no vehicles spare. It was clear that the GWR was already under pressure, having to hire outside vehicles while suffering from complaints from the public about delays in delivery. The Traffic Research Committee finally agreed to submit their findings to the Road Transport Department for them to consider any remedies that were possible

Plenty of platform barrows around for parcels and 'small' goods traffic in this c.1934 view.

An outside-framed 0–6–0PT, believed to have been No. 1075 of the '1016' class from Ludlow shed, seen here at Cleobury Mortimer c.1934. The first two coaches were a borrowed Birmingham 'B' set often seen in use over the branch in the 1930s. This view shows how the goods yard was at a higher level than the running lines.

0–6–0PT No. 6430 on the 4.40 p.m. Kidderminster–Woofferton train at Cleobury Mortimer, and the connecting 5.20 p.m. CM&DP train awaiting departure to Ditton Priors on 10th September 1938. The siding in the foreground dated from Light Railway days and was still laid with flat-bottom rail dog-spiked to the sleepers.
W. A. Camwell

A Ditton Priors branch train awaiting departure from Cleobury Mortimer in 1938. The GWR 'pagoda' replaced the original shelter when the down platform was altered to accommodate the Ditton Priors branch when that line was opened to passengers in 1908. More usually associated with small halts, the pagoda was the only one to be found between Bewdley and Woofferton. *C. L. Mowat*

Ex-Cleobury Mortimer & Ditton Priors 0–6–0PT No. 28 waiting at Cleobury Mortimer with a mixed train to Ditton Priors c.1932. The spare carriages in the distance were stabled on the 'Monkey Road', so named because the coaches were used for a regular school train, which staff associated with mischievous pupils. *P. W. Robinson*

No. 2197 *Pioneer*, formerly of the Burry Port and Gwendraeth Valley Railway, was used for a time on the CM&DP, whilst ex-CM&DP No. 28 was being rebuilt at Swindon. It is seen here at Cleobury Mortimer in 1931.

*S. H. P. Higgins
Nat. Railway Museum*

From 1936 (and a sign of things to come) diesel railcars appeared at Bewdley on Kidderminster triangle workings. However, in 1936 the Ditton Priors traffic was not holding up very well. Various problems at Abdon Clee came to a head and culminated in the quarry plant closing. The demand for the blocks of stone known as setts had dropped off dramatically, and all the dhu-stone cap had been removed, making quarrying much more difficult and expensive. The quarry company's asphalt plant at Ditton Priors preferred road transport to carry the material direct to where it was needed. As the quantity of stone now being quarried was easily and more conveniently carried away in fleets of lorries, only two mixed trains per day were run on the Ditton branch in 1936. By the end of 1937 the incline from Abdon Clee down to Ditton Priors had closed, and equipment on Abdon Clee had been cut up for scrap by the Sheffield firm of Simms-Lewis.

This was just the beginning of the rundown on the Ditton Priors line, for the passenger service ceased on 24th September 1938 after thirty years of operation. The official announcement had been made in July 1938. The trains to be cancelled were the 9.30am, 2.24pm (Wednesdays only) and 5.20pm from Cleobury Mortimer to Ditton Priors and in the reverse direction those at 11.10am, 3.50pm (Wednesdays only) and 6.23pm. The last train was witnessed by an unexpectedly large band of devotees, including Mr R.K. Cope whose report appeared in the *Railway Observer*.

'The morning train from Cleobury Mortimer contained a fair number of passengers, some of whom were observed to make a round trip, but the 5.20pm from Cleobury Mortimer and the corresponding return trip were of course the focus of attention. Reservations had been made in advance for parties from various districts, including a strong contingent from Birmingham and as a result No 28 had behind her a train of twice the normal length i.e. four four-wheelers, Nos 954 and 2657 (each three thirds, plus guard and luggage) and Nos 6308 and 6482 (each two thirds and two firsts) filled to capacity including most of the space for the guard. Little time was lost at the junction, but at the first stop, Cleobury Town Halt, the enthusiasts descended in force and there was an appreciable delay for photographers.

'Proceeding at the usual somewhat leisurely pace not increased by similar requirements of the photographic element at other halts, Ditton Priors was reached nearly half an hour late. Here the scene was amazing. Barely had the train halted when it disgorged its load of enthusiasts and a forest of tripods appeared. The hour was late and the weather almost at its worst, but enthusiasm was undampened, if clothes were wet. It was absolutely impossible to get all on board again until their photographic appetites were sated, and so again the departure was delayed until prolonged whistling forced the delinquents into their compartments. There were cheers from a few local residents as the train moved off, but so far nearly all the interest had appeared from elsewhere.

'Having other means of transport available, the writer was able to anticipate the arrival of the train at the junction by about fifteen minutes. The train for the Bewdley direction was waiting and had to be kept over time until a faint whistle at the nearest level crossing heralded the approach of the branch train.

'As it came round the curve it was seen that the carriages were unlit, but this state of affairs was remedied when a row of roman candles on the station railings burst into flame. At the same time No 5518 on the Bewdley train moved forward a few yards, exploding half-a-dozen fog signals and setting up a fierce whistling.

'Being now 7.45pm the light was too bad even for the most optimistic photographer and the passengers transferred to the Bewdley train after bidding farewell to the staff of the last train that is ever likely to convey passengers from Ditton Priors.

'After the departure of the Bewdley train, No 28 shunted her carriages into their siding for the last time and shortly after 8pm departed light for Kidderminster shed. It is understood that the shed at Cleobury Town Halt is now closed and the one week day goods train will be worked by No 28 or No 29 running light from and to Kidderminster.

'This train (according to notices posted at the halts on the branch) will leave Cleobury Mortimer at about 2.30pm each week day, arrive at

Ditton Priors at 4.45pm and return at 5.00pm reaching the junction at about 6.45pm'.

Another eye witness reported from the year 1938 comes from former railwayman Mr H.D. Bradley:

'I joined the GW and LMS Joint Railway in 1938 as a junior clerk and started work at Tenbury station. The station master was then Mr Harper and shortly afterwards he moved on promotion to a larger station. His successor was a Mr Roy Manning who remained there for most of the war years. When I started, the booking clerk was Mr N.J. Bowers, whilst in the goods department Mr A.J. Griffiths was the chief clerk. Mr Charles Bradley (no relation) also worked in the goods department along with Mr Cound who worked part time at Tenbury and part time at Woofferton.

'I worked a shift system with Mr Bowers. On early shift I worked from 7.45am – 5.30pm; on late shift I worked from 10.30am – 9.00pm. On the early shift I was in the passenger office from 7.45am – 10.30am when Mr Bowers came on duty, and I then went round to the goods department for the rest of the day. On the late shift I worked in the goods office until 5.30pm and then took over the passenger office. My salary then was £2 per week and we worked six days.

0–6–0PT No. 28 at Cleobury Mortimer, waiting to depart for Ditton Priors on 2nd September 1938. The Ditton Priors line curved away from the junction up a 1 in 60 gradient through the edge of the Wyre Forest to Cleobury Town station. *R. E. Tustin*

The nearer of the two bridges across the Bewdley Road was built in 1908 to carry the CM&DP whilst the other one in the distance bore the Tenbury branch on its way through the Wyre Forest. *R. K. Cope*

0-6-0PT No. 28 with a train from Ditton Priors shortly after arrival at Cleobury Mortimer in September 1938. *R. J. Buckley*

'Cash taken during the day for tickets, parcels etc, had to be balanced with the ledgers at the end of each day. The money was placed in a leather pouch and locked in the safe overnight and then dispatched on the 9.30am train to Shrewsbury. The monthly accounts which were sent out and the wages sheets had to be copied in a very interesting but archaic method. They were written out in Indian ink on the bill heads etc. To copy them there was a large book of very fine paper similar to tissue paper. A page was wetted with water and then, with a waterproof sheet between the wetted page and the remainder of the book, it was placed in an iron press and left for a short time till one judged that the paper was moist but not too dry. The book was then taken from the press and the documents to be copied were placed on the wetted pages and the pressing was repeated. The result was that you either got a badly smudged document and copy if the paper was too moist, or no copy at all if the paper became too dry!

'Most of the goods required by the shops in Tenbury and the farms in the surrounding countryside were carried by the railway at this time. Perishable goods were carried by passenger train; non perishable goods, coal, animal feedstuffs, timber, sugar beet, and all types of fruit were the main consignments in the goods department along with cattle and sheep after special markets. Loads of shoddy arrived for use as fertiliser in the hop yards. The local canning factory (then called the Worcestershire Packers and Growers Ltd) dispatched canned fruit throughout the winter and spring. Two Thornycroft lorries operated from Tenbury station for the collection and delivery of goods. They alternated doing one week on town deliveries and one week on country deliveries. Beer from Burton-on-Trent came by rail for some of the local pubs and this was quite a perk for the lorry driver who happened to be on town delivery.

'The porters who worked on the passenger parcels side were Ted Mills and Jack Chapman, later joined by my namesake Jack Bradley (again no relation). In the goods yard was Tom Lucas. Porters were Dick Brown and Ernie Morris who did all the shunting. The lorry drivers were Reuben Martin and Sam Dyer, known to everyone as 'Clapham'. In the weighbridge office was George Jones. There were two signalmen, Edgar Price and Dick Jay. Dick was very deaf and trying to talk to him on the railway telephone was extremely difficult. There was also a permanent way staff numbering about eight. Some of the names I remember were Mr Hardisty, Mr Matthews and Mr Wright.

'From time to time a relief clerk was sent and one I remember was very fond of the cider and perry that was sold at the nearby Rose and Crown Inn. The locals had christened these brews 'Stunum' and 'Tanglefoot'. This particular relief clerk would go to quench his thirst at dinner time but, after two pints at 4d a pint, he would not be capable of much work when he returned.

'There were three coal merchants at Tenbury station, Messrs Henry Edwards and Company run by Harry and Bill Arnett, Messrs E. Parton and Sons run by Charlie and Cecil Parton, and the third merchant was Mr Bill Davies. Mr Davies employed Mr Tipton, known to everyone as 'Kruger'. He would be at the station at 8.30am, fill thirty or forty 1cwt coal bags and then load them on to the lorry. Bill would appear between 10 and 10.30am when 'Kruger' would tell him in no uncertain terms what he thought of him for leaving him to do all the hard work.

'Lever Brothers had a depot at Tenbury station where the animal feeding stuff was stored. Mr Crump was for many years their agent and he used to bring in the orders from farmers for the railway lorry

BETWEEN THE WARS

to deliver. Worcestershire Farmers (now M.S.F.) also had a small depot. Frank K. Sharp, an Evesham fruit merchant, had an office at the station. This was run by Mr Collins who organized the despatch of all the fruit.'

The reference to 55XX 2-6-2T No 5518 on the Bewdley-bound training waiting for the returning CMDP last train special reflects Kidderminster's passenger motive power on the branch at the time. These 2-6-2Ts had, as anticipated, proved masters of their task and as well as No 5518, four others of the class were regularly seen in 1938. Nos 4586, 4594, 4596 and 5574 worked from Kidderminster shed, helped out by 57XX 0-6-0PTs Nos 8701, 8718, 8727 and 8731 plus 64XX class No 6430 and 48XX class No 4863.

Ludlow shed, responsible for the bulk of workings on the Woofferton to Tenbury line, had a varied selection of motive power from 1938 supplied by Shrewsbury, its parent shed. 'Metro' 2-4-0T Nos 3562 and 3563 appeared from time to time along with an 0-4-2T of the '517' class

A 55XX at the head of a Kidderminster to Woofferton train at Cleobury Mortimer in September 1938. *P. J. Garland*

No. 4586, one of Kidderminster's fleet of small Prairie tanks, pulling away from Cleobury Mortimer with the 4.40 p.m. Kidderminster–Woofferton train on 11th May 1938. *R. K. Cope*

'Large Metro' No. 3563 approaching Easton Court on its way from Kidderminster to Woofferton in October 1939. The line here ran close to the Kidderminster–Woofferton (A456) road, and the gradients were very easy as the line followed or used the old canal bed at many points hereabouts.
S. H. P. Higgins, National Railway Museum

'3571' class 0–4–2T No. 3577 and a two-coach Ludlow set leaving Cleobury Mortimer and heading towards Prizeley Cutting with a Tenbury Wells and Woofferton train on 13th September 1938. At least half the class of these handy engines are known to have worked the branch. The Bayton Colliery sidings were behind the vegetation in the background. *S. H. P. Higgins, National Railway Museum*

No 1442, but the most prolific performers were 0-4-2Ts of the '3571' class which more commonly were used around Chester and Birkenhead on Wirral services. At least five of the class of ten (Nos 3573/74/75/78/79) were either allocated or loaned to Shrewsbury for Ludlow-Kidderminster services, usually working along with the 'Metros' and '517' class on the morning turns. The afternoon turns, and Tenbury-Ludlow midday Joint Goods, were usually worked by new 57XX panniers such as 3702, 3745, 3762 and 3788 although older Dean types, such as Nos 1741 and 1803 appeared from time to time and occasionally 45XX 2-6-2Ts. Stourbridge shed was still providing 'Aberdare' 2-6-0s for its regular goods turn along the branch, in particular Nos 2603, 2608, 2620 and 2655, whilst Hereford shed used Dean Goods Nos 2325 and 2471 along with Aberdare No 2680 for the trips to Tenbury.

The 1938 official figures for passenger booking through stations along the branch showed the gradual decline continuing, though for Cleobury Mortimer the drop in numbers was more dramatic following the final Ditton Priors passenger service. The figures compiled for Cleobury Mortimer included bookings made at the CMDP halts, but even so the decrease from 6,006 in 1938 to 2,402 was surprising, for it brought Cleobury Mortimer down to the same level as Neen Sollars (2,309 in 1939) and Wyre Forest (2,304 in 1939) and below the bookings at Newnham Bridge (4,441 in 1939).

Passengers Booked 1935 – 1939

	1935	1936	1937	1938	1939
Wyre Forest	2,801	2,902	2,699	2,466	2,304
Cleobury Mortimer	11,117	9,524	7,887	6,006	2,401
Neen Sollars	2,457	2,457	2,188	2,375	2,309
Newnham Bridge	6,438	6,211	5,705	5,058	4,441

The crew of 0–6–0PT 1749 peeking ahead from under the storm sheet as they near Tenbury Wells on a mid-morning Kidderminster–Woofferton train in the winter of 1939.
S. H. P. Higgins, National Railway Museum

BETWEEN THE WARS

The ropeway route from Bayton Colliery down to Cleobury Mortimer, idle since 1924, was finally dismantled for scrap in 1938. The base of the angle station remained as a marker, and still does, having resisted attempts to blow it up. One of the standards was left intact for some time for use by Sir Walter Blount as a hide in the game season.

The changing nature and location of the quarrying industry at Ditton Priors left a gloomy future for the 'Gadget' following the closure of the passenger service. The quarry company's concrete works and asphalt plant were still in business at Ditton Priors terminus but neither now gave the railway much custom. The elderly Abdon Clee Quarry Company locomotives had become redundant and had been cut up and carted away for scrap.

When Cleobury Town shed closed, Drivers J. How and J. Clutterbuck transferred to Kidderminster shed, as did

Kidderminster 'Prairie' No. 4578 at Tenbury Wells in 1939, with a Woofferton train made up from a motley assortment of coaches including an auto coach. The Dean goods in the down platform was waiting for the single line.
S. H. P. Higgins, National Railway Museum

Signalman Dick Jay passing the time of day with the crew of '3571' class 0-4-2T No. 3578 at Tenbury Wells before departing with the 1.50 pm Kidderminster to Woofferton on 15th June 1938.
G. A. Hookham

Selwyn Higgins stood on Prizeley Bridge looking down into the cutting to take this photo of an unidentified Dean Goods climbing out of Cleobury Mortimer towards the summit at Prizeley Cutting on a Stourbridge-Tenbury Wells goods on 15th September 1938.

0-6-0PT No. 3782 passing through Easton Court station towards Woofferton with a train of vans from Tenbury, probably full of produce from Tenbury Market. The mature woodlands of Easton Court Estate make a pleasant backdrop. October 1939.
S. H. P. Higgins, National Railway Museum

A light load for 0-6-0PT No. 3788 of Ludlow shed near Easton Court with the 3.5 p.m. Tenbury–Ludlow Joint goods (RR weekdays only) in October 1939.
S. H. P. Higgins, National Railway Museum

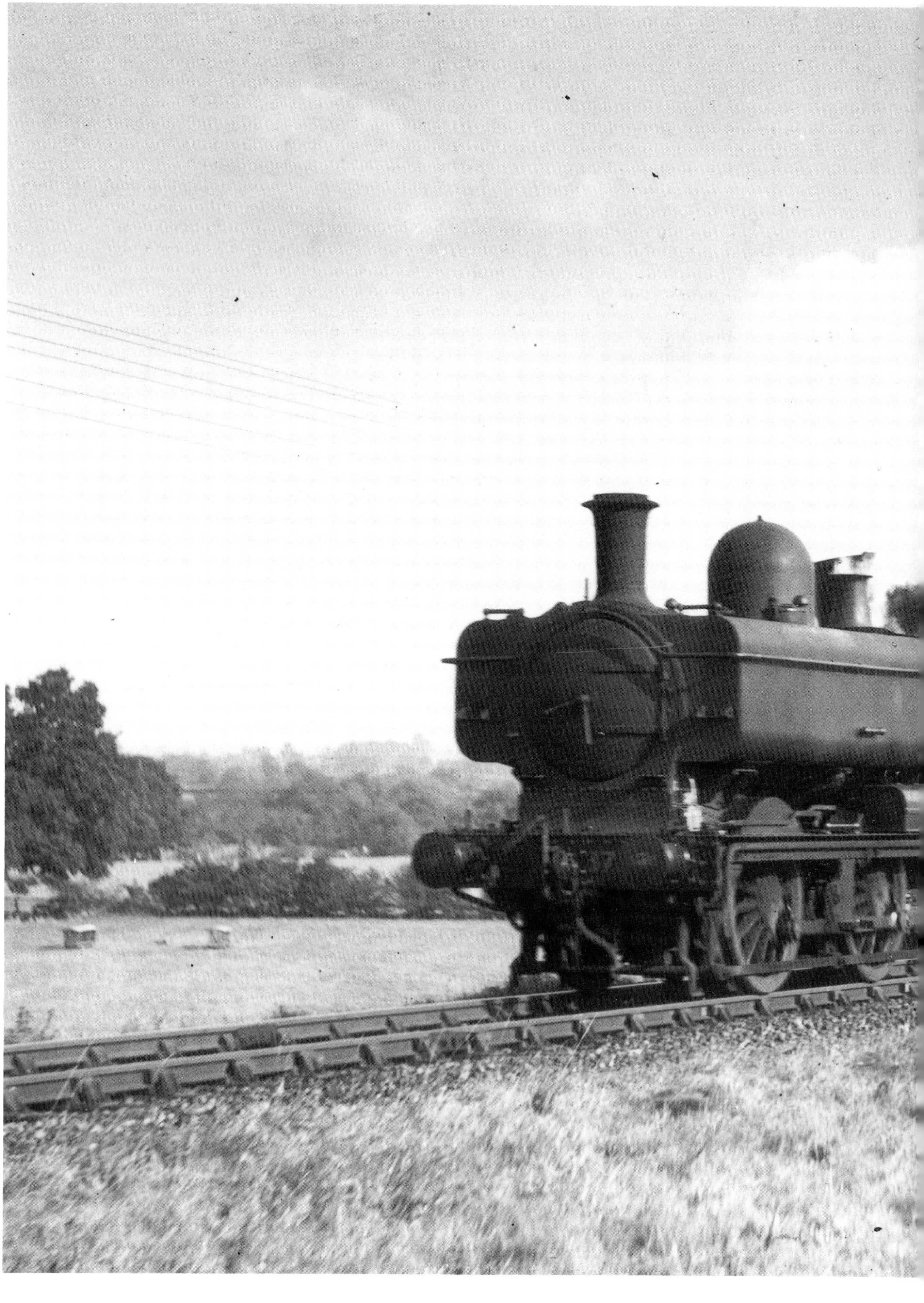

0–6–0PT No. 3782 near Woofferton on the 2.5 p.m. Saturdays-only Tenbury Wells–Woofferton passenger train on Saturday, 21st October 1939. *S. H. P. Higgins, National Railway Museum*

0–6–0PT No. 3782 of Ludlow shed approaching Woofferton on the 1.10 p.m. Ludlow–Tenbury Wells mixed train, in this case with only the Ludlow brake van in tow, on Saturday, 21st October 1939.
S. H. P. Higgins, National Railway Museum

Fireman W. Breakwell, whilst Driver T. Dowding retired. Mr Fred Harvey transferred from station master at Cleobury Town to the staff at Cleobury Mortimer station, whilst two of the men formerly employed on Ditton Priors duties, Guard F. Summers and N. How, took to the roads driving GWR lorries from Newnham Bridge and Cleobury Mortimer respectively.

However, the ensuing turn in international events was destined shortly to give a new lease of life to the Ditton Priors line and with it a tremendous boost to traffic on the Tenbury and Bewdley line as a whole. Since the Munich crisis of 1938, an active search had been made for locations suitable for ammunition storage. Ideally the sites needed were those that were isolated but not without

0–6–0 Dean Goods No. 2325 of Hereford shed at Woofferton with the 12.5 p.m. Hereford–Tenbury goods on 15th June 1938. After arrival at Tenbury at 4.5 p.m., engine and crew worked the 4.35 p.m. joint passenger to Woofferton, returning as the 5.15 p.m. to Tenbury. The goods later went forward (with a Stourbridge crew) as the 6.0 p.m. Tenbury–Stourbridge goods.
G. A. Hookham

0–6–0PT No. 3782 at Woofferton shed just prior to running light to Ludlow after working the Saturdays-only 2.5 p.m. and 2.30 p.m. Woofferton–Tenbury joint passenger on Saturday, 21st October 1939. Woofferton shed was built in 1862 to house the Tenbury engine, a 2–4–0WT of 1856 by Jones & Potts, Newton-le-Willows. It passed to the WMR in December 1862 and then to the GWR in 1863 (GWR No. 228). It was withdrawn in 1872. As the Tenbury Railway was operated by the LNWR (from Ludlow shed) from 1st December 1862, Woofferton shed was closed but used as a watering place for locomotives until the branch closed in 1961.
S. H. P. Higgins, National Railway Museum

access. The Ditton Priors line fitted the requirements very well and Nissen huts for temporary storage purposes were placed along the route as soon as the passenger services ended. The Admiralty were responsible for this development as a fore-runner to the establishment of a Naval armament depot at the Ditton Priors site.

Elsewhere in the Tenbury district excursion traffic continued to tempt the travelling public into using the railway. For instance, on 28th January 1939 an evening trip was run to Birmingham for the pantomime with a choice of two theatres to visit. The train left Woofferton at 4.40pm calling at all stations along the branch. A half-day excursion to Birmingham in the same month was advertised from Tenbury Wells at a cost of 3/2d return. In June 1939 the seaside trips continued, a popular one being to Barry Island with a sea trip across to Ilfracombe (all for a fare of 10 shillings) on the excursion leaving Tenbury Wells at 10.05am on a Sunday. The B.M.M.O. (Midland Red) were still wooing customers as well, advertising during that July, their services, No 414, Worcester-Tenbury-Ludlow with connections from Birmingham, and No 191, Birmingham-Kidderminster on Monday, Thursday and Sunday. The bus fares were Tenbury-Birmingham 2/10d single, 4/9d return. Two unusual excursions ran over the Tenbury line in August, the first on the 9th from Worcester, Shrub Hill, via Droitwich, Hartlebury, Bewdley and Tenbury to Barry Island and back, avoiding the main lines which were becoming congested with troop specials conveying army personnel to dispersal camps. Thirty-five Tenbury men of the Worcestershire Regiment had already joined one such special at Kidderminster on the 6th August with 480 officers and men of the regiment bound for Ludgershall on Salisbury Plain. The second excursion on the 11th ran from Birmingham (Tyseley) to Ludlow taking under-privileged children from the grimy city air, out into the countryside. These commendable trips were organised by a charitable organisation known as Children's Country Holiday Fund (C.C.H.F.) which to this day still does similar charitable work. One particular feature of this excursion was the formation of the train, being similar in make-up to the hop-pickers trains, gas-lit non-corridor stock, and doors kept locked! The last Shrewsbury Floral Fete that there was to be for some time, as usual attracted a GW/LMS joint excursion from Tenbury Wells in August 1939 (fare 4/2d on the 9.40am departure, 2/2d on the 11.15am or any train after 12 noon). Fowler 2-6-2Ts had now arrived at Ludlow and were seen on this type of working. The gardeners amongst the staff at Woofferton station carried off a district prize for their flower bed display in 1939 but it was to turn out to be the last chance they would have to compete for this award for a while.

Even before war had been declared, children were being evacuated from Birmingham, and a special evacuee train arrived at Newnham Bridge. At the same time hop-pickers made for Newnham Bridge and Tenbury Wells as they had done for many years before. However, within a month of the outbreak of World War IIs an emergency timetable came into force and the commercial freight service on the Ditton Priors was suspended (from 11th September). Ex CMDP 0-6-0PT No 29's chimney was fitted with a spark-arresting cowl at Worcester works and was quickly sent back to work ammunition van trains to Ditton Priors.

'850' class 0-6-0PT No. 2001 at Worcester on 12th March 1939. This engine was Kidderminster shed's favourite replacement for the regular CM&DP locos on the Ditton Priors. It was regularly borrowed from Worcester shed for this purpose over a period of 40 years.
Collection R. C. Riley

CHAPTER TEN
1940–1945

'J25' No. 2051 at Worcester on 8th April 1940, soon after arriving on wartime loan to the GWR. No. 2051 ended its time on the GWR at Kidderminster before being sent back to Darlington in November 1946. *A. G. Ellis*

VERY little changed around Tenbury and South Shropshire during the so called 'phoney war' period. The nearest the war came for most people then was when a German Junkers 88 plane crashed in a wood on the nearby Brown Clee Hill, killing all four crewmen. In May 1940 Tenbury Baths opened for the summer season business as usual — but only for the hot baths, the spa water business having finally ended when the wells had been filled in during the previous year.

The summer of 1940 was long and hot, resulting in bumper crops of hops and fruit, and the season extended into October, the consequent congestion at Tenbury Wells and Newnham Bridge putting pressure on the station staff who were valiantly trying to get the produce away before it spoiled. A notice appeared in the *Tenbury Advertiser* on 24th August 1940: 'Notice to fruit growers. The GW and LMS Railway Companies give notice in consequence of the exceptional conditions prevailing, growers and others concerned will be well advised to rail their fruit early in the day at Tenbury Wells station and Newnham Bridge station to admit despatch by 4 p.m.'

There were problems in the hop fields, too, for many of the women who would normally be expected to arrive in the Teme Valley were now working in munitions factories closer to where they lived — a similar shortage of pickers had occurred during the 1914-18 war. Hop-pickers' specials were still scheduled by the GWR, though, and in many ways the branch services remained very much the same as pre-war.

The morning Ludlow to Kidderminster trains were still almost exclusively hauled by the '3571' class 0-4-2T Nos 3575/78 and 79. 'Metro' 2-4-0T No 3563 also appeared (now the lone member of its class at Ludlow shed, since its sister engine No 3562 was working in the Wolverhampton area at this time) and on at least one occasion '63XX' class No 6365 was noted heading two coaches towards Kidderminster on a morning train through the Wyre Forest. The afternoon duties to Kidderminster continued to be worked by '57XX' 0-6-0PTs whilst Kidderminster shed still used '45XX' 2-6-2Ts for its work along the branch. As ever, the Stourbridge–Hereford freights and seasonal fruit specials brought greater variety of locomotives to the branch workings, but from mid-1940 LNER 'J25' 0-6-0s began to appear. Forty of these engines (on wartime loan to the GWR) were stationed in the Worcester and Wolverhampton divisions, but, as few of them were vacuum fitted, they were only used for local freight trips. Half of the total were noted at some time or other on the

GWR 0–4–2T No. 3575 of Ludlow shed waiting in the refuge siding at Kidderminster before working the 10.16 a.m. Tenbury train on 16th August 1941. This was the last day of steam working over the branch from Ludlow. From Monday, 18th August 1941, Worcester-based diesel railcars took over most of the through turns, and Leominster-based auto-fitted 48xx 0–4–2Ts worked the 'short section' Woofferton–Tenbury trains.

Cleobury Mortimer in 1942-3. The camp coach was stationed there to house naval personnel involved in guarding ammunition trains (ex-CM&DP line). The man on the left was Fred Harvey (ex-CM&DP staff).
Authors' collection

Tenbury and Severn Valley lines working from Stourbridge, Kidderminster, Worcester, Hereford and Shrewsbury sheds.

The arrival of the 'J25s' coincided with increased traffic into Cleobury Mortimer station in connection with the setting up of the Royal Naval Armament Depot close by the Ditton Priors terminus. By the end of 1940 the two-coach branch trains were often strengthened to six or seven, with heavy corridor stock conveying military and government personnel involved in the setting-up at Woofferton of a B.B.C. radio station which, among other things, broadcast coded messages to European agents and Resistance fighters.

By 1941, the railways were very much involved in the war effort and the Tenbury line played its part with four ammunition trains arriving daily at Cleobury Mortimer from where 0-6-0PTs Nos 28 and 29 would take over for the haul up to Ditton Priors. By mid-1941, Messrs Bryants of Birmingham had completed their construction work at the RNAD and, to enable the storage areas to be filled more quickly, another loco, 0-6-0PT No 2001, was transferred from Worcester shed, having first been fitted with a spark-arresting cowl similar to those on Nos 28 and 29. These locos ran light each morning from Kidderminster but were stabled at Cleobury Mortimer all day in order to save the time taken running backwards and forwards to Kidderminster for servicing. The crews had to coal by hand from conveniently placed loco coal wagons before setting off, at times double-headed, with train loads far exceeding anything seen previously on the Ditton Priors branch. Cleobury Mortimer was also the stabling point for three clerestory coaches which in peace-time had been used as camping coaches but were now pressed into service as accommodation for naval reservists and marines, some of whom had been posted to mount guard over the ammunition trains that were waiting in the sidings including the sidings once belonging to the Bayton Colliery Company.

Saturday 16th August 1941 saw the last day of steam working between Kidderminster and Ludlow, Worcester-based diesel railcar No 33 taking over these workings as from Monday 18th August 1941. The diesel railcars had been working into Bewdley since 1936 but their use on the Tenbury branch was restricted as the earlier types were not capable of hauling an extra coach up the gradient in the Wyre Forest. In 1941, two of the later variety (Nos 25 and 33) able to pull two coaches if required, were working from Worcester along with railcars Nos 6 and 7. In July 1941, the railcars had taken over the Kidderminster auto-workings to Highley and Bridgnorth on the Severn Valley line, and, following clearance tests over the Tenbury branch, they were passed for service as part of the GWR's economy measures in replacing certain steam services. With this move, Ludlow shed's long involvement with the motive power for the T&B came to an end. This sub-shed had been associated with working through Tenbury via Woofferton since 1862 but now the loco crews were responsible only for the Clee Hill branch, Church Stretton locals and the Ludlow–Hereford freight (dep: 6.55 a.m., arr: Hereford 11.07 a.m.) on which they returned as the Hereford–Tenbury portion of the Hereford–Stourbridge goods, being relieved at Woofferton by Hereford men. Leominster-based auto-trains took over the 'short section' workings. Kidderminster shed's contribution to the wartime running of the branch remained the same except for the curtailment of the Thursdays and Saturdays only Birmingham–Tenbury train.

Just as Ditton Priors had been selected for the RNAD because of its isolation, Tenbury was also chosen as a factory site as part of the war dispersal programme away from the West Midlands. A firm called Richard Lloyd came from the Nechells area of Birmingham in 1941, completing a new factory building close to Tenbury Wells station in 1942. This company made special tools for the machine tool industry including milling cutters for use in aircraft construction. They recruited workers from as far away as Hereford and Leominster, many travelling to Tenbury on the 7.27 a.m. auto from Leominster, a train which was soon given the nickname of 'The Bomber'. Whether the important nature of the company's product had any influence on railway operations is not known, but at the time the Woofferton–Tenbury section of line was upgraded to a 'red' route to allow much heavier engines to work as far as Tenbury Wells. At the same time the first recorded appearance of the 28XX class 2-8-0s on the branch took place, working from the Bewdley end, hauling the heavy ammunition trains destined for the RNAD at Ditton Priors. These 2-8-0s were in place of the LNER J25s, nicknamed 'Spitfires' or 'Graf Spees' by the local enginemen. The 0-6-0s were doing excellent work in the main but stalled on occasions on the Wyre Forest–Neen Sollars section, with the result that the trains had to be divided, the front portion going on to Cleobury Mortimer whilst the rear waited for the engine to return and collect it.

One of the Class J25s, No 2061, damaged the permanent way at Wyre Forest when a 'big end' broke while hauling the 11.0 a.m. goods train from Kidderminster to Newnham Bridge on 14th December 1944. The loose casting dropped, striking and damaging twenty-seven sleepers before the train came to a stand near milepost 142m 20 chs. The line was blocked for just under an hour and a half, the 1.50 p.m. diesel railcar service from Kidderminster to Woofferton suffering the most delay. The broken casting was eventually loaded onto one of the ex-CMDP Light Railway engines which left Cleobury Mortimer at 7.22 p.m. only to lose it 'overboard' on its way to Bewdley. The line then became blocked again for 35 minutes whilst an ultimately successful search for the missing item took place!

Ex-Railwayman, Cyril Morris relates that his wife worked at Newnham Bridge station during the war when the staff were kept busy with traffic consisting of fruit, coal and animal feed. On the occasions when there was an air raid taking place over the Black Country, ammunition trains heading for Ditton Priors would be shunted into the goods loop in Newnham Bridge station to await further instructions. Three other women who are remembered

Yugoslav refugees boarding Charles Motor Service buses at Cleobury Mortimer station during the Second World War. They were bound for Cleobury Mortimer village, to be billeted at the old workhouse.
N. How

1940 – 1945

A Dennis delivery lorry photographed near the weigh machine at Cleobury Mortimer station, with driver N. How, during the Second World War.
Cty. N. How

working alongside Mrs Morris were Mrs Mary Hodges, Mrs Molly Butcher (from Mamble) and Miss Cruxon. The first two were employed as porters, whose duties included not only unloading wagons but delivering parcels and goods in the district using the station lorry. Miss Biddy Cruxon worked in the office and later married the Newnham Bridge station master's son, Ben Lane. Women porter/guards also took the place of men on some branch passenger services at this time.

At Neen Sollars during the war, Charlie Carpenter was signalman, with his wife employed to assist him in these duties. Prior to Charlie's transfer to Tenbury, the Carpenters lived in Neen Sollars station house, and, following the closure of Neen Sollars box, Charlie had a spell as leading porter there. Another young signalman at Neen Sollars during the war was Gordon Harris whose father had been signalman at Cleobury Mortimer. Newnham Bridge had two young men on the staff by the end of the war, Maurice Downes who went on to be relief signalman at Kidderminster, and Brian Williams who became a passenger guard at Worcester. Cyril Morris remembers Messrs Case, Hitchen and Lench working the branch as goods' guards from Kidderminster and a passenger guard at the same time was Mr Frank Beal, and later Bert Savage.

Shortly after the war, Mr Dennis Espley was a porter at Newnham Bridge before moving to Bridgnorth as relief signalman. Also at Newnham Bridge for some years in the postwar period were Jack and Ernie Haycock, the latter moving to Kidderminster parcels depot at the station's closure.

Cyril Morris's own job on the railway was as a relief signalman based at Bewdley, covering both the Severn Valley and Tenbury lines. He often took over from Harold

A Thornycroft delivery van outside the Talbot Hotel, Cleobury Mortimer during the Second World War. In earlier years, a horse-drawn vehicle operated from the Talbot Hotel carrying passengers to and from Cleobury Mortimer station over 1½ miles away.
N. How

Thomason at Cleobury Mortimer or Bewdley North box. Harold is also remembered throughout the district as landlord of the Blount Arms, just by the road entrance to Cleobury Mortimer station. At other times, Cyril relieved at Tenbury box and recalls one time on a Saturday when he had a token failure and had to appoint the Tenbury porter as pilotman. Later, this porter, Jack Tong, was promoted to signalman at Ludlow and then went on to Craven Arms, Central Wales Junction, before retiring.

One ex-employee, Mr John Morgan, even rejoined the GWR during the war at the age of 73! (Mr Morgan is seen on the Tenbury staff photograph of 1924). Born near Craven Arms in 1868, Mr Morgan began his railway career (aged 13) at his local station, moved to Leominster, then Birkenhead, before transferring to Tenbury Wells as chief goods clerk. He retired in 1932 after fifty years service and settled at Easton Court. In 1941 Mr Morgan returned to work as Grade 1 porter at Easton Court station and worked there on his own until he was 78, with the claim to fame that he was the oldest railway employee 'in harness' in the country. He retired again to live on until 1952 in Easton Court station house.

Wartime fuel rationing meant that private motorists had to forsake their cars for public transport. The Midland Red ran a daily bus service from Cleobury Mortimer village to Kidderminster and Charles Motor Services of Cleobury Mortimer operated some bus routes in direct competition with the railway. However, rail transport was being urgently recommended to sugar beet growers as an alternative to the movement of their crop by road.

In 1942 the Tenbury Baths was still in business but now only for an experimental period and manned by volunteers, since the building had been taken over by the local council as an 'emergency gas cleansing station' for treatment of victims in the case of enemy gas attack. Fundraising events for the upkeep of the baths demonstrated Tenbury's wish to hold on to this amenity, and a dance held at the Bridge Hotel in July 1942 raised £11 6s 4d.

Mawley Hall, close by Cleobury Mortimer station and former home of the influential Blount family, was taken over by the Government to house Italian POWs who were put to work on various tasks, including farm work near to the Ditton Priors branch line and its 'secret' ammunition trains. Little is known of any accidents to these trains — they were subject to some wartime censorship — but a story persists about one runaway in Wyre Forest which eventually derailed itself near to the station. The ammunition, thankfully, did not explode, but the fireman broke an ankle when he bailed out (along with his driver) and landed in a tree.

Mr A. H. (Howard) Lane came to be station master at Newnham Bridge in 1943, whilst Mr Maurice Bott (ex Tenbury Wells) retired as station master at Leominster in the same year. Mr Lane had transferred from Leigh Court station on the Bromyard branch and, with similar traffic there, he was already well versed in fruit, hops, and not least the hop-pickers.

Wartime necessity was bringing many more unusual locos to Bewdley, albeit mostly destined for Bridgnorth on the Severn Valley line where an RAF training camp had been established. The upgrading of the Severn Valley line to 'blue' enabled heavy troop train movements to be routed around the Kidderminster triangle. 'Manor' class 4-6-0s appeared, as did LMS 'Crab' 2-6-0s and LMS class 5 4-6-0s on specials originating from Padgate (Near Warrington) and Cardington (Bedfordshire). Probably the most unexpected type to appear subsequent to the D-Day landing in 1944, was LNER Holden B12 4-6-0s bringing GI casualties to Stourport for an American Hospital at Burlish. A 'Southern Railway locomotive' was also reported to have appeared at Woofferton, presumably one of those on wartime loan to the GWR. The 4-4-0 'Dukes' were frequently seen passing through Bewdley during the war on Shrewsbury–Birmingham and Shrewsbury–Kidderminster workings, including No 3276 and No 3284 *Isle of Jersey*. 'Dukedogs' Nos 3207 and 3224 were also being used on these trains.

The Kidderminster shed allocation for 1943/44 shows little change from pre-war days, although 2-6-2T No 8101 was to have a long association with Tenbury Wells–Birmingham passenger service.

Loco Number	Class
28/29	Ex CM & DP
2153	2021 0-6-0PT (1943 only)
4586	45XX 2-6-2T
4596	45XX 2-6-2T (1943 only)
4625	57XX 0-6-0PT
5110	51XX 2-6-2T
5112	51XX 2-6-2T
5518	45XX 2-6-2T
5538	45XX 2-6-2T (1943 only)
5573	45XX 2-6-2T
8101	81XX 2-6-2T
8718	57XX 0-6-0PT
8727	57XX 0-6-0PT
2134	J25 0-6-0 (LNER on loan)
2142	J25 0-6-0 (LNER on loan)
2051	J25 0-6-0 (LNER on loan)
1994	J25 0-6-0 (LNER on loan)

Worcester shed's allocation in 1943 included diesel railcars 5, 6, 7, 14, 19, 25 and 33. Leominster shed in 1943 had 0-4-2Ts Nos 4845 and 4855, available for the auto service.

A list of locos hauling Stourbridge–Hereford 'Tenbury Goods' over the 1939-45 period gives some insight into the working of this train: 'Bulldog' 4-4-0s Nos 3389, 3432, 3401 *Vancouver* (all HFD), 'Aberdare' 2-6-0s Nos 2608, 2620, 2655 (all STB), 2680 (HFD), Collett 0-6-0s Nos 2279, 2281 (STB), 2286, 3209 (HFD), Deans Goods 0-6-0s Nos 2349, 2513 (STB), 45XX 2-6-2T 4534 (HFD), 37XX 0-6-0PT 3601 (HFD), LNER J25 1994, 2053, 2072, 2076 (HFD), 1973, 2043 (STB).

Locos noted on fruit or other special workings: LNER J25 1986, 2043, 2051, 2071 (none on fruit trains), 0-6-0PT 1898, 3649 — cattle specials ex Tenbury Wells, Dean Goods 0-6-0 2515, 2538, 2532, Collett 0-6-0 2211, 2294 — fruit specials, 55XX 2-6-2T 5518, 5573, 4596, 4586.

With the coming of peace there was a slow return to pre-war conditions. The end of the war did not mean the end of ammunition trains to Ditton Priors, for all the explosives now surplus to immediate requirements continued to require storage space. In November 1945, ex-CM&DP 0-6-0PT No 28, after a magnificent war effort, was sent to Swindon for a much needed overhaul, leaving Nos 29, 2001 and occasionally 0-6-0PT No 2044, to deal with the remaining ammunition trains. These locos reverted to the immediate pre-war practice of coming and going every day from Kidderminster but running only to an exchange siding near Cleobury North, well outside a security fence which the RNAD had erected around the depot. From here the RNAD diesel loco collected the consignments and took them into the depot.

With this return to some normality, the LNER J25s were no longer needed for the Tenbury freights, and by November 1946 were all back in the North East, the last one at Kidderminster shed, No 2051 (since renumbered 5704), returning on the 12th of the month.

Mr H. D. Bradley continued his recollections of Tenbury station after his return from the RAF in 1945.

'During my period in the services the railway made up the difference between my service pay and my salary until such time as I was earning more service pay than my salary. When I returned, my salary was £20 per month. We were paid fortnightly and the first fortnight I would receive £10, but the second pay day would have one month's deductions, leaving me with about £7-£8.

'There were several new faces on my return. Mr Ted Lawrence was the station master, Win Griffiths was the booking clerk and Mr Reynolds was chief goods clerk. Jack Chapman returned about the same time as me and became a lorry driver, replacing Tom Dyer. Jack moved into the crossing-keeper's cottage at Little Hereford, and his wife became crossing keeper, supervised (like Little Hereford station) from Tenbury. Only once can I recall a collision with the gates when the auto from Woofferton came into contact but with no injuries.

'I finally left the GWR in 1947, the traffic suffering badly from lorry competition at the time. I went to work for Messrs Beatty Bros who made bicycle mudguards, and as I was responsible for despatch which still mostly went by rail, I did not entirely lose contact with Tenbury station until I left Beatty Bros in 1950.'

'Bulldog' 4-4-0 No. 3386 of Hereford sheds leaving Kidderminster goods yard with the Stourbridge–Tenbury–Hereford goods in 1946.
P. F. Curtis

No. 7023 *Penrice Castle* on a Hereford to Shrewsbury stopping train at Woofferton on 10th September 1949.

H. C. *Casserley*

CHAPTER ELEVEN
THE POSTWAR YEARS

45XX 2–6–2T No. 4596 in the bay platform at Woofferton Junction with a Kidderminster train in June 1951. The bay was taken out of use in 1957.
D. B. Clayton

THE October 1946 timetable showed that the schedule for working of coaches on the Tenbury branch from Kidderminster had not altered since the war, but by February 1947, the late evening Thursdays and Saturdays-only through train from Birmingham to Tenbury Wells was being run again, although the through train to Leominster had been taken off as a temporary measure, the national coal supply situation presenting problems to the railways. The 6.25 p.m. Kidderminster–Woofferton railcar which formerly returned to Worcester via Bromyard, now worked back to Kidderminster (dep. Woofferton 7.45 p.m., Tenbury Wells 7.57 p.m., arr. Kidderminster 8.45 p.m.), then empty to Worcester.

The 23rd August 1947 was the retirement day of one more of Tenbury's long-serving railwaymen, Dick Jay, who worked for the Joint Railways for thirty-eight years. Leaving his father's farm, he began as porter at Aberdovey for a wage of 15s per week. Then, after a short spell in the pits, he came to Tenbury in 1911. He became signalman and remained in that position for the rest of his working life. It was reputed that Dick Jay was the reason for the single needle instrument being kept on at Tenbury signal box long after they had become redundant elsewhere. Dick was very deaf but could pick up the vibrating bell beats by placing his ear next to the instrument!

On 1st January 1948, there were major changes in organization as the branch passed on nationalization into British Transport Commission hands. Amazingly, the Tenbury Railway had remained a nominally independent company, still paying out dividends. From 1st January 1948 it was vested under the BTC by the 1947 Transport Act. Compensation was paid to shareholders in British Transport 3% guaranteed stock. The Tenbury Railway Company was not finally dissolved until 2nd April 1949. At the end of 1947, the Woofferton–Tenbury section was organized by the GWR acting on behalf of the LMS/GWR Joint Committee. This situation had been the rule since 1st March 1932 when Mr J Ratcliffe, Joint Superintendent at Shrewsbury, retired, and his office closed. At this time the whole of the Shrewsbury and Hereford Joint Line and all branches therefrom were transferred to the GW Superintendent at Chester. The London Midland Region of the newly created British Railways, did not become involved for long with its theoretical inheritance of the joint ownership of the old Shrewsbury & Hereford Railway. The LMR officially relinquished all interest in the S&H and Tenbury Joint lines from 5th September 1948, the lines thereafter being part of the Western Region, controlled from Chester as before. From the outset, the Bewdley–Tenbury section was managed by

A panoramic scene, looking north towards Ludlow, with the late afternoon sunlight casting shadows over Woofferton Junction in 1953.
P. J. Garland

0–4–2T No. 1461 with the 4.5 p.m. Craven Arms–Ludlow–Tenbury Wells auto-train on 20th April 1957. The new branch signal and indicator, allowing branch trains to run 'wrong line' as far as the junction, can just be discerned (in both views) at the top of the signal post in front of the goods shed door.
M. Hale

Woofferton railcar W26 on the 12.10 p.m. to Bewdley with 'County' class 4–6–0 No. 1026 passing in the opposite direction with a north to west express on 2nd January 1959.
J. Dew

the GW Divisional Superintendent at Worcester Shrub Hill, whose area was virtually the former West Midland Railway system of 1860.

In March 1948, various people from around the Teme Valley travelled to Birmingham to attend a meeting of traffic commissioners. They were witnesses to support an application for an extended bus service between Tenbury Wells and Ludlow and between Tenbury Wells and Leominster. The witnesses included a clergyman, a JP, a farmer's wife and a member of Tenbury Chamber of Commerce. The main application was for the extension of the service already running between Tenbury and Ludlow, by adding an early-morning bus to ensure all schoolchildren on the route got to school on time, and to enable all employees working in Ludlow to reach their workplace punctually. The application was granted by the commissioners to Yarrantons Buses of Eardiston, who were supported by Tenbury RDC but opposed by Midland Red, Messrs Bengry of Leominster and the newly-formed British Railways. The Tenbury RDC representative pointed out the nuisance of changing trains at Woofferton for schoolchildren making the outward journey to Ludlow on the 8 a.m. dep. Tenbury Wells and similarly on the 4.23 dep. Ludlow return journey. BR therefore lost some regular customers to Yarranton's Bus Company but regained some lost revenue by the reinstatement of day, half-day and evening excursions.

The December 1948 *Railway Observer* refers to the Tenbury Goods as a Hereford shed '2251' class working, but noted that Hereford's 'Aberdare' class 2-6-0s Nos 2651

S&HR buildings at Woofferton Junction. The waiting shelter in the upper photograph was similar to the one at Tenbury Wells.
G. Hookham

Passengers joining a Kidderminster train in the bay at Woofferton Junction on 10th September 1949. Only remnants of the prize-winning platform gardens remained at this time. The goods shed (on the left) was similar to the one at Tenbury Wells.

H. C. Casserley

Two views of the Tenbury bay platform at Woofferton, the lower one showing 2–6–2T No. 4586 of Kidderminster shed waiting with a four-coach train to Kidderminster on 10th September 1949.
H. C. Casserley

and 2680 had appeared at times along with sister engine No 2655 (STB) and Dean Goods 0-6-0 No 2541. Nevertheless, the use of the Collett 0-6-0s on a more regular basis was an updating of motive power for these long-standing workings. From 1948 the number of RNAD trips to Ditton Priors could no longer employ both ex CM&DP locos, so No 28 was sent from Kidderminster on loan to Hereford shed, whilst No 29 still kept active in its usual surroundings.

From 1st January 1949 walking-tour day tickets and touring tickets were revived, aimed at members of rambling and cycling organizations. Wyre Forest and Neen Sollars stations were always attractive starting points for these special ticket holders and benefited from the custom accordingly.

At the same time, an announcement by the Midland Red bus company signalled a return to direct competition between road and rail in the area. Since the end of 1947, the GWR and Midland Red companies had formed an alliance and issued combined rail and road tickets. However, on 28th January 1949, notice was given that bus service No 409 Hereford–Tenbury–Kidderminster–Birmingham would run on Tuesdays, Thursdays and Saturdays. This service departed from Hereford at 8.15 a.m., which gave an arrival at Tenbury at 9.30 a.m. and allowed the bus to depart earlier than the Birmingham

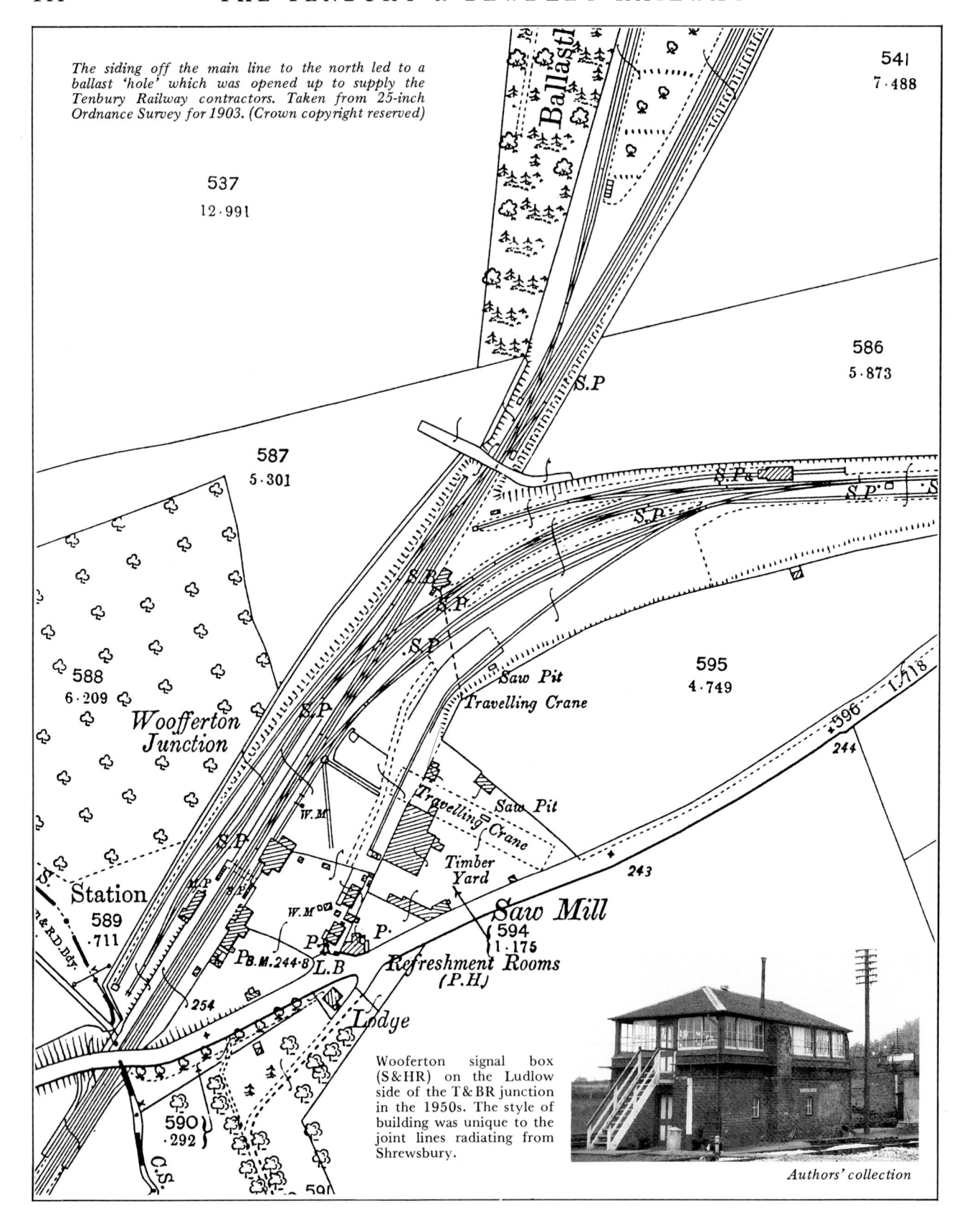

THE Tenbury & Bewdley Railway

The siding off the main line to the north led to a ballast 'hole' which was opened up to supply the Tenbury Railway contractors. Taken from 25-inch Ordnance Survey for 1903. (Crown copyright reserved)

Wooferton signal box (S&HR) on the Ludlow side of the T&BR junction in the 1950s. The style of building was unique to the joint lines radiating from Shrewsbury.

Authors' collection

THE POSTWAR YEARS

A 1960 photograph of Woofferton Junction featuring the disused cattle pens on the right. By this time the connection to the Tenbury bay platform had been taken out along with other trackwork. The bay platform line was retained for use as siding accommodation.
J. H. Moss

The 4.30 p.m. Woofferton to Tenbury leaving the junction on 20th April 1957. The siding in the foreground led to the saw mills. *M. Hale*

Woofferton shed c.1960, derelict and vandalised but still in use as a watering place for branch engines, hence the 'fire devil' stove used to thaw out the water pipe in frosty weather.
M. Lloyd

Easton Court opened to passengers and goods on 1st August 1861 and finally closed within a day of celebrating its centenary on 31st July 1961. It became an unstaffed station from September 1954.
Cty. Harry Heath

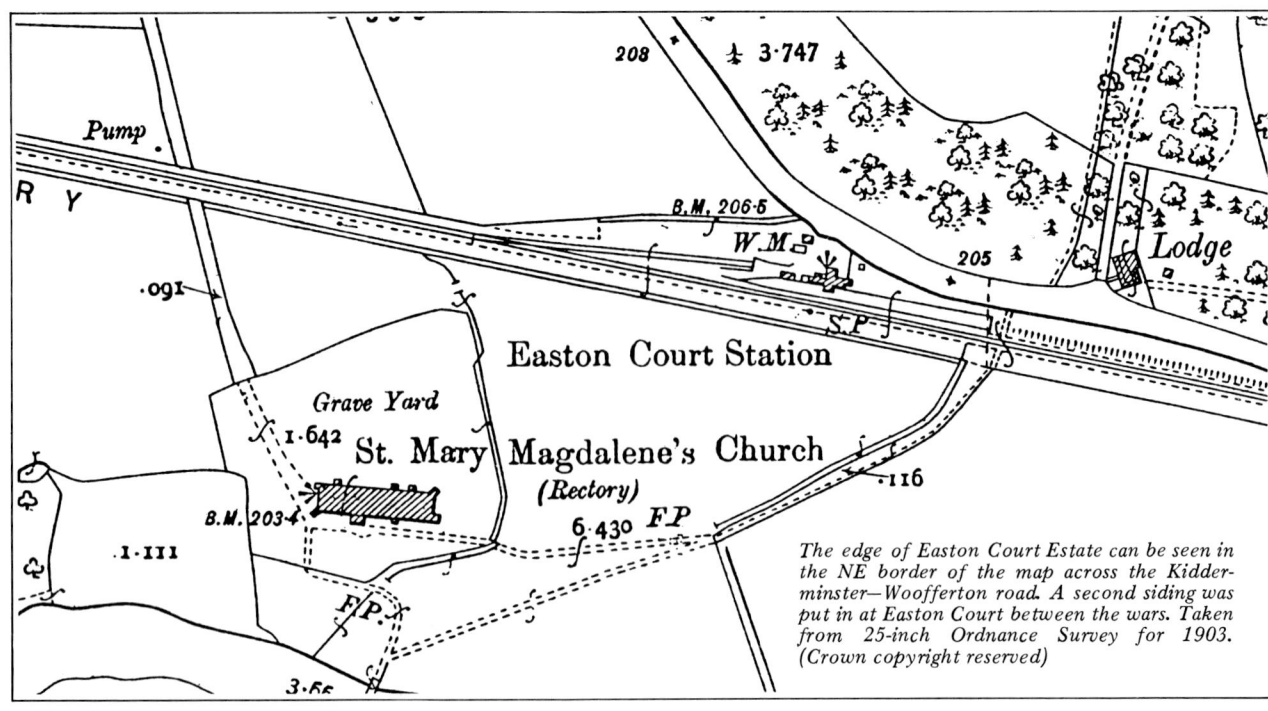

The edge of Easton Court Estate can be seen in the NE border of the map across the Kidderminster–Woofferton road. A second siding was put in at Easton Court between the wars. Taken from 25-inch Ordnance Survey for 1903. (Crown copyright reserved)

THE POSTWAR YEARS

train by half an hour. Running via Newnham Bridge, Cleobury Mortimer and Bewdley, the bus returned from Birmingham two hours sooner than the evening train and was thereby preferred by many people in spite of being more costly.

Excursion traffic continued to provide the bulk of passenger revenue, with late season evening pantomime trips to Birmingham and fishermen's specials much in evidence. The 45XX 2-6-2Ts maintained their predominance on the passenger traffic in 1949, Nos 4578, 4586, 4594, 4596 being regulars, with 4599 (ex Machynlleth shed) and 5518 appearing on occasions.

There was an interesting development in the excursion trains over the branch in mid-summer 1949 when Kidderminster Co-operative Society showed commendable enterprise by chartering the first of many 'Co-op Specials' which ran around the Kidderminster triangle and also over the Tenbury branch. The inaugural train was on

Easton Court was the only station between Tenbury and Woofferton on the Tenbury Railway. This picture, taken on 21st July 1956, shows 0-4-2T No. 1445 with the late afternoon auto for Tenbury Wells.
Gregory

A familiar sight to users of Easton Court station during 1960/61 was the caged parrot which belonged to Mrs. Lucas, the lady who lived in the station house at this time. *B. Barnes*

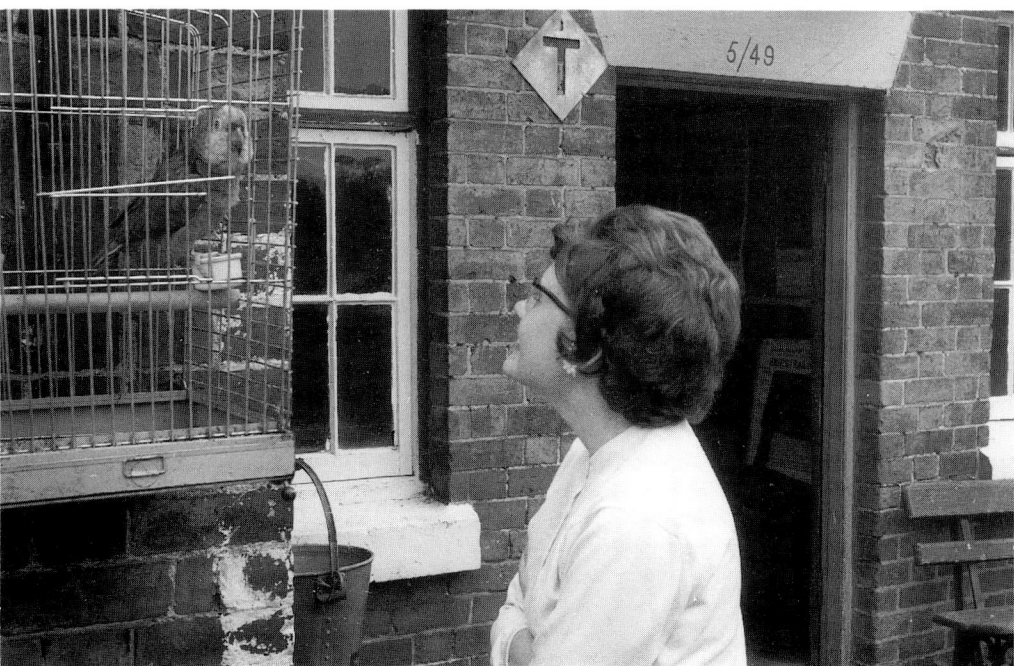

14XX No. 1445 of Leominster shed propelling a Tenbury–Woofferton–Craven Arms autocoach about a mile west of Tenbury on 15th August 1959. The line at this point was routed over the bed of the old Leominster Canal. *M. Mensing*

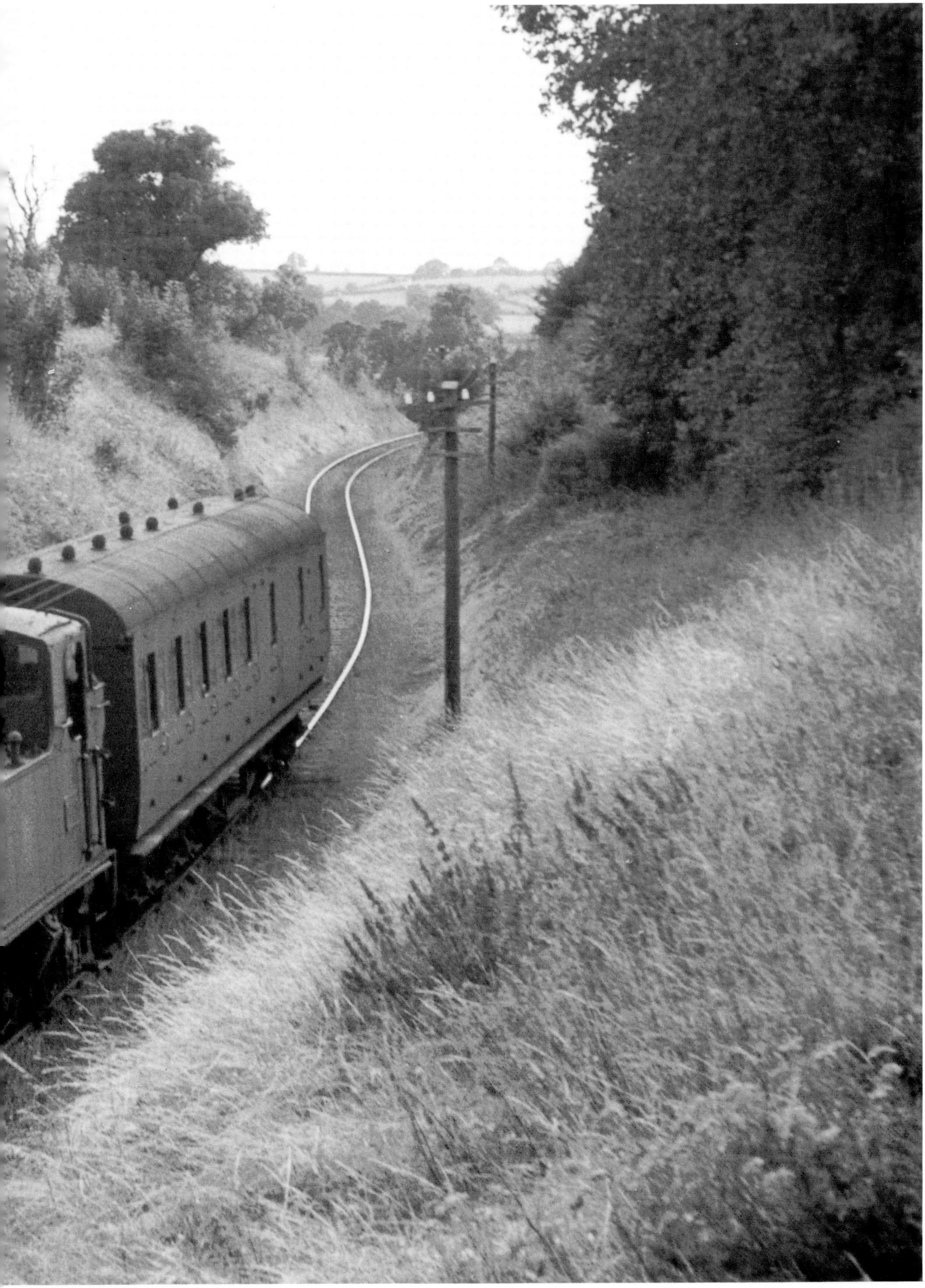

150 THE TENBURY & BEWDLEY RAILWAY

A glimpse of the track layout at the Woofferton end of Tenbury Wells in the early 1950s. *J. H. Moss*

No. 1445 arriving at 4.40 p.m. at Tenbury Wells with the 3.27 p.m. auto from Leominster via Craven Arms. *G. Bannister*

THE POSTWAR YEARS

11th June 1949, a trip to Blackpool from Stourport, Bewdley and Kidderminster, for which Worcester shed turned out 'Star' class 4-6-0 *Swallowfield Park*. In summer 1949, the destination of two such excursions over the Tenbury line was Barry Island, and although the motive power is not known, the 63XX class Moguls had established themselves on these duties by the following year.

Another excursion 'first' was the Birmingham Loco Club's trip on 2nd July 1949. This special, organized by the late Eric Tonks, travelled in diesel railcar No 14 from Snow Hill to Woofferton en route to Welshpool via Craven Arms and Shrewsbury. The Tenbury branch was chosen especially for its scenic attraction. These scenic railcar specials became popular and many more were run.

This picture shows the single-armed tubular-post home signal which replaced the wooden bracket shown opposite. Note the timber pedestrian crossing.
J. H. Moss

When first opened to passengers and goods on 1st August 1861, the station was simply named 'Tenbury'. The 'Wells' was added from 14th November 1912 following a request from the parish council to advertise the town as a spa. *R. Pearson*

The wide station drive leading up to Tenbury Wells station also served as the entrance to the large goods yard. The ladies waiting room extension of 1913 can be seen at the end of the station building on the right in this photograph taken on 30th September 1960.

H. C. Casserley

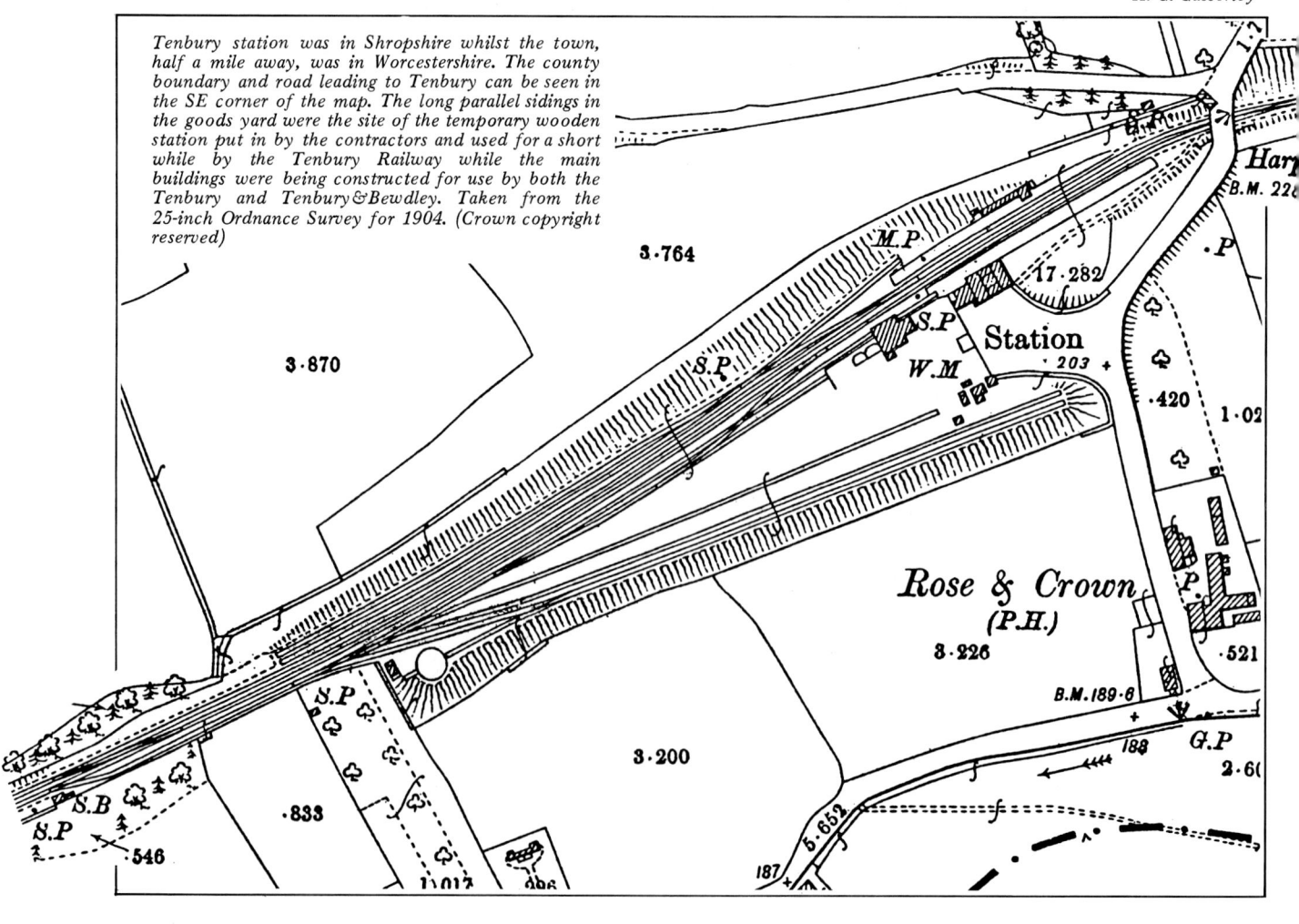

Tenbury station was in Shropshire whilst the town, half a mile away, was in Worcestershire. The county boundary and road leading to Tenbury can be seen in the SE corner of the map. The long parallel sidings in the goods yard were the site of the temporary wooden station put in by the contractors and used for a short while by the Tenbury Railway while the main buildings were being constructed for use by both the Tenbury and Tenbury & Bewdley. Taken from the 25-inch Ordnance Survey for 1904. (Crown copyright reserved)

THE POSTWAR YEARS

Tenbury station was built partly on the bed of the Leominster Canal. The bridge at the end of the platforms replaced an earlier one which had spanned the canal at this point, the house alongside having been a canalside cottage. In later years, it was occupied by Charlie Carpenter, the last Tenbury signalman.
J. H. Moss

Up platform waiting rooms and signal box at Tenbury Wells, showing S&H Joint line architectural influence. The signal box, built in 1878, was of the LNW/GW Joint Type No. 1 but with the hipped roof pitched higher than others. Opened as Tenbury 'A', it was known as 'Tenbury Wells' after the abolition of the 'B' West box in 1928. A plan for a signal box on the station side was never implemented. The box closed on 28th April 1963.
J. H. Moss

The afternoon auto to Woofferton about to depart on a hot summer's day in 1955.

Gregory

THE POSTWAR YEARS

Ever-increasing transfer of rail traffic to the expanding road haulage led to the first of many economy measures on the branch. The working of the Stourbridge–Hereford freight, so long a feature of the Tenbury scene, was cut back in September 1949 to work only between Kidderminster and Woofferton return. At the time of this curtailment two regular locos on the duty, 0-6-0PT No 3601 from Hereford, and Collett 0-6-0 No 2281 of Stourbridge, were both transferred to Kidderminster shed (23rd September 1949) especially to work the new train, the local 'Aberdare' 2-6-0s having all been withdrawn by this stage. Ex-CMDP 0-6-0PT No 28 was in open store at Kidderminster in late 1949 through lack of suitable employment, but No 29 was still busy on the Ditton Priors

Originally Tenbury only had one platform, on the down, station side. However, with the opening of the other platform and the Kidderminster loop in 1878, up and down directions on the Tenbury branch were reversed; Woofferton–Kidderminster up trains then became down trains. From 1948, under BR, directions were restored and this 1950s view shows left, the 'restored' down, and right, up platforms.
J. H. Moss

Looking towards Bewdley in August 1928. The white post in the middle distance marked the limit of the GW/LNWR Joint working. This was the junction of the T&B with the Tenbury Railway (4 chains from Tenbury station). The site of Tenbury's canal wharf was not far away around the bend, and the wharf house still stands, but hidden now by housing development.
J. Bott

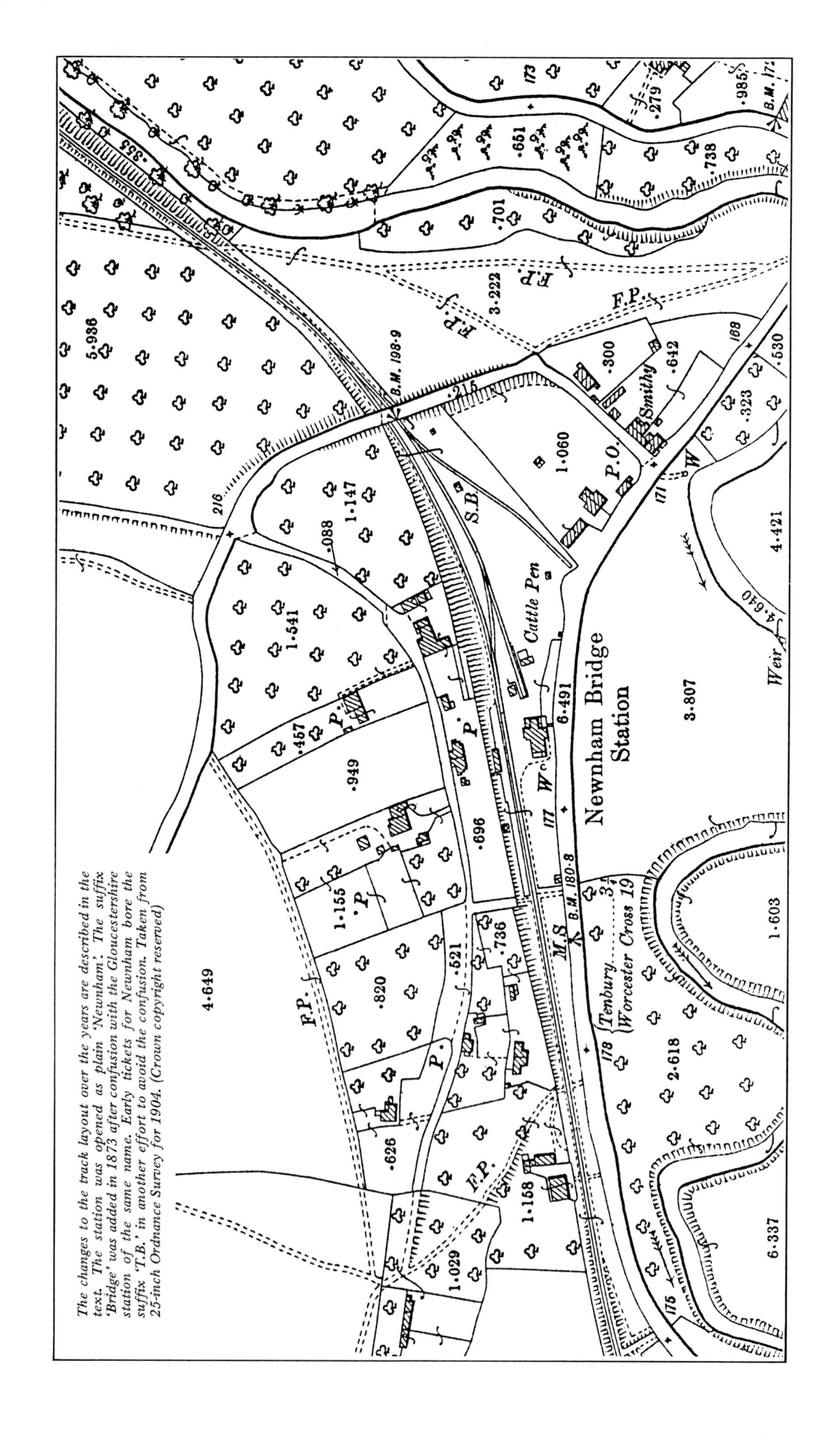

The changes to the track layout over the years are described in the text. The station was opened as plain 'Newnham'. The suffix 'Bridge' was added in 1873 after confusion with the Gloucestershire station of the same name. Early tickets for Newnham bore the suffix 'T.B.' in another effort to avoid the confusion. Taken from 25-inch Ordnance Survey for 1904. (Crown copyright reserved)

THE POSTWAR YEARS

81XX class 2–6–2T No. 8101 was a regular loco on the branch. Shedded at 85D, it worked the more important passenger trains until the final days of steam. This picture shows it at Newnham Bridge on 29th August 1959 with a train for Tenbury Wells. The occupational crossing served a group of houses, above the station, which were a former Leominster canalside settlement. *John Marshall*

trains. A new loco of the 51XX 2-6-2T class (No 4175) arrived ex works in November 1949, indicating the eventual phasing out of the older Churchward 2-6-2Ts which had given so much useful service. In February 1950, Kidderminster was given the BR shed code 85D. The Kidderminster allocation during 1950 included the following locos, the Collett 0-6-0 having been transferred away:

Class	Loco No		
Ex CM&DP 0-6-0PT	28	51XX 2-6-2T	4153
Ex CM&DP 0-6-0PT	29	51XX 2-6-2T	4175
2021 0-6-0PT	2051	51XX 2-6-2T	5110
2021 0-6-0PT	2101	57XX 0-6-0PT	3601
45XX 2-6-2T	4578	57XX 0-6-0PT	4625
45XX 2-6-2T	4586	57XX 0-6-0PT	7700
45XX 2-6-2T	4594	57XX 0-6-0PT	8718
45XX 2-6-2T	4599	57XX 0-6-0PT	8727
45XX 2-6-2T	5518	63XX 2-6-0	6382
51XX 2-6-2T	4100	81XX 2-6-2T	8101

In September 1950 yet another timetable change took place. From 28th September, the early morning Worcester railcar was diagrammed to work empty to Ludlow via Shelwick Junction and the Shrewsbury & Hereford main line, a distance of approximately 49 miles compared to 36 via Hartlebury and Bewdley! At this time the railcar worked all the passenger trips on the Tenbury branch with the exception of Kidderminster's one morning and afternoon steam working and the Leominster auto-train turns. The usual return route to Worcester off the branch for the empty railcar was via Leominster and the Bromyard branch, until this route closed on 15th September 1952.

Lamp above the entrance to the ticket office. *Lens of Sutton*

Ex-GWR railcar W32 in green livery at Newnham Bridge on the 11.10 a.m. Bewdley–Woofferton on 7th May 1960.
J. Dew

The position of the original bay window on the station master's house can be seen in this 1950s view. Newnham Bridge station house was unusual in not being on a platform. For reasons yet to be discovered, it was also set back from the running lines. It may well have coincided with projected plans such as those of the Teme Valley Railway in 1866 whereby a double track of rails would have been laid between Newnham Bridge and Tenbury. However, if that was the case, intending passengers would have needed steps to enter the carriages as the station was at ground level.
Lens of Sutton

Although the goods loop on the left was installed in 1914, Newnham Bridge was never a crossing place for passenger trains. However, it was equipped with an intermediate electric token instrument to enable goods trains to be shut in the siding to keep the main line clear for passing trains. There was also an occupation key provided to protect the running line while road vehicles were using the timber crossing to load and unload goods from the platform. Strict instructions were given in the working timetable with the added rider that 'the practice of backing vehicles to the platform must not be resorted to when it is possible to avoid it'.
Lens of Sutton

The railcar then reverted to previous practice and returned to shed via Woofferton and Kidderminster as it had done in 1947. Ludlow shed, no longer servicing the Tenbury line, closed completely on 29th December 1951, with men and duties transferred to Craven Arms shed.

Throughout the 1950s many specials were organized, mainly worked by Kidderminster shed's 41XX/51XX 'Prairies' and 63XX Moguls, usually double-headed as far as Woofferton, where Shrewsbury line coaches were sometimes attached and the 2-6-2T dropped off. The Kidderminster Mogul would then take the train on to such seaside destinations as Barry Island, Porthcawl and Weston-super-Mare (Locking Road). Some excursions started from Hagley and were well patronised by the time they reached Tenbury Wells, picking up at Bewdley passengers who had travelled via the Severn Valley line. Easton Court was the only station omitted from the stops on the Tenbury branch for these trains. Some were loaded to ten coaches, including a buffet car; one was noted with a Gresley LNER 1st class coach included in the mixture of BR and ex GWR stock. On occasions 4-6-0 'Manors' were used including No 7805 *Broome Manor* of Hereford shed. On the return journey the Shrewsbury portion was detached at Woofferton, the Kidderminster portion then going forward up the branch. Normally, the branch was closed on a Sunday but on these occasions staff would have to be on duty. Once at Neen Sollars, a porter waited late for the return of just two passengers picked up from there on the outward journey, only to find that no-one got off. In spite of a thorough search of the train, the missing couple were nowhere to be seen and the porter must have thought the lonely vigil a complete waste of time! Another Bank Holiday special which ran in the early 'fifties was one

Howard Lane, Newnham Bridge station master from 1943 until closure in 1962. He was a most respected man and usually smartly turned out. When asked to pose for the camera, he was concerned about his jacket which was grubby. He suddenly remembered his new uniform had recently arrived in a parcel from Worcester, so he quickly ripped it open, and put the jacket on. It was not until later that he realised just how much the jacket was creased, especially the sleeves, and, to make matters worse, he hadn't buttoned up the top two buttons!
Ct. Mrs. H. Parkinson

Worcester-based railcar W20W at Newnham Bridge on 20th April 1957.

M. Hale

THE POSTWAR YEARS

The prize track length sign at Newnham Bridge was a reminder of past glories and the 'Railway Tavern' buildings above the station could tell some stories too. Whilst the platform garden still attempted a spring display, weeds were colonizing everywhere. The line of wagons in the siding in the far distance were the precursor of a future much larger use of the Newnham Bridge site for storage. *T. R. Jay*

A 'Large Prairie' leaving Newnham Bridge with a train for Kidderminster on 23rd May 1961. *B. T. C. Good*

View from diesel railcar leaving Neen Sollars for Newnham Bridge c.1952/3. *J. H. Moss*

Neen Sollars, looking towards Tetstill Farm overbridge, with a railcar arriving from Newnham Bridge. The signal box dated from 1878, but its size and wooden construction were identical to the specification of the original 1864 T&B south box at Bewdley. Combined with photographic evidence of a similar box at Much Wenlock, there is a strong possibility that this may have been the south box at Bewdley, dismantled in 1878 and re-erected here as part of the alterations carried out for the opening of the Kidderminster loop line. *W. Potter*

Neen Sollars from the Cleobury Mortimer end on 20th June 1953. The signal box and staggered platform put in in 1878 can be seen in the distance. The station buildings were an exact mirror image of those at Newnham Bridge (on page 158) and this was a familiar feature of William Clarke's work on other lines he engineered.   *L & GRP*

organized by BR staff from the Stourbridge and Kidderminster areas and known unofficially as the 'Platelayers Special'. This was one of the twice-yearly outings taking (mainly) platelayers and their families to Weston-super-Mare via Tenbury, Woofferton and the Severn Tunnel. On one trip 4-6-0 'Grange' class No 6804 *Brockington Grange* of Oxley shed was used. At the time, BR carried out deflection tests on Dowles Bridge, but, from evidence obtained, decided against the use of these 'Red' route 4-6-0s on this excursion traffic. However, some other 'Granges' did work through and at least one other type of locomotive, officially banned, a 66XX class 0-6-2T, arrived at Cleobury Mortimer from Woofferton around this period on a ballast train.

In the early 'fifties, increased mechanisation in the hop-yards meant less hand labour being required in the season, and a decline occurred in the quantity of hop-pickers specials. For years these trains had run, bringing generations, from grandmothers to grandchildren, to Knotts Farm, Kyrewood or around Newnham Bridge and Lindridge. Camps were set up in barns or converted outbuildings near the Talbot Hotel, Newnham Court Farm and by the Nag's Head on the Lindridge road. Mr Alma Edgington, one of the Dawley 'hoppers', remembers, as a schoolboy after the war, coming to work in the hop-yards and, like all the children who had arrived, being 'looked at' by the nurse for head lice and then being ordered to take the compulsory shower just to make sure! The Railway Tavern Inn at Newnham Bridge was the focal point for both railwaymen and hoppers, especially at the height of the season when 'hoppers friends' specials arrived, the adults accompanied by dozens of noisy children suddenly let loose into the

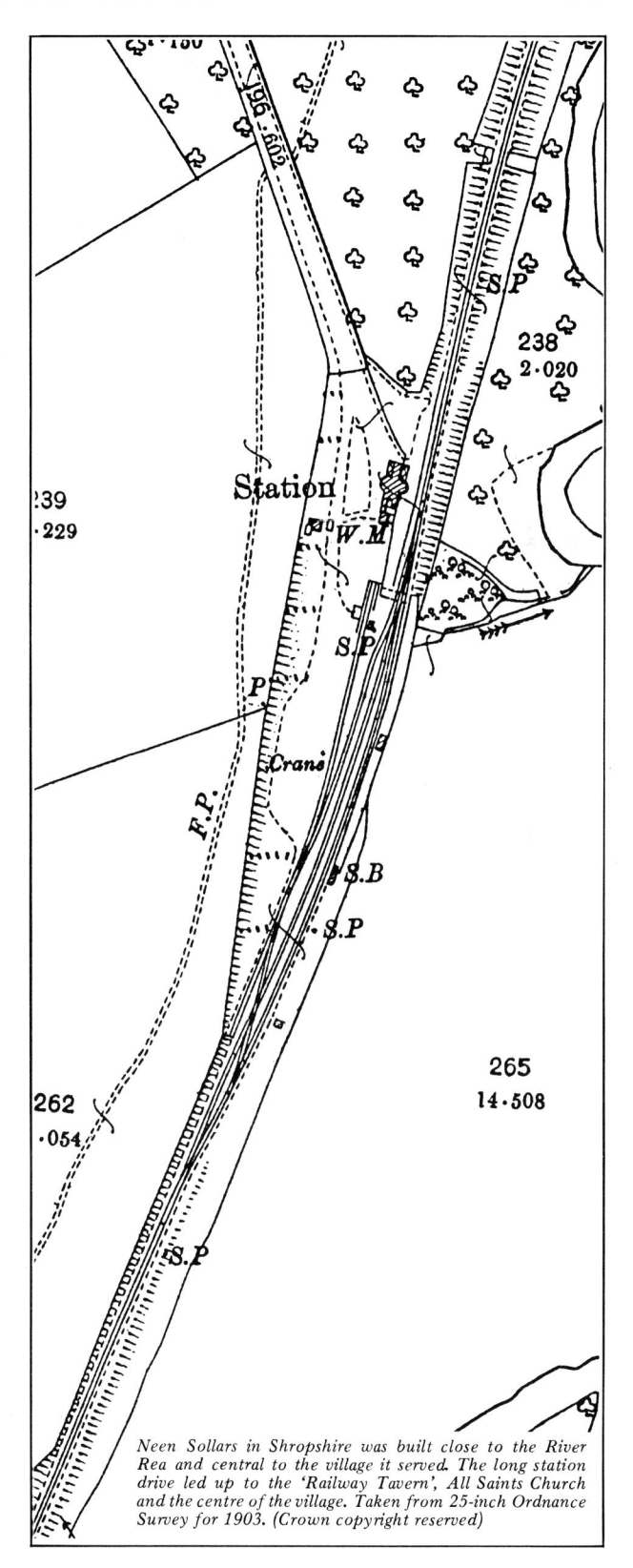

Neen Sollars in Shropshire was built close to the River Rea and central to the village it served. The long station drive led up to the 'Railway Tavern', All Saints Church and the centre of the village. Taken from 25-inch Ordnance Survey for 1903. (Crown copyright reserved)

A springtime view of Neen Sollars station, with a diesel railcar about to depart for Cleobury Mortimer c.1952/3. *W. Potter*

Another view of Neen Sollars from the cab of a railcar, this time featuring the up loop, platform and signal box before they were closed in 1954 when the line through the station was singled. *J. H. Moss*

THE POSTWAR YEARS

open space of the countryside. The day that the season finished was something to behold. The railway staff would try to get the celebrating pickers, who had settled comfortably in the Railway Tavern, out and onto their train which was waiting to return them home. People remember how the local policeman had to be called sometimes to insist on their departure so that the station could be cleared. Although the season was only three weeks long on average, Newnham Bridge alone would dispatch 3,000 pockets of hops, each weighting 1½cwt.

By May 1953 it was clear that even more economies were called for. The passenger traffic continued to fall away in spite of the heavily advertised excursions and the odd bonus, like the parties of boys from all over Europe

In the late '50s, Kidderminster Co-operative Society chartered summer excursions to the seaside. Here a Co-op special to Porthcawl, hauled by Nos. 4153 and 7307, is seen passing under Prizeley Viaduct on 10th August 1958. The specials were often loaded to ten bogies and a buffet car and were very popular trains for some years.
B. Moone

regularly travelling by train to Tenbury to take part in adventure courses held at nearby Nash Court, which had been presented to the Association of Boys Clubs in 1948 as a gift from South African children to their counterparts in Britain. Richard Lloyd's factory had continued to operate in Tenbury after the war ended, having been asked to stay on because of the possible effect on the local economy if it closed, which meant the incoming traffic in steel and oil and the outgoing scrap and swarf would continue.

The economies of the summer of 1953 included a new diesel railcar working, replacing the long-standing steam-hauled 8.50 a.m. Kidderminster to Woofferton and 10.05 a.m. return through working to Birmingham. The railcar off the 8.07 a.m. from Worcester was rostered for this turn

An early 1950s view from a diesel railcar, looking towards Prizeley Cutting, Cleobury Mortimer. The gate to the former Bayton Colliery siding can be seen to the left of the vans in the siding, whilst the end of the ex-CM&DP Light Railway sidings also features to the right of the telegraph pole. *J. H. Moss*

Cleobury Mortimer Junction signal box was built in 1908 to replace the earlier McKenzie & Holland one, put in in 1878 as part of the alterations required when the Kidderminster loop was opened. The vans in the background probably contained consignments of ammunition awaiting movements to and from the armaments depot at Ditton Priors. This picture was taken on 4th July 1959. *M. Hale*

No. 4586 on the 11.55 a.m. from Woofferton taking water at the Bewdley end of Cleobury Mortimer station on 10th September 1949. The Woofferton goods train in the opposite platform was hauled by No. 2286. *H. C. Casserley*

A closer view of No. 4586 on the same occasion. *H. C. Casserley*

The siting of Cleobury Mortimer station on the edge of the Wyre Forest is evident in this late 1950s view which shows the Ditton Priors line curving around into the middle distance and the line to Bewdley disappearing to the right over the road bridge. This picture also shows the weighbridge at the rear of the station buildings.
National Monuments Record

A closer view of the concrete shed at Cleobury Mortimer. *Authors' collection*

On the T&B, only Tenbury Wells had a purpose-built goods shed. Wyre Forest had nothing, but the others had a variety of structures including this old Holden coach body in use in Cleobury Mortimer yard in May 1955. *Dr. J. Hollick*

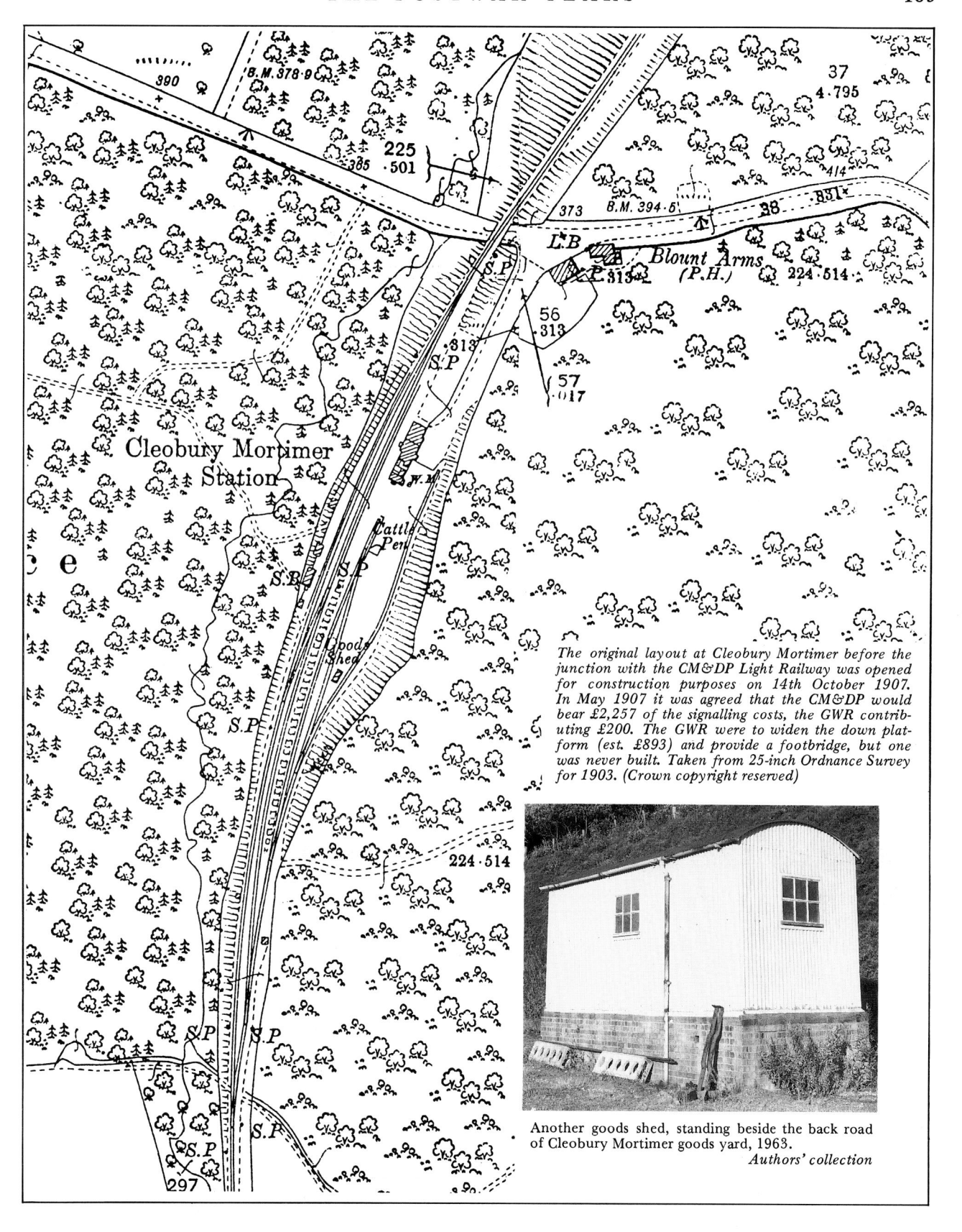

The original layout at Cleobury Mortimer before the junction with the CM&DP Light Railway was opened for construction purposes on 14th October 1907. In May 1907 it was agreed that the CM&DP would bear £2,257 of the signalling costs, the GWR contributing £200. The GWR were to widen the down platform (est. £893) and provide a footbridge, but one was never built. Taken from 25-inch Ordnance Survey for 1903. (Crown copyright reserved)

Another goods shed, standing beside the back road of Cleobury Mortimer goods yard, 1963.
Authors' collection

Kidderminster Pannier No. 2144 starting a freight out of Cleobury Mortimer bound for the Admiralty Armament Depot at Ditton Priors, on 23rd February 1954. The spark arrester was fitted, as a safety measure, to all locos used on the RNAD trains to Ditton Priors.

G. Bannister

An ex-GWR railcar pausing at Cleobury Mortimer on its journey to Kidderminster on 20th May 1961. The horse-box body on the right was in use as a lock-up shed and the water tank behind fed the columns at each end of the up and down platforms.

National Monuments Record

Another railcar pulling away from Cleobury Mortimer towards Wyre Forest. The building on the right was the 'Blount Arms'. D. K. Jones

from May 1953 but terminated at Kidderminster on the return trip from Woofferton, intending passengers for Birmingham having to change at Kidderminster. The only steam passenger over the branch, working from Kidderminster shed, was the 4.48 p.m. to Woofferton, returning as the 6.35 p.m. Woofferton to Stourbridge and Birmingham. At this time 2-6-2T No 8101 was a regular on this train hauling a two-coach non-corridor set. The service was advertised that summer to work through to Leominster which it had already been doing in the winter without being advertised in the public timetable.

Following long periods in store and a brief swan-song at Newport Dock Street, ex-CM&DP 0-6-0PT No 28 was withdrawn at the end of 1953, whilst No 29 lasted until February 1954, being active until its last days on the Ditton Priors line trains on which it had worked for 46 years. The 2021 class 0-6-0PTs, as often in the past, replaced the Manning Wardle rebuilds, Nos 2101 and 2144 being used on the Ditton Priors freight in spring 1954, with No 2034 replacing No 2101 at 85D from April 1954 onwards. The freight services up to Ditton Priors were now run 'as required', usually one but sometimes as many as three trips per week. The Admiralty intimated to BR that its depot would be kept going and would continue to need rail access. This caused the BR operating staff a problem, for the remaining 2021 class locos were run down and being condemned, making their continued availability very uncertain, but one of their lightweight successors, the relatively new Hawksworth 16XX 0-6-0PTs, No 1629, was conveniently already allocated to Worcester shed and was successfully used on the Ditton Priors for a short while in July 1954.

Next BR looked for economies in staffing, and in 1954 came the first of the cuts to have an effect on station operation. Easton Court was 'unstaffed' as from 20th September 1954 and tickets had to be bought by passengers at the termination of their journey. There was also a problem with the water supply there, as the station well, which had supplied drinking water from early days, had become polluted. Two empty water urns had to be sent daily by passenger train to Tenbury Wells for filling up, and these were returned on the next available train. There was also a similar situation at Neen Sollars, for which supplies were provided by Cleobury Mortimer. (These water urns looked very similar to milk churns and are sometimes mistaken for them when seen on photographs.)

Extracts from a wagon checker's book highlight the continuing variety of goods in and out of Tenbury in the middle 'fifties. All goods in wagon or multiple wagon loads:

Goods outwards:
Canned goods to Liverpool, Plymouth, Truro (including fruit and paint)
Farm feed cake to Avonmouth
Holly and mistletoe to Newcastle, West Hartlepool, Paddington, Wakefield, Batley, Goole
Cattle to Wolverhampton, Shrewsbury, Shifnal, Wellington
Swarf to Pontardawe and Round Oak (Brierley Hill)
Potatoes to Newport Docks

The road approach to Wyre Forest station, looking across to the grounds of Goodmoor Grange, on 18th March 1961.
National Monuments Record

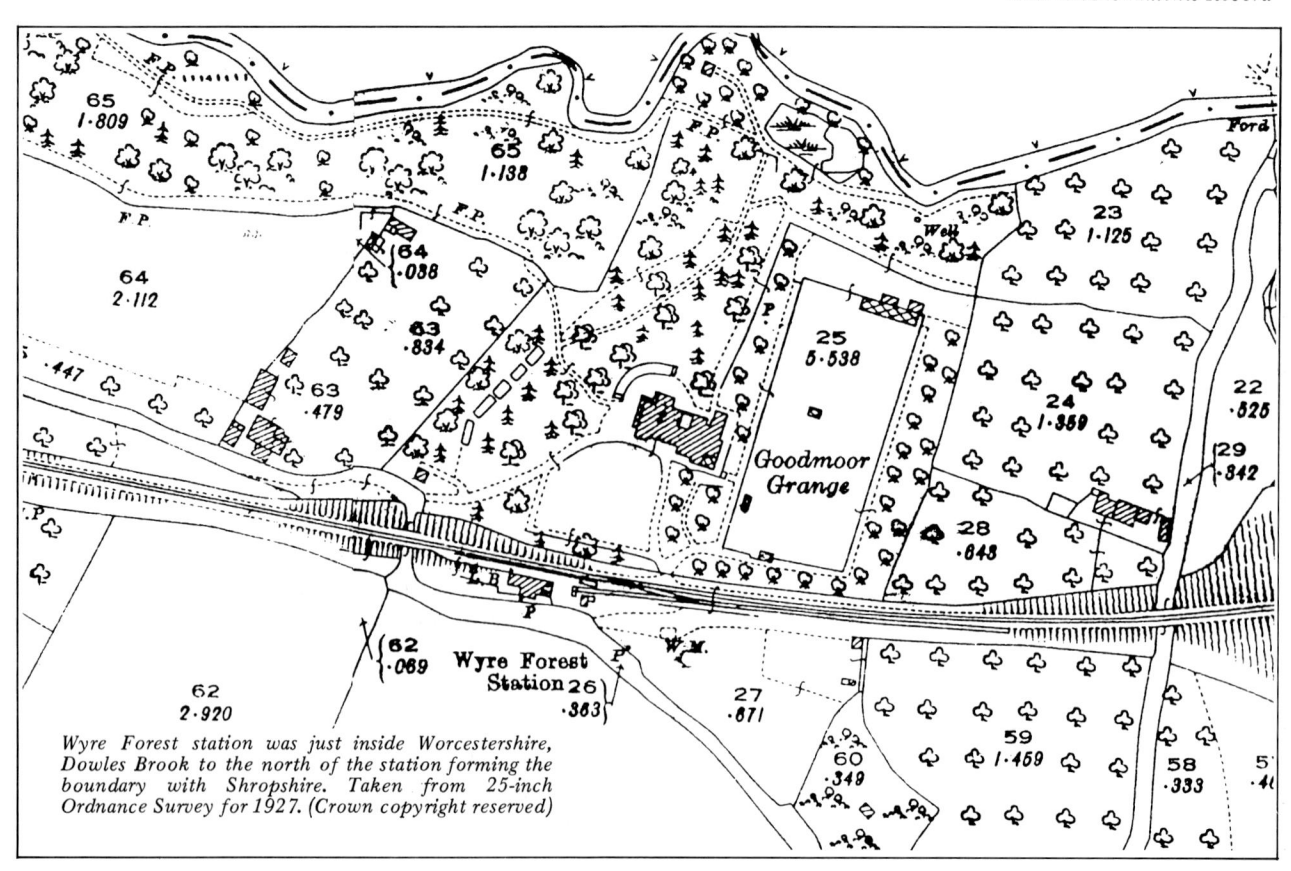

Wyre Forest station was just inside Worcestershire, Dowles Brook to the north of the station forming the boundary with Shropshire. Taken from 25-inch Ordnance Survey for 1927. (Crown copyright reserved)

Only one potential customer for W20W as it called at Wyre Forest before travelling on to Cleobury Mortimer with the 4.10 p.m. Kidderminster to Tenbury Wells on 30th April 1960. *D. A. Johnson*

Wool to Worcester
Parsley to Manchester
Sheep to Alrewas

At this stage cattle trains were made up of no more than eight wagons, and some may have been attached to the 'Tenbury goods' working.

Goods into Tenbury:
Coal for Messrs Parton from Highley Pit
Coal for Messrs Edwards from Littleton Colliery, Cannock or Highley
Coal for Gas works from Holditch Colliery
Meal for Worcestershire Farmers
Garden sheds
Cake, Lever Brothers
Cartons for Worcestershire Packers and Growers, Tenbury
Tins for Glazebrooks (Permaglaze paint factory, Tenbury)
Manure for Worcestershire Farmers
Bricks
Fencing
Farm implements for Burgess and Co
Tins for Worcestershire Packers and Growers
Oil for Richard Lloyd's from Runcorn
Steel for Richard Lloyd's from Worcester
Paper for *Tenbury Advertiser* from Grimsby
Slag for Worcestershire Farmers
Cases for Richard Lloyds
Paint Powder for Permaglaze Paints.

Tenbury Wells and Newnham Bridge continued to move huge quantities of fruit and hops in season, but by 1954, the hop-pickers specials appear to have been discontinued. Neen Sollars station continued to make use of its siding. Messrs Monkleys had erected a corrugated shed alongside this siding before the Second World War to avoid the cost of paying for the time wagons were in the Neen Sollars siding awaiting unloading, and goods were moved immediately into the shed for future delivery around the district. Monkleys ran the only shop in Neen Sollars and before the war goods were taken around nearby villages on a horse and cart driven by the late Harry Palmer, and a Model T Ford lorry was also used for a similar role. Coal came to Neen Sollars from Littleton Colliery, and the local cherry harvest still went away largely by rail. 1954 also saw the closure of the signal box at Neen Sollars, on 29th August. The up loop was removed, making the second platform unavailable to the public and the siding connection was thereafter worked by a new groundframe, locked by key on the electric staff.

Work at Leominster shed, already reduced through the closure of the Bromyard line, was again affected by the clo-

Wyre Forest from the Bewdley end, with W20W awaiting the 'right away' before travelling through the western edge of Wyre Forest to Cleobury Mortimer on the 4.10 Kidderminster to Tenbury on 30th April 1960. The gate on the left provided access to the short goods siding. *J. Dew*

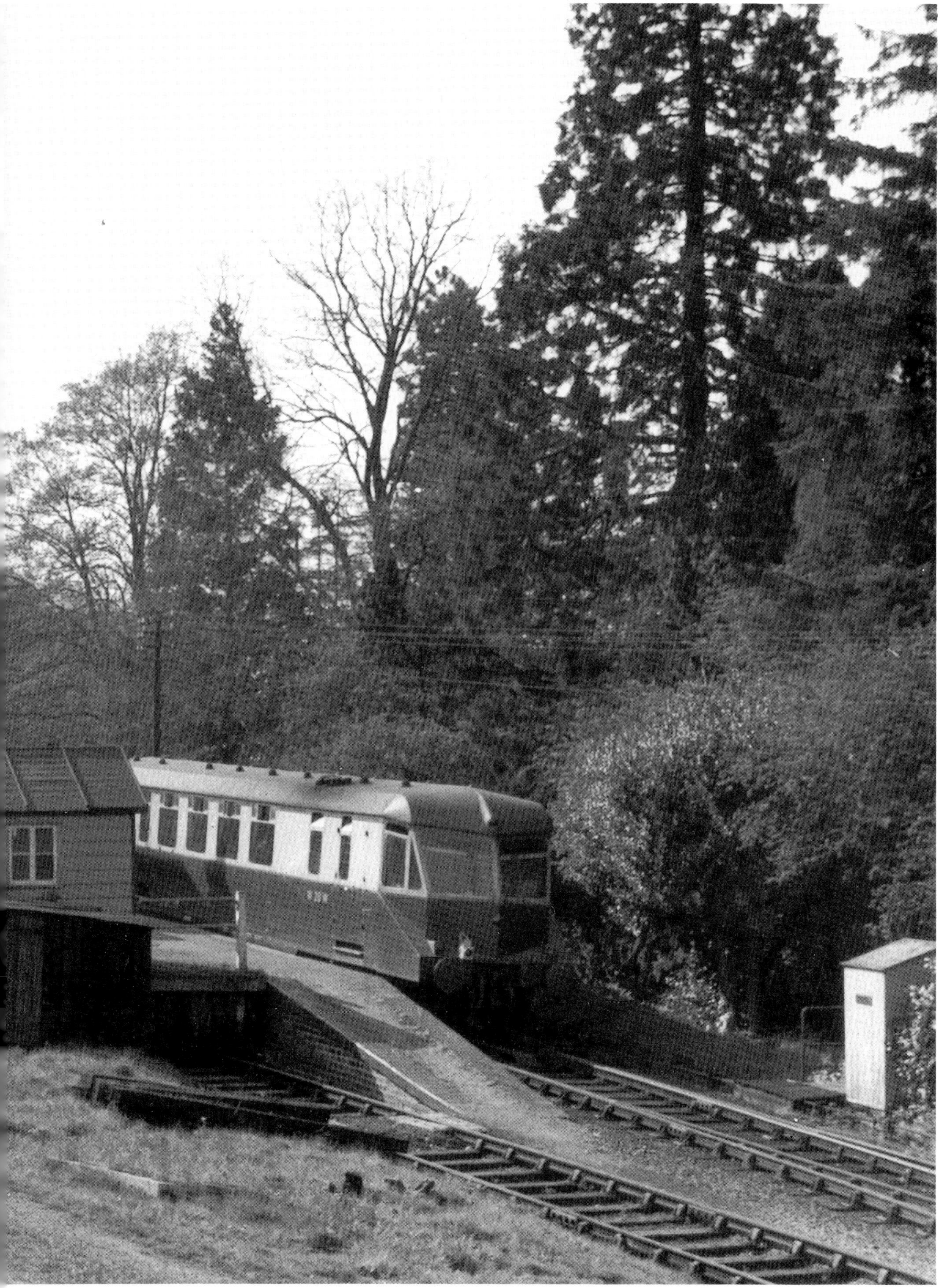
W 20 W

sure of the Kington branch passenger service from 7th February 1955. As far as passenger turns were concerned, this only left the Tenbury Wells auto. After representation by the shed staff, extra duties came into being from March 1955. From then, the Leominster auto worked 6.45 a.m. Leominster–Ludlow, then 7.22 a.m. Ludlow–Woofferton–Tenbury Wells (both previously Worcester railcar workings). Following this the 7.58 a.m. Tenbury Wells–Woofferton and a return trip to Tenbury Wells. In the afternoon there was an innovation when the auto working was extended beyond Ludlow to Craven Arms. Locos of the 14XX 0-4-2T class available at Leominster shed were Nos 1445, 1455 and 1461, whilst 0-6-0PT 7437 was known to be used if no auto was available. Other timetable changes included the early-morning empty ex-Worcester via Bewdley railcar terminating at Tenbury Wells and the retiming of the ex 4.48 p.m. Kidderminster–Woofferton–Leominster to 4.10 p.m. dep Kidderminster and return at 4.58 p.m. from Woofferton. Hence there was now no longer a through service to Leominster from Bewdley. This retimed train plus the 11.00 a.m. and 6.38 p.m. ex Kidderminster were all steam-hauled in the summer of 1955. 0-6-0PTs were now often used on these workings, including Nos 8718, 3601 and 4629 in addition to the more familiar 2-6-2Ts Nos 4175 and 8101. Even a BR standard would appear, such as No 82008 noted at Easton Court hauling the 11.00 a.m. ex Kidderminster on 2nd September 1955 and again on 5th September. There was no longer enough cattle travelling by rail from Tenbury to keep the cattle specials running regularly and the only freight of the day was the 'Tenbury Goods', leaving Kidderminster at 11.40 a.m. working as a 'pick-up', dropping off any traffic for Ditton Priors at Cleobury Mortimer. On 2nd September 1955 0-6-0PT No 8731 was noted on this duty at Neen Sollars. Other locos used around this time on the Tenbury Goods included 2-6-2Ts Nos 8101, 4578, 5518, 4175 and 5110.

Earlier in 1955 No 1661, the 16XX 0-6-0PT that was due to take over the work of the Ditton Priors line, arrived at Kidderminster. The authorities had provided a brand new loco from Swindon works to replace the ancient 2021 class No 2034, and No 1661 was put to work from March 1955.

An event which enlivened the scene on the Ditton Priors was the SLS West Midland branch line tour of May 1955 which brought 0-6-0 Dean Goods No 2516 into Cleobury Mortimer. Ditton Priors branch ex-regular loco No 2144 (2021 class) worked the train on as the first ever train of bogie passenger stock over the old Light Railway. It journeyed up the branch as far as Cleobury North transfer sid-

From the mid-'50s it was rare to see steam-hauled passenger services on the branch other than on the 11.00 a.m. Kidderminster–Woofferton, 12.12 p.m. Woofferton–Kidderminster and the 6.38 p.m. Kidderminster–Woofferton, 7.50 p.m. Woofferton–Kidderminster which were rostered steam turns. This picture, taken on 4th August 1956, shows No. 8718 on the 11.00 a.m. Kidderminster–Woofferton. Deep in the forest the train would have passed over Ford Lane Crossing which was put in in 1866 to give access to Park House on the Alton Woods Estate of W. Lacon-Childe. Although only on a forest track, it was the only public vehicular level crossing between Bewdley and Tenbury. The 1924 GWR No. 13 sectional appendix refers to it as worked by a gatekeeper, indicator, and bell, the bell being operated by passing trains. The gatekeeper lived in a lodge especially built for the purpose, and would open and close the gates for traffic, which included timber from the forest. The gatekeeper was probably dispensed with after the 1926 strike for there is no longer any reference to Ford Lane in the appendix from that time. The lodge and crossing survived until closure. *B. Moone*

0-6-0 Dean Goods No. 2516 about to cross Dowles Bridge before tackling the steep climb through the forest to Cleobury Mortimer with the SLS Special on 21st May 1955. *H. F. Wheeller*

ings. This turned out to be No 2144's swan-song as she was withdrawn the following week. Not long after this trip, interesting plans were announced for the future of the Ditton Priors line when in December 1955 the British Transport Commission Bill provided for the takeover of the line by the Admiralty at a cost of £40,000.

The excursion traffic along the Tenbury branch continued into the second half of the 'fifties, the 63XX and 51XX classes still in use on Co-op specials, double-heading the trains through to Woofferton. A note in the *Railway Observer* records that on 1st October 1955, the Leominster autocoach was No W67W hauled by loco No 1460. The report adds that since 19th December 1955 only two Kidderminster trains worked through to Woofferton, the 11.00 a.m. and 6.38 p.m. ex Kidderminster, both steam-hauled. The 4.53 arr and 4.58 dep Tenbury — previously a steam working (4.10 p.m. ex Kidderminster) — consisted of W7W, the early ex GWR railcar type not so frequently seen on the branch as the later version. The usual railcars (W19W, W20W, W22W, W23W, and W32W) did require deputising from time to time, and another type new to the line, standard 2-6-0 No 78008 of Worcester shed, sometimes performed as stand-in for a failed diesel by hauling an autocoach. The *Railway Observer* report also mentioned the derisory number of passengers using the service on that day, a dozen passengers inward to Tenbury but only three on the return trip!

Although the British Railways DMUs worked the neighbouring Severn Valley line, none worked over the Tenbury line except for a single unit in the 55XXX series on a district officer's special which reversed at Bewdley, having arrived from there from the Severn Valley direction.

On 16th February 1957 further contraction of the branch took place when the Tenbury line bay at Woofferton was taken out of use, branch trains thereafter terminating in the down main line platform. This alteration obviously involved some new movements and a new signal and indicator were provided on the footbridge allowing Tenbury-bound trains to depart from the down platform, working 'wrong line' as far as the junction.

Woofferton was a calling point for a special on 27th July 1957 when No 1445 of Leominster shed hauled a commemorative train celebrating the centenary of the Leominster–Kington line, and during the day ran two coaches to Tenbury Wells and back.

In November 1957 more alterations were made at Woofferton as part of the run-down of maintenance work. The connections to the up branch sidings and the engine shed sidings were taken out, thereby making the ground frame and associated point work redundant. For most of the lifetime of the branch, water had been available to steam engines from the supply at the long-closed Woofferton shed. It had been the rule that if a loco passing Tenbury towards Woofferton required water, a message would be sent ahead via the signalman to the station staff at the junction. Someone would then walk over to the shed and start the petrol-driven pump to fill the tank over the shed entrance in readiness. A signalman who once worked

Dowles Bridge with an unidentified 2–6–2T heading towards Bewdley during the final years of steam.

D. A. Johnson

THE POSTWAR YEARS

A view looking across the Dowles Bridge, showing to good effect the 15 mph curve leading up to the Severn Valley line on 24th August 1959.
John Marshall

at Woofferton Junction remembers the use of the water supply in an emergency by a 'King' class loco shortly after the class had been permitted to run over the S&HR.

The admiralty took official control on the Ditton Priors line on 1st May 1957, though it was not until 30th September 1957 that they provided their own motive power, two Ruston and Hornsby 165 h.p. 0-4-0 DM shunters. Cleobury Mortimer-bound trains off the Ditton Priors now had to be brought to a halt at a stop lamp 21 ch from the Junction signal box, the Admiralty guard obtaining a key from the signalman to operate a ground frame catch point giving access to the BR station where the traffic was exchanged.

The relaying of track all the way from Bewdley to Tenbury, including replacement concrete sleepers along some stretches, caused much speculation. Many thought the ulterior motive behind the move was to prove once and for all that the line cost too much to keep open any longer.

The first reported accident on the branch for many years occurred on Saturday, 24th January 1959 when the 7.58 a.m. autotrain from Tenbury Wells to Ludlow, propelled by 0-4-2T No 1445, hit the buffer stops in Tenbury yard and sank into the soft earth. On weekdays the train was used by children going to school in Ludlow, but on this morning there was only one passenger, Mr Ben Bowkett. He was flung into the opposite seat by the sudden crash, and though shaken made his way back to the station on foot where his fare was refunded. From there he continued

2-6-0 No. 6364 passing Bewdley distant signal with a coal train on 29th May 1963. The Tenbury branch dropped down on the left with a 15 mph speed restriction as it curved away to cross the River Severn by the Dowles Bridge. *B. Moone*

his journey to work at a bank in Ludlow by bus. The driver of the train was Mr Tom Lloyd of Leominster and the accident was his only one in 47 years service which he had begun with the Barry Railway. It seems that the auto from Leominster normally arrived in Tenbury Wells and stopped by the signal box before running forward under the road bridge and reversing into the up platform. The

This picture, taken on 27th August 1962, shows the crossovers used by the Tenbury branch trains running in and out of the back roads at Bewdley. The Tenbury line was on the left.
M. Lloyd

Bewdley, looking towards Tenbury.
J. H. Moss

empty diesel railcar from Bewdley arrived at 7.47 a.m. and waited in the down platform by the signal box for ten minutes before leaving for Bewdley at 7.57 a.m. Its departure was immediately followed by the auto at 7.58 a.m. bound for Woofferton and Ludlow. On the morning concerned it was particularly dark, cold and frosty, so much so that the auto's crew were unaware that the turnout points from the up platform to the 'main' had frozen. The signalman, unable to warn them in time, could only watch in horror as the train moved away to the inevitable crash. The engine was more or less unscathed but the coach (which was leading) was badly damaged. Both were retrieved by a breakdown train later in the day. An enquiry was later held at Swindon but no official conclusion has yet been discovered.

By 1960 rumours were rife about the likely withdrawal of the passenger service on the line. These local suppositions were soon translated into a firm proposal from British Railways to close the line completely. The West Midland Transport Users Consultative Committee met in March

Bewdley from the Tenbury end, looking towards Kidderminster.
J. H. Moss

Contrasting liveries in Bewdley. W20W still in crimson and cream and about to head to the Tenbury branch. The railcar in the opposite platform was in green with cream lining, 'whiskers' and a white roof.
Courtesy Bob Marrows

A 2–6–2 tank drifting into Bewdley with a Kidderminster-bound train.

Lens of Sutton

THE POSTWAR YEARS

A view of Bewdley, looking south-east off the footbridge. *Authors' collection*

An unidentified 57XX 0–6–0PT shunting at Bewdley. *J. H. Moss*

A glimpse of the goods yard at Bewdley. *B. Barnes*

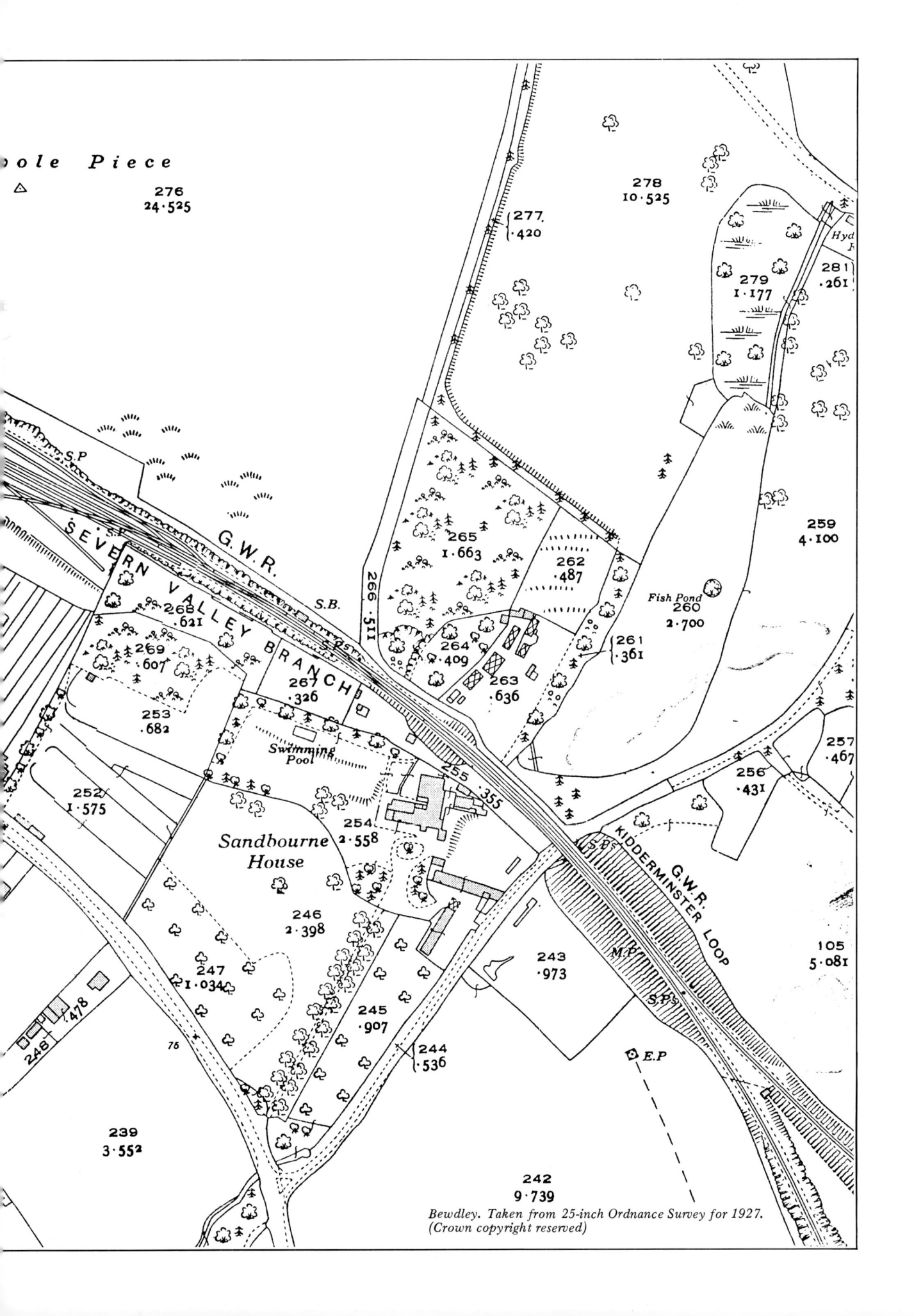

Bewdley. Taken from 25-inch Ordnance Survey for 1927.
(Crown copyright reserved)

186   THE TENBURY & BEWDLEY RAILWAY

At holiday times, the GWR railcars on the Tenbury and Severn Valley branches were replaced by steam-hauled trains, as shown in this 1960 August Bank Holiday picture, which shows Kidderminster pannier No. 4629 heading a Woofferton–Kidderminster local past the 'rifle range' on the loop between Bewdley and Kidderminster on 2nd August 1960. The driver was Claude Robinson, the last shedmaster at Kidderminster when it closed in August 1964.
B. Moone

Foley Park Halt on the Bewdley loop, looking towards Bewdley and Foley Park tunnel. The siding to the left of the picture was part of the rail complex of the British Sugar Corporation factory.
Collection Bob Marrows

THE POSTWAR YEARS

Kidderminster shed, looking towards Bewdley on 13th July 1958. The locos stored alongside the Bewdley line were 22XX class 0–6–0s Nos. 2247, 2277, 2301 class No. 2367, and 63XX 2–6–0 No. 6367.
B. Hilton

Kidderminster shed on 14th June 1953, with a trio of Tenbury branch regulars, 2–6–2T No. 4153, 0–6–0PT No. 2144, and 0–6–0PT No. 29, formerly of the CM&DP. The spark arresters were fitted to locomotives working ammunition trains to Ditton Priors (via Cleobury Mortimer) on the former CM&DP branch. Coded 85D under BR(W), the Kidderminster shed code changed to 84G (1st January 1961) and then to 2P (9th September 1963) on being transferred into the LM region. When the shed finally closed on 10th August 1964, the engines were transferred to Stourbridge shed, by then coded 2C in the LMR.
B. Hilton

The Tenbury branch diesel railcar, with tail load, signalled towards Bewdley. Kidderminster Junction box replaced a wooden structure which was demolished in an accident on 7th June 1953.
Authors' collection

A sunny view of Kidderminster station on 14th April 1957. The signal box survived until 1972, three years after the station was demolished.
Lens of Sutton

Most Tenbury line and Severn Valley line trains were stabled in the up refuge siding at Kidderminster awaiting turns. This picture shows 2–6–2T No. 5151 waiting there with the 10.40 to Bridgnorth on 17th June 1961.
M. Hale

W20W waiting in the refuge siding at Kidderminster.
C. Berridge

1961 to consider the possible results of the closure to the area. It was said that the line was losing approximately £15,000 p.a. against an income of just £4,000 p.a.

However, the hardships that closure of the line would cause, especially to schoolchildren who relied on the trains, prompted a rethink and a compromise was reached whereby after the complete closure of the Tenbury Wells to Woofferton section (the old Tenbury Railway), from 31st July 1961, one passenger train each way per day would run from Kidderminster to Tenbury Wells for a trial period of one year.

The last through train was run from Woofferton on Saturday, 28th July 1961. This was the 7.50 p.m. return working of the 6.38 p.m. ex-Kidderminster which for the past year had been the only steam passenger working on the branch except for the auto on the short section.

The Leominster News reported the proceedings under the heading 'The Bluebell Line':

'Cheers rang out from about 300 people at Woofferton railway station on Saturday evening as the 6.38 p.m. train to Tenbury Wells steamed in behind an immaculate little green tank locomotive. But the cheers from railway enthusiasts from all over the Midlands and Wales . . . marked a rather sad occasion . . . the closure of another of Herefordshire's fastly diminishing branch railway lines.

'Just three days before the Woofferton to Kidderminster line was due to celebrate its centenary, the Woofferton to Tenbury Wells section has been closed to passenger traffic and the Kidderminster to Tenbury section reduced to one train in each direction a day.

'With the withdrawal between Tenbury and Woofferton, the few trains on the Hereford to Shrewsbury line stopping at Woofferton have also been withdrawn and the station closed. As a result, Mr G. Dickens, stationmaster at Woofferton for the past five years, has been made redundant. Goods traffic will be continued.

'The closure of this lovely line follows similar action in recent years on the Leominster to Bromyard line, the Leominster–Kington line, the Titley to Eardisley and Presteigne lines, the Ross to Monmouth line and the Ledbury to Gloucester line.

'To mark this historic occasion, British Railways laid on a special train to cater for the hundreds of railway enthusiasts who invariably attend the closure of such lines as this.

'The platform on the Hereford line at Woofferton was packed with about 200 people from all over the Midlands and Wales as the six-coach train entered the station for the last time, crowded with a further 300 enthusiasts.

'As driver C. Austin, and fireman David Jones, both of Bewdley and based at Kidderminster, took engine No 6144, a Western Region tank engine, itself 30 years old, out of Woofferton and collected the token, used for single line working, from the signalman, hundreds of people

Ex-GWR railcar in BR green livery, entering Bewdley with a Woofferton–Kidderminster working, on a grey, murky December day in 1960.
Cty. Express & Star

This picture of Bewdley shows one of the public notices which read 'On and from Monday 31st July 1961 the following services will be withdrawn: 9.05 a.m. to Tenbury Wells, 11.10 a.m. to Woofferton, 2.30 p.m. SO to Tenbury Wells, 6.30 p.m. to Woofferton, 10.20 a.m. to Kidderminster, 12.53 p.m. Sats ex to Kidderminster, 1.52 p.m. SO to Kidderminster, 3.44 p.m. SO to Hartlebury. *B. Barnes*

along the line paid a last royal farewell to a line which has served this rural community so well.

'All along the five miles to Tenbury people lined the route and waved white handkerchiefs as the engine steamed past with a continuous blast on its whistle.

'As the train pulled into the tiny station at Easton Court, Herefordshire's only station on the line — Woofferton is in Shropshire and Tenbury in Worcestershire — Mr W.R.J. Alloway the 'unofficial Mayor of Little Hereford', as he called himself, and scores of other local residents crowded onto the platform to pay their last respects.

'In my compartment, first class, by courtesy of British Railways, I had the good fortune to find myself sitting next to a former station master of Woofferton, Mr N.J. Davis of Ashford Carbonell, near Ludlow.

'Mr Davis who has been station master for 11 years until his retirement in 1956, said he could remember the time in 1910 when the return fare between Tenbury and Woofferton was 5d, the old penny a mile charge. Now, the single fare is 1/3d.

'Sitting next to Mr Davis was Mr J. Butcher, of Mill Street, Ludlow, who can claim 41 years service with the railways and who, for 19 years, was a driver based at Kidderminster.'

'For Mr Butcher, it was an extra sad occasion, for he frequently drove one of the small engines through the Wyre Forest between Kidderminster and Woofferton. "I know this line quite well. In fact I know every inch of it", he said.

'One traveller treated the matter light-heartedly, however. He was Mr Reg Mytton, of Brewery Cottage, Tenbury Wells, who was suitably dressed in top hat and tails, bow tie and an umbrella handle without an umbrella; for "a bit of nonsense".

'As the train pulled into Tenbury station, the station master, Mr E.E. Savory, of Kingsland, met the train, took the token from the driver and handed it for the last time to the station signalman, Mr C. Carpenter, of Station Cottage, Tenbury Wells.

'The line is now overgrown with weeds; it is obvious that little maintenance has been carried out. Because of the closures, the engine shed at Leominster, which supplies motive power for some of the trains, has also been affected, and some men are redundant.'

The loco in use that day, 61XX 2-6-2T No 6144, was a class new to the line and one more used to London commuter traffic. It had been transferred to Kidderminster shed from Southall (81C) along with sister engine No 6128 on 20th July 1960, surplus to requirements once DMUs had become established in the London area. This last train was much photographed, but not so the last auto which left earlier in the day. This was the 5.40 p.m. Tenbury Wells to Craven Arms hauled by 14XX No 1445 of Leominster shed. One who did take notice was the elderly lady living at Easton Court station who drew her curtains as if a funeral was expected to pass.

The last train was the 7.12 p.m. Kidderminster–Tenbury diesel railcar, which eventually arrived back at Kidderminster with the last ever regular passengers off the Tenbury and Bewdley branch. So ended twenty years of railcar service along the line.

Before the last day, letters had appeared in the local press — notably from a Mr Harman of Southampton, who suggested a scheme for running the line, with others, on a private basis. Support was expressed by the then MP for Kidderminster, Mr Gerald Nabarro, who said he could get in touch with Transport Minister Ernest Marples to find ways of obtaining a lease. Support came also from Jasper More, MP for Ludlow, but the scheme came to nothing and was soon forgotten.

The schoolchildren's train, steam-hauled, started the following Monday 31st July which was rather odd as it was the start of the school holidays. Nevertheless, two empty carriages were brought from Kidderminster to form the 7.55 a.m. departure from Tenbury Wells. The return working was 4.10 p.m. from Kidderminster, arr Tenbury 4.53 p.m. These trains were allowed to run mixed if required and often did. BR did try to interest other passengers in using these school trains, advertising cheap day tickets

Between 1957 and 1961 the Tenbury branch was used for commissioning trials of Diesel Multiple Units built at the Birmingham Carriage and Wagon Company at Handsworth, Birmingham. This 1961 photograph shows a 3-car set entering Cleobury Mortimer from where it reversed and returned via Bewdley and Kidderminster. This particular set (BR 110 class) was destined for use on the Eastern Region Calder Valley line between Southport and Bradford Exchange.
John Dew

THE POSTWAR YEARS

Fireman Borbery of Kidderminster shed leaning out of the cab of 0–6–0PT No. 3619 as it squealed round the curve approaching Dowles Bridge with the last passenger train to Tenbury Wells on 31st August 1962. Also on the footplate was the Reverend Selwyn Frost, a former Kidderminster fireman, who, a year earlier, had also been in the cab of 6144 on the last through train to Woofferton. Even his divine presence could not have halted the branch's closure!

The experimental passenger service, mainly for the benefit of schoolchildren, ran for just over a year. It ceased on Saturday, 31st August 1962 and this picture shows 0–6–0PT No. 3619 at Newnham Bridge on its way to Tenbury Wells with the last passenger train.

from Tenbury Wells to Birmingham for 8/3d return and connecting with the trains in service on the branch. However, the early start and inconvenient train changes at Kidderminster did not apparently appeal, and the eventual loading of 20-30 schoolchildren mainly bound for Kidderminster Girls' High school was not enough to warrant a continuation beyond the trial period.

It came as no surprise, therefore, to locals that BR proposed to close the remainder of the route to all passenger traffic, from 1st August 1962.

The last steam-hauled train left Kidderminster at 4.20 p.m. on 31st July 1962 with 0-6-0PT No 3619 and two coaches. Driver D.M. Lamb and Fireman G. Borbery took a leisurely run and arrived at Tenbury Wells thirteen minutes late at 5.05 p.m. Many people had gathered at Tenbury Wells to pay their last respects; some were local residents witnessing the passing of a familiar scene into history, others were enthusiasts who had travelled long distances to say goodbye to an old friend. One poor harrassed passenger had got on the train at Bewdley by mistake and, as he explained to reporters, as he looked round the crowded station, all he wanted was to get back home.

It was anticipated that the three local bus companies would benefit from the demise of the railway, and when the line closed the Midland Red put on a bus which departed from Kidderminster station at 5.47 p.m. and ran to Tenbury. Yarranton's Buses ran a Newnham Bridge to Tenbury service whilst Bengry's advertised a Tenbury to Leominster service. It is interesting to compare fares on the bus routes with what had been charged by BR for journeys between Kidderminster and Tenbury. The bus fare in July 1962 was 3/- single whereas the train fare had been 4/9d return, with the bus trip taking an hour and a half against forty-five minutes by train. The hopes of the bus

Neen Sollars had become partially unstaffed in 1958, then unstaffed in 1961, although its public siding remained open for goods. Luckily, it suffered little vandalism after closure and is now a private dwelling. This view shows the station in early 1963 when the only train using the line was the daily Tenbury Goods. In the final years the water pump at the station failed and water for the staff had to be brought in by train. It was quite usual to see small churns on the platform awaiting collection for refilling. *R. Keights*

Wyre Forest station viewed from a brake van, looking towards Bewdley in the summer of 1965. The station became unstaffed and closed for goods in July 1961. *A. Muckley*

companies did not materialise and many buses were little used. There were unavailing calls from local people to bring back the trains, but the age of private motoring had arrived and it became clear that the demand for public transport had severely diminished.

After closure, a goods service was retained on the branch only as far as Tenbury, Easton Court having closed completely on 31st July 1961. All connections with the S&H main line had been removed at Woofferton on 12th November 1961 although the main line goods facilities did not cease until 7th October 1963. Wyre Forest station completely closed from 1st August 1962, having been unstaffed and closed to goods since 31st July 1961.

In December 1962 the stationmaster at Cleobury Mortimer was withdrawn. Mr Fred Harvey, an ex CM&DP light railway employee, was kept on until 1965 to supervise the remaining goods and Ditton Priors branch traffic as events began to gather speed to a final closure.

In the meantime, Leominster shed had closed during April 1962 having been left with only the Kington freight

0–6–0PT No. 3619, with the Bewdley brake van in tow, passing by the peaceful waters of the River Rea, near Neen Sollars, with the Kidderminster-bound return working of the Tenbury Goods in 1963. In order to avoid building a viaduct over a loop in the river between Newnham Bridge and Neen Sollars, a long embankment was constructed, beside which the river was diverted into a new channel. The old water-filled loop can still be seen today in a meadow to the west of the trackbed. It is known to local people as the 'dead Rea'.
R. Keights

Claude Robinson, the last shedmaster at Kidderminster, surveying the sad scene on the day of its closure, 10th August 1964.
Kidderminster Times

trips to service. Tenbury Wells station made the national newspapers on 30th August 1962 with a scathing report in the *Daily Telegraph* under the headlines 'A twelve staff station with no passengers and only one goods train a day', but this staffing complement soon dwindled. The signal box closed on 28th April 1963 and the following day the electric token working was withdrawn and replaced by a wooden staff for one-engine-in-steam working.

From January 1963 both the Severn Valley line and the Tenbury had become part of the London Midland Region but little changed. Kidderminster shed (still responsible for working the Tenbury goods) was now coded 2P under the LMR after briefly being 84G (from 85D) following the Western Region's reorganization of January 1961. The Severn Valley line lost its passenger service when the last scheduled passenger train between Bewdley and Shrewsbury ran on 7th September, followed by the end of the through freight workings on 30th November 1963, leaving only the line south of Alveley open for coal traffic from the colliery.

The daily Tenbury goods lingered on until Saturday, 4th January 1964, officially withdrawn from the 6th. On 10th January BR began dismantling operations around Tenbury Wells with one or two trips being made to clear away a few remaining wagons. The line from Tenbury Wells to Newnham Bridge was then used as a storage area for condemned wagons, some 1,000 being estimated as being there at one time. Gaps were left in the long rows of vehicles where occupation crossings required access, though on numerous occasions complaints were made about brakes being let off and wagons buffering up, causing much inconvenience to those whose right of way across the line was blocked.

Kidderminster shed closed on 10th August 1964, its eight remaining engines, Nos 3601, 3607, 3619, 8718, 4147, 4153, 4173, 4175, being transferred on 8th August to Stourbridge, which then became responsible for the infrequent goods to Cleobury Mortimer for Ditton Priors branch traffic. Another closure which passed virtually unnoticed in 1964 (although not as a result of the railway's demise) was that of the Bayton Colliery Brickworks at the south end of Cleobury Mortimer yard, following the owner's retirement. By early 1965 the freight trip to Cleobury Mortimer was being 'run as required', the Admiralty having announced its intention of closing the depot at Ditton Priors. The engine on this trip sometimes had an extra job, working further down the line to retrieve batches of condemned wagons from Newnham Bridge, and on one occasion an ex-LMS 2-8-0 8F (probably from Stourbridge) was seen heading some wagons along the branch towards Bewdley.

The inevitable end came on Good Friday, 16th April 1965, from which date all traffic on the branch ceased. From 8th May 1965 electric token working was withdrawn between Cleobury Mortimer and Bewdley North box, and the wooden staff withdrawn from Cleobury Mortimer to Tenbury. The whole line was then worked as a siding. Points were clipped at Cleobury Mortimer to give a single line through the loop whilst the Admiralty cleared away materials through the junction. At this stage the section of track between Woofferton and the western end of Tenbury Wells yard had already gone. The dismantling had been

THE POSTWAR YEARS

0–6–0PT No. 4646 of Stourbridge shed at Cleobury Mortimer in March 1965, having exchanged wagons with the Admiralty diesel seen behind the water column.
A. Muckley

Another view taken on the same occasion, showing Admiralty diesel DP Yard No. 35 (Ruston & Hornsby Class 165 DS) about to depart from the former Light Railway platform at Cleobury Mortimer.
A. Muckley

Wrekin Roadways' Scammel-hauled trailer backing into Newnham Bridge yard in July 1965. The Hunslet 0-6-0 diesel No. 3 from Aldridge was used on the demolition train between Newnham and Cleobury Mortimer. *B. T. C. Good*

carried out by George Cohen Sons & Co Ltd of Wood Lane, London, and had been completed by April 1964. A year later the demolition contractors Henry Boot and Sons (Railway Engineering Ltd) of Sheffield were waiting to start removing the Tenbury–Cleobury Mortimer section.

Worked commenced on 24th June 1965. An 0-4-0 diesel was brought by road to Newnham Bridge from 'Pittsteel', Aldridge, Staffordshire, to work the demolition trains between Newnham Bridge and Cleobury Mortimer. The diesel was not rated very useful, however, and was returned by road from whence it came. Another diesel, a BR shunter in the D39XX series, was later seen at Wyre Forest station heading a demolition train towards Bewdley.

While the demolition was in progress, a group of local enthusiasts were trying to set up a preservation scheme, and considered the ex-CM&DP line. A tentative enquiry to the Admiralty resulted in a figure of £12,000 being quoted. However, the many restrictions imposed on the working of the branch, plus the impending rail isolation, caused the group to divert their attention to the Severn Valley line. The lifting of the section to Cleobury from Newnham Bridge was completed by November 1965. The contractors for the next section to Bewdley started work on 19th November 1965 having set up camp in Cleobury Mortimer yard. This firm, Leonard Fairclough (London) Ltd, Gospel Oak Station yard, London NW, were also responsible for the demolition of six bridges including the Dowles Bridge across the River Severn. This operation required much expertise for the spans had to be lowered onto pontoons moored on the river and in fact the last span slipped into the river, from which it had to be retrieved. The final dismantling of the bridge took place in March 1966 but not before much heated correspondence in the press from those like Councillor J. Wardle, former driver at Kidderminster shed, who had wanted the bridge to remain and be converted to a roadway. Despite a last-minute telegram to BR, the bridge did come down and by May 1966 the contractors had finally taken the Tenbury and Bewdley branch apart. The ballast was left *in situ* for disposal along with the land, and station buildings by British Railway's estates surveyors, leaving only the supports of the Dowles Bridge standing in the river as a memorial.

Passenger trains to Bewdley via the Kidderminster triangle finally ceased in January 1970, the closing of the Bewdley–Hartlebury section severing the last link with the Tenbury, Bewdley and Worcester Junction Railway.

THE POSTWAR YEARS

A final reminder of happier times with 'Manor' 4–6–0 No. 7810 *Draycott Manor* easing over Dowles Bridge with a ballast train of steel hoppers on 2nd July 1955.
A. Turley

Dowles Bridge being dismantled in March 1966.
Kidderminster Times

The scene today, the centre piers of the dismantled Dowles Bridge emerging ghostlike from a mist-shrouded River Severn. The spirit of William Norris lives on . . .

Wyre Forest District Council/Bewdley Museum

CHAPTER TWELVE
POSTSCRIPT

Cleobury Mortimer in 1971 still as it was in railway days apart from the accumulation of rubbish and a sign by the white fence denoting the fact that Banbury Buildings Ltd had use of the site. The station still stands today, in isolation, some miles away from the town it was supposed to serve, newcomers to the area not even being aware of its existence. It still holds fond memories, however, for the older folk who used it when railways were perhaps part of a better era. *Authors' collection*

IF William Norris and Lord Northwick were alive today they would, without doubt, be sadly disappointed to find 'their' railway route rapidly merging back into the landscape. However, they and the other pioneering directors of both the Tenbury and the Tenbury & Bewdley Railway certainly achieved their first ambition. The Teme Valley was duly opened up to trade and local people were consequently more likely to share in the improved prosperity and living standards of the times. The soft fruit industry in particular thrived as never before once the railway was there and able to carry produce away on the same day that it was picked. The hop yards flourished with a huge seasonal labour force only a short train ride away. Tenbury's age-old Tuesday market grew in importance and value, giving the speciality holly and mistletoe traders a national instead of local market to supply.

The second ambition, to make Tenbury into a spa town equivalent to Droitwich or Leamington, never really happened. The reasons were two-fold, the lack of suitable hotel accommodation and the image of spas which had become slightly old-fashioned, even more so by the time moves were made for Tenbury's revival in the 1930s. The Tenbury Baths did not survive the 1939-45 war, although the Bath House stands, the iron panelling sadly neglected and rusting away. The building has been the subject of several attempts at preservation in recent years after having been used as a café and for a while the WI's market place. The Tenbury Baths Company carried on as TBC (Garages) Ltd at its other premises in Oxford Street, Kidderminster, becoming part of the Lex Motor Group before closure in 1972, many people being unaware of the historical significance in the initials. The Corn Exchange in Teme Street, scene of many Board meetings, still survives, occupied by Bedford Instruments who, like Richard Lloyd, came from Birmingham during the war.

Of the stations on the line, Easton Court, Neen Sollars and Wyre Forest (which were sited to suit individual demands rather than serve a local population) are now private houses. Cleobury Mortimer was so far from the town of the same name that the original intention of naming the station 'Cleobury Road' might have been less misleading to the travelling public. The activities on this site since closure have centred around the construction firm, Banbury Buildings, and as a caravan site.

Cleobury Mortimer station was involved not only with the independent CM&DP Light Railway, and later the Admiralty, but with a rail outlet for the South Shropshire Coalfield. The inability to exploit the coal reserves to the full was a continuing frustration to various owners and one which the railway did not overcome in the way it was once hoped.

Bewdley station always seemed slightly apart from the rest of the branch. Separated by the River Severn, it was both the gateway to the West Midlands and the key to the establishment of the line as a through route when the link with Kidderminster was made. It shared its Tenbury line interests with the working of the Severn Valley line to Shrewsbury as well as the Stourport side of the 'triangle' and today plays a big part in the railway preservation scene, a reminder, too, that it could very easily have been the line to the Tenbury direction that was preserved rather than towards Bridgnorth.

Newnham Bridge station no longer comes alive at hop-picking time but presently serves as a garden centre, the site having also been used as a local council depot.

Tenbury Wells station was occupied after closure by a firm of seismic explorers in an unsuccessful search of the area for oil and natural gas. They moved away in 1964 when the buildings were refurbished on behalf of the long-established Tenbury family soft drinks firm of Robinsons who remain there today, bottling (amongst other items) an aerated mineral water product — ironical given the history of the early days of Tenbury's saline springs.

The old stations remain the most obvious artefacts, particularly as much of the track has been taken back into farmland, but there are small farm accommodation bridges like the one leading to Tetstill Farm and nearby derelict mill, Neen Sollars or the larger, still impressive Prizeley Viaduct carrying traffic from the Bewdley Road to Clows Top. In places the course of the old Leominster Canal can still be traced and some remnants survive, in particular the former canalside settlement at Newnham Bridge and the nearby aqueduct over the River Rea. At Easton Court an occupation bridge can still be seen alongside the main road whilst at Little Hereford the Teme Aqueduct still stands although its centre span was blown up in September 1939.

The Tenbury Branch, like other rural branch lines, was a community affair. The station staff were known to everyone throughout the district and the station master was a respected local figure. To employees the 'company' inspired a sense of loyalty well after the change at nationalization. It was a community spirit that William Norris would have wanted.

The line was a way of life for many of the staff. The platelayers formed close-knit gangs up and down the line, keeping it in good order and the rabbit population in check. The lineside huts were apparently as warm, inviting and as well-stocked as any gentlemen's clubroom.

During and shortly after the last war, any duty which took staff over the Tenbury line was always popular and particularly remembered at Stourbridge shed. Home-grown produce, no longer available in the town in days of rationing and shortage, could be had with luck and a little bargaining in the Rose and Crown at Tenbury.

The memory of many travellers over the Tenbury line has to do with the variety of scenic beauty throughout the seasons. Always outstanding in people's minds was the ride through the ancient woodland of the Wyre Forest, especially in early spring with huge clumps of primroses, followed by cowslips in flower along the embankment, and sheets of bluebells in the woods. In May the T&BR really lived up to the nickname of the 'bluebell line'. In late autumn, travellers recall the pungent, sulphurous smells of hop-drying coming from the oast-houses set amongst the most northerly hop-yards in Europe. These were scenes remembered, too, by Frances Brett Young in the novel *Portrait of Clare*. It is an irony that the towns of Tenbury Wells, Cleobury Mortimer and Bewdley have each grown out of all proportion since the closure of the railway and far more rapidly than they ever did when it was in operation and private car ownership was enjoyed by only a small minority of the population.

ACKNOWLEDGEMENTS

Only when a list is drawn up is a true realisation of how many individuals and bodies of people have helped, many of whom have played their part in the foregoing history. We would like to express our thanks to the following: W. Arnett, R. Bannister, A. Barfield, B. Barnes, G. Bedford, R. Blount, J. Bott, B. Bowkett, G. Bramhall, J. Britton, I. Button, C. Carpenter, R. Carpenter, A. R. Croall, T. Davies, N. Davis, R. Davis, G. Dickens, J. Edgington, H. Evans, R. Evans, G. Farmer, Rev. S. Frost, B. Good, B. M. Good, M. Hale, F. Harvey, H. Heath, A. Higgins, B. Hilton, E. Hitchen, G. Hookham, H. How, T. R. Jay, G. Kendrick, H. Lane, M. Lloyd, E. Lowe, R. Martin, T. Mills, B. Moone, C. Morris, D. Parkes, G. Parton, R. Pearson, D. Postle, E. Price, J. Pritchett, B. Roberts, C. Robinson, L. Shingles, A. Turley, members of the HMRS, Lens of Sutton, staff at the Worcester, Hereford and Shropshire County Records Offices, staff at Shropshire Local Studies Library, also at Dudley, Stourbridge, Kidderminster, Worcester and Hereford Reference Libraries, staff at the *Tenbury Advertiser* and the *Kidderminster Times and Shuttle*, the Tenbury Wells Civic and Historical Society, and last but not least, our typist Mrs. D. V. Griffiths.

BIBLIOGRAPHY
Navigable Waterways, L. T. C. Rolt, Longmans
Philips Inland Navigation, 1805
Leominster and Stourport Canal, Cohen, RCHS 1957
History of Tenbury, Tunstall Evans, 1840
Worthies of Worcestershire, Miss E. O. Brown & Rev. J. R. Burton, 1916
Worcestershire's Agriculture, 1939
Cleobury Mortimer and Ditton Priors Light Railway, Smith and Beddoes, OPC 1980
When There was Steam, A. Barfield, Bradford Barton 1976
Locomotives of the GWR, RCTS
History of the GWR, MacDermot (revised Clinker) Vol. 1, Ian Allan

We have also consulted *Commercial Motor* (18th January 1906), *Worcester Herald*, *British Chronicle*, *Hereford Times*, *Hereford Journal*, *Shrewsbury Chronicle*, *Eddowes Shrewsbury Journal*, *Wellington Journal*, *Ludlow Advertiser* and *Tenbury Advertiser*.